Steve Kilbey began his professional music career when he was 17. He played in several bands before forming The Church in Sydney in 1980. After some initial success, Kilbey and The Church shot to international fame in 1988 when their album *Starfish*, featuring the song 'Under the Milky Way', rose to the top of the music charts in both Australia and the US.

Kilbey has collaborated with a vast array of musicians on various projects and has produced a number of solo works as well. He is also a painter, poet and music producer.

In 2010 The Church was inducted into the ARIA Hall of Fame.

Steve Kilbey currently lives in Bondi, Sydney.

SOMETHING QUITE *peculiar*

STEVE KILBEY

SOMETHING QUITE *peculiar*

THE CHURCH. THE MUSIC. THE MAYHEM.

hardie grant books
MELBOURNE • LONDON

Published in 2014 by Hardie Grant Books

Hardie Grant Books (Australia)
Ground Floor, Building 1
658 Church Street
Richmond, Victoria 3121
www.hardiegrant.com.au

Hardie Grant Books (UK)
5th & 6th Floor
52–54 Southwark Street
London SE1 1RU
www.hardiegrant.co.uk

A Cataloguing-in-Publication entry is available from the catalogue of the National Library of Australia at www.nla.gov.au
Steve Kilbey: Something Quite Peculiar
ISBN 978 1 74270 831 7

Cover design by Mark Campbell
Cover photography by Scott Davidson
Text design by Patrick Cannon
Typeset in 12/17pt Adobe Caslon by Cannon Typesetting
Printed and bound in Australia by McPherson's Printing Group

The paper this book is printed on is certified against the Forest Stewardship Council® Standards. FSC® promotes environmentally responsible, socially beneficial and economically viable management of the world's forests.

To God, for giving us so much unbearable talent!

Contents

INTRODUCING ...

IT'S 2010, AND I'm sitting here at the ARIA Hall of Fame induction ceremony. My band, The Church, is being let in. They've even brought the famous journalist George Negus to induct us into the non-existent hall. I'm sitting between my mother and my brother Russell; I'm here reluctantly I must admit. I'm not looking forward to proceedings. I don't as a rule like award ceremonies. I've always felt as if I didn't need some boozy industry accolade to justify my contribution to Australian rock, whatever the hell that means. Yet here I am, sitting at a big table in the Hordern Pavilion, trying to cope with the not-very-good vegetarian option, and also looking after my old mum and making sure she's having a good time. I'm chatting with everyone as they drop by our table to offer up congratulations. You know what? That isn't really my cup of herbal tea either ... all that back-slapping and stuff? All that fakery and big noting? What has that got to do with music?

No, I haven't been looking forward to this at all. My band and I haven't talked about it much between us – we've been offered it a few times before and turned 'em down, but now everyone reckoned it behove us to do it. So here I am. Everyone in the band has said we shouldn't have a speech, so I don't have a speech. OK, that was the easy part, not having a speech …

But as the awards progress all the other inductees make very gracious and heartwarming speeches that go down a treat. And it's becoming increasingly obvious that we'll be considered churlish if we don't at least say something. It's not going to be good enough to let the music do the talkin', as we'd planned. The occasion demands a speech. And it's going to fall on my bony shoulders to deliver it! Tim Powles – our drummer and the 'new boy' in The Church – has perceived exactly the same thing: the necessity of a speech. He takes me backstage and pours me a tiny nip of my favourite liqueur, Unicum Zwack from Hungary. A little drop goes a long way in refreshing your attitude.

'You're gonna have to say something!' Tim says. Yes, fuck it all, I am! The only reason I came here is because they said I wouldn't have to give a speech and now, with about fifteen minutes to go, it's become very apparent that a speech is expected. A speech that's funny, and engaging, and all the other stuff an occasion like this warrants. Slightly emboldened by the Zwack, I sit back down between my mother and brother and go to work in my head trying to construct the perfect acceptance speech. Time is running out as I hurriedly try to chuck together in five minutes what I should've been composing over the past five months. Typical Kilbey, typical The Church. The final nail in the coffin of my perfect speech is Lindy Morrison, good friend and drummer in The Go-Betweens. Seeing me sitting there slack-jawed and still as I mentally try to get a magnanimous and eloquent speech together:

'You better say something!' Lindy says in her no-nonsense manner.

'I will,' I reply, trying to ignore her well-meaning interruption.

'What are you gonna say?' she asks.

'Um, I dunno ... something.' I mumble, trying to concentrate.

'But what will it be?' she asks again.

'I dunno! I'm trying to think of something!!'

We go on like this for a while until I notice George Negus motioning us up to the stage. There are cameras and lights and people shaking my hand and slapping me on the back. Suddenly I'm up at the old podium being handed my pointy triangular golden award; I turn and face the audience. I can see my mum and brother wondering what I'll say. Will I ungraciously and ungratefully blow it? I can see other musicians and managers and agents and publishers and hangers-on, and the merely curious onlookers who've paid to get in. All of 'em sitting there waiting for the last guys up to explain themselves and accept their award. There is absolutely no way a simple 'thank you' will suffice.

So I just start saying the first thing that comes into my head, and I keep going for fifteen minutes and then I stop. Somehow I manage to wax forth, and my words make them all laugh and clap and cheer. And in the middle of the whole thing Michael Chugg, who once managed us, yells out a very pertinent question as he observes all the mirth and merriment my speech is causing: 'Why couldn't you have been like this 25 fuckin' years ago?!' he demands to more cries of laughter.

Yes, that's a very good question. Why does it take someone so long to arrive and be what they could've been all along? Chuggy had managed me during my insular, confused, sulky stage, which preceded my arrogant and blasé stage, which gave way to my ugly junkie phase, which in turn begat my eccentric uncle phase – the one I'm currently in.

The answer to Chuggy's question is perhaps blowing through the pages of this book.

PART I

'Don't write about your fucking childhood,
no one wants to read that!'

– Greg Dulli, 2013

1

IT'S A BOY, MRS KILBEY, IT'S A BOY!

Just before Christmas in 1960 I had a deep lucid dream that I was flying around our neighbourhood on a warm night at about eleven o'clock. In the dream I felt such an incredible deep sense of warmth and satisfaction; I felt something so beautiful, so comforting that I will remember it until I die. It was a dream of my true home, whatever that means.

MY MOTHER AND father met in London just after World War II. My father, at 23, had seen action in Europe and just been demobilised from the Royal Marines. My mother (Joyce Bennett, no middle name) was sixteen and had spent the last five years dodging bombs. She was one of eight children, and her parents were working-class, left-leaning, no-nonsense types. She had a crowded, damp, cold and scruffy war-torn childhood, and was a bit frustrated because she had more going on inside her than would ever have been possible for her to realise in those days.

My father was Leslie John Kilbey and nobody knows much about his childhood – not even Joyce; I've quizzed her on it a few times. He was one of two kids and his father (Stephen John Kilbey) died when Les was only sixteen. Les taught himself the piano and drums and photography and painting, as well as how to fix stuff like washing machines and fridges. He was also a bit of a comedian with such great lines that I still use many of them to this day, and they're getting as good a laugh as ever.

My mother's initial opinion of my father wasn't that high; she thought he was a pushy type with tickets on himself. (Who does that remind you of, already?) When I see photos of Joyce as a young woman I can easily see why Les fell for her: she was quite a curvy buxom old-style stunner. Les was a handsome devil too, no doubt about it. They both looked a bit like film stars – I was always very proud of them when they turned up at school for open day.

Well anyway, I got myself born on the 13th of September 1954 in Welwyn Garden City, Hertfordshire. But maybe you already knew that. They brought me home to their little house that contained my ailing paternal grandmother Jessie Bellette, whom my father adored and my mother also became very attached to, and a big vicious Alsatian dog called Duke who took it upon himself to guard little Steven – yes, they named me Stephen after my mysterious grandad but thought the 'v' was the way to go because people were just going to shorten it to Steve anyway. And while I do prefer it with the 'v' myself, most people who really know me call me Steven, not Steve. It's strange that that little 'v' and that extra little syllable make so much difference.

My first real memory is this: my mother used to give me this stuff called Milk of Magnesia, which I realise now was probably quite good for me. But although it looked like milk it sure didn't taste like bloody milk. To little Steven's two-year-old palate this stuff tasted like a chemistry set had just exploded in his mouth. Plus I hated my mother making me drink it. It outraged me to have no control over my own body. (I resented having my hair washed too.) Having been big sister to five other kids, my mother didn't mollycoddle me – ever. I wasn't that kind of child: I was a bit hard to love, I think. Precociously intelligent. As soon as I could talk I was arguing with grown-ups or being cheeky, which was very much frowned upon in those days. One simply did not answer back. But I did, immediately I think. I always had something to say.

So on this particular day I sat there waiting for my mother to come home from shopping. And I knew she'd be buying Milk of Magnesia. And I wasn't gonna take it anymore! She came in and put the bag down – I can still see the sunshine framing her in the doorway, all of 28 years old. Quick as a flash I got that Milk of Magnesia out of the bag and sprinted away down the long dark hall where I was gonna stash the foul white stuff. But as I ran I tripped up and the bottle smashed ... and I achieved my end. My first truly rebellious act.

My next memory is also a rebellious one. Mum and Dad had decided to leave the damp misery of Blighty for the sunny climes of Australia, where things were verily good and a man like my father could find a future for his little family. We paid ten pounds to migrate on the good ship *The New Australia*. I would've been about three but already I was questioning all the grown-ups' rules – in fact my whole life has been (and still is) about attacking those 1950s British assumptions about the world, neatly contained in little aphorisms like 'children should be seen and not heard'. Although the 60s hadn't yet dawned on the grim post–World War II world, I was already yearning for some slack from the paradigm.

So there I was, sitting up on deck with my mother, when I asked her about her wristwatch and if I could hold it. She didn't want me to because she thought I might drop it but I talked her into it ... 'No mummy, I'm not going to drop your watch' ... She handed it over and quick as a flash I tossed that pretty little girly gold piece into the roiling churning ocean. It was my first big statement: an open act of rebellion and trickery and pure mindless destruction. My mother was shocked, my dad was angry and I was ... I'm not sure ... satisfied, I suppose. I'd got my mother back for all the Milks of Magnesia and shampooing and combing that I'd endured. And I made the ship's newspaper under the headline, 'Now the sharks can tell the time'.

We went to Wollongong, New South Wales – where all Dad's friends and relations were – and suddenly I had a heap of new uncles and aunts. At first we stayed with my father's sister's husband's sister and her husband (phew!), Aunty Ivy and Uncle Chas. They had a son called Ray who had a drum kit; I remember sneaking into his room and gazing at it in wonder. But my dad listened to him play and pronounced him a dud. My dad loved his drummers and Ray didn't have a Gene Krupa-esque bone in his body.

Once Dad was on his feet we moved out of that backyard caravan and rented a house in the suburb of Fairy Meadow. Dad had a record player but only a couple of records: one was Frank Sinatra's *Only the Lonely*, an album of torch ballads that we'd listen to over and over. Those songs became my first musical turn-on as I wallowed in the sadness and melancholy of such beautiful numbers as 'Angel Eyes' and 'One More for the Road'. That record is an exquisite treatise on love lost and hearts broken as Frank visits another lonely place and laments to the bartender or the sea or the trees or anyone who's listening. Lamenting to me, the little brown-haired freckle-faced kid who was absorbing all this music. The arrangements were by Nelson Riddle and each song was recorded live: Frank and the orchestra at the same time. The instruments illuminate the voice with little flourishes and things to help you get the picture, so you can see it all clearly in your head. Frank's voice is mellifluous and suave.

Frank was a real crooner, and that record is so unbelievably smooth. It had a deep and profound effect on me. Even as late as the *Seance* days I was saying in interviews that I wanted to make a record like that, but nobody makes records like that anymore. It's a lofty ambition I can never realise – but in my heart of hearts the *Only the Lonely* numbers remain a yardstick by which I judge songs.

When my parents went to work they dropped me off with a lady I called Aunty May who had a huge influence on me. Aunty May was impossibly glamorous, with jet-black hair and tanned skin and bright red lipstick. She was married to Uncle Norm and they had two grown-up kids. Aunty May was English and quite theatrical and we watched the matinee movie together every lunchtime, with her explaining it all to me. She loved the musicals and wasn't above a good cry and then little Steven would cry too because he had very thin skin and these things often overwhelmed him. After the movie Aunty May would have one of those headache powder things that she slipped into her mouth and washed down with a cup of tea. I wonder what was in them because then Aunty May and I would have our afternoon lay-downs. When I couldn't sleep I would just lie there very still next to her as Aunty May could get rather cross if children wriggled around while she was having her sleep.

Oh how I loved and adored my Aunty May! But she wasn't blinded by whatever charm I possessed as a little kid. One day I watched an episode of *Lassie* where the poor dog became lame. Well the next day when little Steven got up he couldn't walk and it sent his parents into paroxysms of fear – these were the days when poliomyelitis still stalked the wild frontiers of a parent's anxiety, and there I was, unable to walk. Undecided, and both having to go to work, they drove me over to Aunty May's place and Dad plopped me down on the floor. 'Do you think it's polio?' they implored. But having seen the *Lassie* episode Aunty May quickly assessed the situation and commanded I get up or she'd kick me up the bum! I saw her foot swing back menacingly, ready to call my bluff with a sharp kick to the rump. Immediately I was on my feet. It was a miracle in Mount St Thomas, Wollongong.

Another geezer who had a huge impact on me was my dad's old corporal from the marines whom I called Uncle Dennis. He was from Bristol in England and was a radical-atheist sarcastic ironic kind of bloke. Being locked in cupboards as a kid and then witnessing the carnage of World War II had rendered Uncle Dennis a peculiar character. He was my dad's best friend and had migrated here because my dad migrated here and they had a wartime camaraderie that was far closer than most other friendships. There's not a time in my life when I can't remember Uncle Dennis's voice intertwined with my father's as they held one of their long, usually silly, jokey conversations – although Dennis always brought a more bitter side to it than my dad. Think of him as Peter Cook to my dad's Dudley Moore – especially with my dad playing the piano too. They talked about blokes from the war and blokes they'd worked with back in England. Blokes with names like Wanky Wheeler. Between themselves my dad and Uncle Dennis were slightly contemptuous of Australia and Australians, although they'd certainly found it to be a land of plenty as advertised. But they never stopped being English and thought the Australian accent was comical and colloquial and I was starting to get confused about this even at that early age. I felt like my allegiance was to nobody, neither country.

You can hear Uncle Dennis and me on a record I put out called *Addendaone*. Dennis would teach me poems, which I would regurgitate, and then all the grown-ups would sort of have a laugh at my expense. A very mild laugh but a laugh nonetheless. I was never exactly sure what they were laughing at, and funnily enough I don't think they knew either. I was a right little ponce at four years old already and it amused them to trot me out to recite my poems – some of which were from World War I, spooky sobering poems about Flanders Fields with words from dead soldiers' mouths that affected me deeply and strangely. An incredibly precocious pretentiousness was beginning to manifest in spades: an intrinsic desire to perform and be rewarded.

Eventually my parents bought a block of land in a suburb called Dapto, which was bordered on every side by bush. On it they built a modest two-bedroom fibro home (which had an outdoor loo, but thank God it wasn't a dunny can like all the neighbours there had in 1959), with the bush just one street away – in a minute you could be in a world of tadpoles and snakes and birds' nests and among other wandering bands of kids. I spent one lovely idyllic year with my mum there before I started school. Not that my mother ever fussed over me, at times she treated me quite brusquely you might say; she didn't think everything I said and did was brilliant, and I don't think that that did me any harm. I don't think a load of flattery would've done me any good as a child, but of course I craved it then and it's made me try very hard all my life to pull something good out of the hat. Mum and Dad and Dennis and his wife Barbara were a hard audience to impress. It set my standards high.

Christmas in our humble little house was truly magical. Mum had brought her decorations with her from England in these cardboard boxes, and as soon as you got them out there was this wonderful Christmassy smell. A smell of puddings and brandy and cigars and an England never known by me really, except maybe as a wee child. We had all the Christmas rituals too like having little silver charms and three-penny pieces in the pudding: 'Now I'll have to wait till tomorrow to find out what I got!' commented Dennis grimly one year after accidentally ingesting one. Funny how random remarks like that stay with you a lifetime. Christmas night 1960, Mum and Dad and Dennis and Barbara and me sitting at the kitchen table on a hot black Australian December evening all pretending it was England in a way. My mother, more than anyone, missed England at a cellular level; it took both of us a while to relinquish our ideas of England and see the real beauty of Australia.

After the pudding and a few cups of tea the men retired to the lounge room to smoke cigarettes and the women to wash up and natter. Dennis smoked Viscount and my Dad smoked Rothmans – they'd already been smoking all their lives I think. They both smoked about two packets a day; they smoked in cars with the windows up when it was cold outside and I was squeezed between Mum and Barbara in our Morris Major on a Sunday drive. Jesus, I must've passively smoked a million cigarettes by the time I hit six! My lungs recoil in horror at the thought. No one was saying they were bad for you in those days, other than that they made you short of breath. Most adults smoked, including the teachers and doctors and preachers and cops. It was a cigarette-smoking world. Every home had ashtrays for guests to use. Everyone had cigarette lighters but my dad often used a box of matches, and had the unfortunate habit of sometimes putting used matches back in the box before they were quite extinguished and thus igniting an entire box in a flare-up in his pocket somewhere. Actually, a very Kilbey kind of thing to do!

So I started at Dapto Infants School and on the first day cried so much because I thought my mother would forget to come and get me for lunch. Even though I think I knew deep down she'd come, I manufactured a big panic out of nothing, sobbing uncontrollably until I was sent out into the playground to weep because the teacher couldn't stand the blubbering. Then when my mother turned up I began to laugh hysterically. I've seen this trait in my daughters Aurora and Scarlet who at around four years old used to have savage mood swings that included laughing and crying at the same time. It's funny but this trait of creating a panic has manifested itself in my life many times since, and always with the same voice whispering anxious thoughts inside my head. Thoughts of doubt and gloom. Sometimes I wonder if that's actually the voice of the real devil …

At school I was nothing remarkable. Just another English kid with straight brown hair and freckles, neither fat nor thin, not big or small. You could put me in a dictionary alongside the word 'medium' or 'average' or 'normal' … I gravitated towards other English kids and we made the discovery that the Australian kids were circumcised and the English kids weren't. I wasn't sure how to feel about this: it was quite a dilemma for a five-year-old to have! My mother told me I hadn't been done because my father hadn't.

Anyway, one night when I was about five my mother began reading *Alice in Wonderland* to me and that was the first book to rush into my empty head. It made a huge impression. From that moment on almost everything I liked had to involve some kind of magical marvellous adventure, or something supernatural. After that we moved on to *Alice through the Looking Glass*, which I enjoyed just as much: I felt like both books had been written for me. The episode at the end with the bumbling white knight is so full of melancholic longing and a gentle sense of regret at time passed that it was tangible to me. The nasty queen and the forgetful queen, both of them like aunties of mine; Humpty Dumpty, that famous foolish egg sitting on a wall with all his sophistry, unaware that he's about to crack – a metaphor for Steve Kilbey or humanity itself. The imperious caterpillar, archetype for all smart-arse stoner philosopher guys. The hatter and the hare, and their sleepy wombat-like dormouse: they so utterly illustrate the pointlessness of the whole damn thing. How I longed to join those nutters and take up the endless afternoon tea party! All these characters lived and breathed in my head. The book and all its moods and questions and implications blew my mind.

But my days were spent roaming around the neighbourhood with other kids, of whom there were plenty: Aussie kids, English kids, Maltese kids and various assorted combinations that I never figured out. We climbed houses that were being built and leapt from roofs into sandpits. We played cricket and French cricket and rugby league in the spare lots and big back gardens. We rode scooters and bikes into the hinterlands and explored graveyards and lakes that had huge lizards living on their rocky banks. We got lost in the bush and climbed trees and got swooped by birds. We snuck under barbed-wire fences and got chased by people. We hid and we sought. We chucked stones at each other and fought with sticks. We played with bats and balls and fireworks and marbles and jacks and darts and toy cars and toy trains and billy carts made from prams. We made boomerangs from two rulers and rubber bands and had all kinds of water pistols – I was quite a cowboy with my holsters, guns and cowboy hat and my dad called me Slim or sometimes the Watermelon Kid as he filmed me in slow motion jumping off a wall and getting a flesh wound in the arm yet still standing up and taking a few shots at the baddies. We played with hoses and sprinklers, and in puddles and gutters and drains, and with the tar on the road on a hot day.

Then every Saturday a sweet truck would drive around and we bought musk sticks and licorice cigarettes and cobbers and bullets and those little red frogs on a yellow stick that were sweeter than anything.

And in no time I was in Grade One being taught by the somewhat uptight Miss Dewgood, who whacked you behind the knee with a feather duster if you were unruly. One day she selected me to represent our school in the Under 7 category at a poetry eisteddfod at the Wollongong Town Hall. I had to learn and recite 'Foxgloves' and 'Time You Old Gypsy Man', which were both pretty unappealing and quite meaningless to six-year-old me. Eventually the big day came: my first-ever public gig. There were hundreds of middle-aged ladies with bright red lipstick and there I was with my hair combed and my school uniform all nice and clean and tidy. I was standing backstage with all the other contenders and their mothers and teachers and was so fucking nervous I could've burst and I needed to do a wee-wee really badly too. Yet when I walked onto that stage the nervous energy was transformed into focus and I witnessed my first show biz miracle right there and then. As soon as I was on I was feeling much, much better and I stepped up to the little dais and did my crazy funky poetic thing. (I got rated second last, which made Mum and Miss Dewgood awfully disappointed because they thought I could've done better if I'd tried, but nope, that's as good as I could've done considering I hated the dopey poems that had been foisted upon me.) So that was my first adventure treading the boards: hardly auspicious, but there was something there.

When it came to music, my mum and my dad were on a collision course from Day One. I recently saw some very rare footage of them at a wedding, from years before I was born. There's Dad sitting at a drum kit, a cigarette hanging insouciantly from his lip, and he's tapping away like a real hipster. And then there's my mother looking petulant and disinterested on this silent piece of film. My father begged me from an early age: marry any woman you like as long as she likes music! My father thought music was simply one of the most important things in life and my mother didn't.

It was interesting to watch that dynamic at work. One day in about 1962 Dad brought home two brand new sewerage pipes that'd been fitted at each end with a large hi-fi speaker. He added these to his stereo rig. Man, he was so advanced for his day! My father liked jazz and boogie-woogie and torch ballads sung by Shirley Bassey. He liked the blaring trumpet of Al Hirt and the jazzy improv of Erroll Garner, who used to grunt as he played his piano and mumble and make strange noises along with the music. One day my father turned that stereo most of the way up and some of my mother's plates and knick-knacks fell off the wall or vibrated right off their shelves. My mother wasn't the slightest bit amused. My father could never really turn it up again. For him it was like having a Ferrari he could only drive at 30 miles per hour, yet the pipes remained as remnants of past volume glories.

Life seemed like it would always go on that way: our little house in Billabong Avenue, Mum working in the insurance office of Manufacturers' Mutual and Dad as the foreman of all the mechanics at HG Palmers in Wollongong. When I go back and drive around there now it seems so strange but at the time life seemed so good to me: I loved my mum and my dad so much and I didn't really have any problems. I got in fights at school and fell in love with a rapid succession of girls and knew our neighbourhood inside out. I knew where lizards and frogs were, and how many bottles of milk people got ... the baker even delivered then. And which brand of soft drink people drank and what kind of weeds grew in which spots. I was in a boyish dream and life was very good and uncomplicated.

Even the arrival of my brother Russell didn't slow me very much. We brought him home one afternoon when I was eight and it seemed like he'd always been there. Russell was a lovely baby and grew into a lovely kid, though that didn't prevent me from bullying him mercilessly in all kinds of underhand pranks. He got a lot of love and attention and I can honestly say I wasn't jealous of it at all, it's just that ... Oh hang on, I'm having a cry! Actually Russell was welcome to all the attention from that bunch of red-lipsticked aunties with their helmet-like perms. It was all his ... and he worked them well too – he was a very adorable kid!

2

THE DIFFICULT SECOND CHAPTER

I look around me now sometimes and it's like it never happened. Square kids in square jobs in square suits, believing in the same old stuff. It's like we fought the rock'n'roll war for nothing. Yeah, that's how it sometimes seems to me. I guess there will always be the opposing forces of society: the groovy and the non-groovy. And the non-groovy are usually better organised and seem to always prevail ... That's a real shame, but what are you gonna do?

SO HERE WE are in Chapter Two already and I'm putting myself at around nine years old. I'm living in Dapto, New South Wales, and I've got myself a nice little brother called Russell and life so far has proved to be pretty good. I do OK at school ... I'm in the A class, though I flounder around the middle-to-lower end in all the tests. Everybody tells me I could do better and my general 'cheekiness' is usually cited as the cause for getting a C or D for conduct.

I can't help but be the class clown – I suppose it's an effort to imitate my father, who is such a funny fellow, but I don't make that many kids laugh, just arouse the wrath of my teachers with the flippant and disrespectful remarks I yell out in class. ('Fuck 'em if they can't take a joke!' I say now to my former self who's stuck in 1963 and trying to get on with it.)

One night there was a strange sight on the telly: it was a film clip of the new singing group The Beatles playing a song called 'Love Me Do'. 'Look at their bleeding Barnets,' said my dad – Barnet Fair being cockney rhyming slang for hair. I must admit I didn't undergo an epiphany upon first sighting the Fab Four, though it's sure tempting to write that I did. A few kids came over that evening and they were all talking about The Beatles and how silly their parents thought they were. A few weeks later a friend of mine, who was a bit of a boy genius, turned up with a Beatles magazine and I quickly learned who was who and what instruments they played. I wondered what the difference was between the bass, rhythm and lead guitars and thought if I were to play, it would be rhythm because bass sounded too boring and lead too complicated. My friend Andrew was really excited by the whole thing and could even recite whole bits out of this magazine: what colour eyes the boys liked in a girl, and how they all shared a dislike for something called trad jazz. I also heard him discussing with my mother how JFK had been assassinated over in the US that same day, but it all meant very little to me – The Beatles and JFK seemed like they belonged to another universe compared to sunny Dapto and its little houses where we all lived.

That year we had a great holiday: we drove up to Surfers Paradise and stayed at a place called Stuvon Flats that had a swimming pool and everything. But the thing I remember most is that the owner of the place had a groovy teenage daughter who was already a crazy Beatles fan and had a load of singles by them and a lot of other long-haired bands who looked very similar to the Liverpool lads. This groovy teenager said she spent all her time playing Beatles records or going out to clubs where they played Beatles records all night long. I was struck by her dedication to this new thing that was starting to capture the young people and I made a mental note to check it out more thoroughly.

Soon enough my dad bought *Please Please Me*, The Beatles' first album, and occasionally played it on the Kilbey hi-fi system. I got to know that record pretty well; I got to understand John's gruff shouty voice, and Paul's more smooth singing, and George's sweet and youthful sound. I listened to the words and they made me yearn for love. Oh I didn't care if I got my heart broken like on that song 'Anna' ... I just wanted whatever it was that all this exciting sound was about! I couldn't separate the love from the music: it was all some glorious thing waiting for me out there in the future.

I remember playing Beatles records when my parents were out, complete with stage announcements, miming along on the tennis racquet (this was a bass) or a squash racquet (this was lead), frequently accompanied by my fledgling brother Russell who played a badminton racquet (rhythm). He also wore a pudding bowl on his head symbolising a Beatles haircut – all before he turned two. With my racquet and announcements between tracks ('Thank you, Ladies and Gentlemen, this next track is called "I Saw Her Standing There"!') I imagined myself onstage at my school assembly. There I shocked the boys and delighted the girls with my singing and playing and my brilliant songs. This, *this* was the way forward for me and I twigged it at about age nine. From there on in it was always at the back of my mind that I would escape all the drudgery and work and study and become a pop star somewhere, somehow. I'd pull it off in the end. I told myself that so many times that I began to believe it – I had no doubt the world would catch up with me eventually. (Although it still really hasn't ... or doesn't want to.) That dumb belief would see me through many hard times.

One Friday afternoon at Dapto Primary School in early 1964 I was feeling very contented and pleased with myself: it was lovely weather and we'd finished the day with a game of softball and I'd done pretty well. I'd been hitting and catching the ball like a real good 'un. I felt relaxed and popular and all that stuff that you crave from school but was hard to always get. That certain *cool* feeling. I was pretty happy with my lot I must say. That night though Dad gave us some news that shook up my world – we were moving to Shepparton in the state of Victoria. He'd been promoted and transferred and there was a house that went with the job. It broke my heart to leave Dapto, which had been my home for most of my short life, but there it was.

Shepparton was a whole other trip. It was more parochial, behind the times. And everything was different: different sweets, different soft drinks, different schools, different desks. Even a different way of writing (with pen and ink). In fact, the whole education curriculum seemed different – more focused on art and that kind of thing, that's for sure. My new teacher and I clashed immediately. Mr Scott was about 45 and a bit of a painter in watercolours, and pretty good too. We were too alike to get on I think, in the beginning anyway. The kids in class perplexed me too; I didn't seem able to make any impression on them.

Everything was so weird to me at first: they even played a different brand of football, not the rugby or soccer I was used to, and nobody ever explained the rules to me. Every time I got the ball the whistle would be blown because I'd committed some Aussie Rules blasphemy. Like running with the ball or throwing it to other players or ankle tapping and tackling round the neck. Still, I had quite a vicious streak from playing rugby in Dapto and it amused Mr Scott to let me have a run when we played other schools. A lot of kids had never seen such mayhem as I was liable to cause, breaking all the rules I didn't understand. It was somehow good for the morale of our players to see me go illegally berserk and run through the whole other side clutching the ball, even though the umpire had blown his whistle a minute ago.

Eventually I settled in and Mr Scott took me under his wing and I really flourished. By the end of the year I was dux of the class and had done well in every subject. I painted a picture of one of Mr Scott's paintings and he was tickled pink. He would've been a great mentor for me if we'd remained in Shepparton; he had my measure and knew how to reward me and keep me from misbehaving. I think I was his favourite student, though he still told me off from time to time. But a lot of the stuff he talked about, like Greek mythology, was mostly for my benefit because I was the only one really listening. Suddenly I miss Mr Scott and my classroom in Shepparton; I would never have as good an academic year again. At the tender age of ten I'd done my education dash!

After a great school year and running around at large in the lovely Shepparton hinterlands, Dad once again broke the news that we were leaving – for Canberra, in December. Again I was broken-hearted: Shepparton had treated me well and I was much better for it but Dad had been promoted again and so we moved into a modest three-bedroom red-brick place at 7 Baines Place, Lyneham, which would be my dwelling place for the next ten years.

Canberra, in 1964, was quite small, and Lyneham was right on the fringe of it. So there I was again with the bush right on my doorstep, which proved fertile ground to wander in with its yabby ponds and minor industrial areas with all their engine parts and pipes and bits of machines and other things we didn't even recognise. Lyneham Primary School was different again to Dapto and Shepparton – this was the Australian Capital Territory and they had their own friggin' curriculum, but at least the kids were writing in pen and ink. But now the ink was in inkwells in the desks and every kid was somewhat covered in ink and the blots were everywhere. My teacher was a cat called Mr Ferguson – later on my brother had him too and then he even came across to the high school, following after me! Mr Ferguson was no Mr Scott, that's for sure. For the first time someone applied the label 'immature' to me: 'Steven often interrupts the class with a loud comment, which he regards as smart but is generally immature.' My first really bad review – but of course my comments were immature, I was ten years old!

I made lots of new friends at Lyneham Primary and a few enemies. On my first day I got in a fight with a good-looking kid called Nigel Murray who was a year older than me. (It was a portentous sign that I completely missed – this kid would become the first drummer in The Church and play on most of our first album ...)

I had a crush on a girl at school called Anna, just like in the Beatles song (although one they didn't actually write). Anna was an Austrian girl I think. I mean, I never spoke to her – I just worshipped her from a distance. Anyway, I let on to these three idiots in my class that I was in love with her and one afternoon they concocted a letter that contained the immortal line 'let's have a root and see how many babies we get!' Which they sent to her address. So a couple of days later the headmaster, Mr Slade, a real old crotchety geezer, came into Class 5A and grabbed me by the ear and led me down to his office. And there's Anna's father – a seriously full-on Austrian (not Australian, for you dyslexic types). I mean he's got the accent and the look of a fucking Monty Python-esque

Austrian, and he's beside himself with fury that someone has sent such filth to his ten-year-old daughter. I'd be pretty miffed too; now I've got five daughters myself I understand where Mr Austria was coming from.

Mr Slade let him loose on me and left the room and the guy grabbed me by the chin and yelled all this crazy 'Germlish' stuff at me about his daughter's honour etc. He started dragging me around the room by my chin, which was compounded by the fact that he was using it to lift the rest of me off the floor. Slade came back and they both pulled me about: Slade by the ear and Mr Austria by the chin. At one stage they were having a tug of war with my face, pulling me in different directions. It was uncool to rat on people at my school but eventually I blurted out the names of the kids I suspected were responsible. They were summoned. They confessed and were dismissed, but Mr Austria was convinced they were protecting me and went at me again even harder, cursing me in some guttural nastiness … Eventually Slade let me go, though with no sorry or anything.

Then that Saturday afternoon two cops knocked at our front door. Mr Austria had decided he wasn't going to see me get off scot-free and had dialled the police. So these cops came around to my house to bust me for writing obscene letters, and the first two things they saw were a painting of a nude my father had done (painted from a book) and a copy of the latest *Playboy* magazine sitting on the telephone table. The 60s Canberra coppers were shocked: they were speechless! Their faces began to harden. Then my mother, who'd greeted them at the door, pulled out a real doozy that stopped 'em nonplussed in their oafish tracks. In her best Queen Elizabeth II accent she said, 'We try to encourage our children to be broadminded in this house.' Well, the cops were suitably impressed and left shortly after.

As we (and the neighbours) watched them back down our drive Mum reverted to her normal Burnt Oak accent, and turning to me said, 'You little bugger, if I find out you had anything to do with this ...' And you know what, everyone forever after secretly suspected that I did! But I didn't. I must just have a guilty face.

Meanwhile, I was getting intoxicated with rock music. In class me and another kid sat up the back drawing pictures of guys playing guitars and drums and just generally whispered to each other about our latest favourites all through the lesson. We convened after school a few times and did acapella versions of 'Twist and Shout' and other Beatles numbers.

I became obsessed with The Easybeats and bought their first album; my first-ever LP purchase. When they came to Canberra and played at the Albert Hall my lovely generous Dad got me a ticket and dropped me off and picked me up. My first-ever gig and I'm seeing a bunch of Aussie bands at the top of their game: there was Bobby and Laurie, who had a great song where everybody stamped along; then MPD Ltd, who had a load of hits I loved; then The Easybeats hit the stage and the place absolutely erupted. I was right down the front among a bunch of teenage girls and they were screaming and wetting their pants and everything. As an eleven-year-old boy (and one of the very few males in the joint among all those teeny teary girls) they regarded me with contempt and disdain.

The Easybeats were mind-blowingly brilliant. Little Stevie was only sixteen or seventeen at the time. He was so skinny and quick and he danced around that stage while the chicks had proto-orgasmic spasms, or whatever it was that was happening to them. Easy-mania I suppose. The drummer was flinging out drumsticks into the audience and the girls around me were fighting tooth and nail to get them. Eventually one landed near me. Oh how I wanted that fucking drumstick flung out by Snowy Fleet! I went crawling under the chairs. There it was! As I reached towards it, hypnotised by the mojo it must contain, a face loomed into view. The face of a tearstained convulsing vicious teenybopper girl who mouthed these words over the deafening music of The Easybeats: 'I'm gonna fucking kill you, you little bastard!' She meant it and I stood back up drumstickless. There was no way I was gonna argue with that kind of hysterical teenage female when I was eleven. To tell the truth, I still try and avoid it now at age 59.

The Easybeats had an amazing stage show. At its culmination Little Stevie leapfrogged the three guitarists while still playing. He was agile and he was on fire that night. I wanted all that immediately for myself. A voice in my head said 'this is the life for you' and from that moment on I was more or less plotting, plotting, plotting my move into the big time. I had seen it for real, up close. The sheer adrenaline of loud rock'n'roll by my favourite band as they delivered hit after hit. The crazy girls like frenzied sharks smelling blood. The skinniness and the black bell-bottom trousers of the group, the sparkling drum kit, the different guitars, the sound of the bass, the light show flashing and blinding. Here lay a mystery I knew I could penetrate and from then on I counted on becoming a player. I was envious of The Easybeats and the other bands. I wanted the money and the chicks and the adoration. I wanted it so bad and so fast.

If you'd seen me as my dad picked me up in his Wolseley you might not have recognised a rock star in the making with my short back'n'sides, my freckles and my bermuda shorts. But inside the ideas were already formulating: I was in for the long haul – eventually, I was sure, I was gonna make it happen.

Maybe that's why Mum and Dad decided I should get piano lessons. They got in this young teacher who was using a new method where numbers, which correlated with fingers, represented the notes on sheet music. Everything was fine until the day she took the numbers away; then I was flummoxed. No, she wouldn't teach me to play a Beatles song as I repeatedly requested: she wanted me to play 'Marche Militaire' and it was a horrible piece of music and I had no motivation to try. The teacher sussed out I was a precocious little sod and she knew I had some good music in me but she wanted me to do as I was told and I just wasn't interested in playing classical stuff from dots on paper. I wanted the frigging Easybeats and I wanted it right away! What did this jibber jabber have to do with me? So she went to my parents and tearfully resigned and that was that. I mean I kept horsing around on the piano, but I never got any good – and I'm still not. Now I wish I'd stuck at it because the piano is really the ultimate instrument in my book; the one that's capable of so much and is an indispensable songwriting companion. But I was stubborn. I didn't care that my piano lessons were over.

One day Mr Ferguson asked the class who liked The Beatles and almost every kid's hand shot up cheering. Then he asked who liked The Rolling Stones. I shot mine up again but me and my mate were the only ones who did – the other kids groaned and moaned to think anyone would like those anti-Beatles, who'd just been in the paper for pissing all over a service station in England somewhere coz the toilets were closed. But the Stones were beginning to emerge and I was fascinated by Jagger: there was something urgent and primal and all those other clichés everyone uses to try and describe him. I knew a kid whose father allegedly smashed his TV set with rage when he saw Jagger singing and leering into the camera. I was starting to understand the equation that bad doesn't necessarily equal *bad*. I saw at the early age of eleven that the ideal rock star could embody many new personas that were so different from the heroes we'd previously been offered.

Man, Jagger made guys like Mr Ferguson look so uncool! Jagger implied so much in each of his songs: freedom, rebellion, hedonism, ambiguity, sarcasm and aloofness, all hovering somewhere between the Stones and your ear. 'Paint It Black' slew me. Everyone's used to it now I suppose, but when that hit the Canberran airwaves in 1965 I felt like I'd been knocked into another universe where everything was so fucking groovy it was ridiculous. Mick Jagger and then Keith Richards would become on-and-off obsessions for the next fifteen years: I loved The Rolling Stones. At the time only The Beatles or Dylan could touch them – 'Mr Tambourine Man' really blew my mind.

Eventually of course I got into The Kinks and The Who and The Yardbirds and all the rest. The Byrds too, from America. The airwaves were rich with fantastic songs all competing with each other and adding new innovations and increasingly sophisticated production values. It was a great leap forward for rock'n'roll and things began to get really interesting. I sat at home avidly watching all and any pop shows on the telly. And I began to love it when Mum and Dad started coming out with all the classic comments from those days: 'He's got no bleeding talent in his whole body,' 'They look like they would smell to me,' and 'Why don't they wash their hair?' 'That's not bloody music, that's a racket!' All the things I say to my daughters today. I was enjoying the generation gap. And Mick and Bob and all the others seemed to understand something my parents didn't, something that I'd intrinsically felt my whole life, which was that the 'straight' postwar way of life was a farce and a charade. And that something much hipper was about to come along and try to obliterate it.

Meanwhile at school I was coasting along, doing OK. All my reports said I could've done better but they didn't understand that I could only do well in the subjects I was interested in – I wasn't interested in doing projects on the Snowy Mountains Hydro-electric Scheme or the fruit growing regions of Victoria. One day Fergo-fart, as we called him, wasn't there and Slagger Slade (the headmaster, remember? called Slagger because he used to slag on the boys he was yelling at) took over proceedings. Slade started asking us about Greek mythology and was astounded that I knew all the Greek names and their Roman counterparts. He was even more astounded when he found that I knew a whole heap about Norse mythology, and then I really took the cake when he realised I also knew my Celtic mythology. When he asked me to name the four ancient counties of Eire and I did so correctly he was utterly gobsmacked. I could see he was clearly fucking impressed. The rest of the class sat there bored and clueless but I'd been devouring every book I could find on mythology since I was first let loose in a library and had such a proclivity for the stuff that it was almost like I was remembering it, not learning it for the first time. I had an incredible affinity with the ancient world: in some ways I felt like I would've been more at home there than in Canberra, Australia, in 1965, which was hot, dry, barren and philistine all the way. Slagger Slade looked at me carefully: I was an impertinent little git who probably wrote dirty letters to little girls ... but fuck! Did I know my mythology and ancient history?!

1966 came and with it the strange music that The Beatles were beginning to make on *Revolver*. The hair was getting longer and the music weirder. One day I walked into my Aunty Doris's house and out of the radio on top of the fridge came a song I'd never heard before, which was 'Like a Rolling Stone'. A totally new sound and a totally new rock lexicon as Dylan tore strips off some phoney chick with the most delicious sneering eloquence, with his jugglers and clowns and Napoleon-in-rags. Dylan set a new standard for lyrics right there in that very song. Everything about it was a blast to the straight world and all its fakes and bullies. It was a punch in the face delivered as a song. I could never again be happy with the corny stuff from the early Merseybeat days, and apparently neither could Lennon nor Jagger who both began noticeably to sharpen their claws à la Dylan, targetting the hypocrisy of our floundering Western morality and the pathetic double standards of the day. I lapped it all up and took it all in.

The next year I turned up at Lyneham High School one hot morning in late January feeling so fucking sick and nervous that I couldn't believe it. (Backstage at the Sydney Opera House recently someone came up to me and said 'boy I bet you're nervous' and I thought nope, I'm not nervous like going to Lyneham High that first day. That was NERVOUS! This was just a walk through the park compared to *that*!)

At high school, things intensified. It was a lot more violent and I saw kids get black eyes and kids getting their teeth knocked out. Suddenly I lost my taste for fighting: I really didn't want my pretty face messed up forever because of some playground scrap. Unfortunately I had a big mouth, which meant I was often on the receiving end of a smack in the head. My mother had warned me it would be my undoing and it was turning out to be true.

High school also made me realise I'd better get with it as far as my clothing choices were concerned, and I became obsessed with fashion for the very first time. I went through a phase of Beatle boots: I had a black leather pair and a brown suede pair, which each cost $15 – a princely sum for a twelve-year-old kid's pair of shoes in those days, but Dad indulged me. I was so in love with my boots I slept with them under my pillow for the first few nights, if you can believe that.

At my first school social I was blown away again – we had some local band playing and I was amazed at the fashionable threads and the music all around me. Something inside me was demanding to be set free and I was frustrated because I didn't know what it was or how to let it out. I was always uncomfortable being in an audience; I felt implicitly that my place was up on the stage making the music not down there dancing around. I stood in front of the bass guitarist who had a pair of incredibly groovy suede boots that went all the way up his calves and sat there plucking this instrument that made a deep mysterious sound you felt more than actually heard. It was so different to the scratchy obvious sound of the electric guitars, as cool as they were. The bass seemed to me to suddenly be the most profound instrument of all, dictating everything with a rich depth that went right through your diaphragm and kicked your arse. I stood there watching this guy play and he looked back at me and winked very slightly – I guess he could see I was really getting hooked. His sound seemed omnipresent. I wondered how a squirt like me could ever master such a majestic instrument and from that night on I began to lean towards the bass guitar. Every time I heard anyone say 'bass guitar', or even if I just read the words, a thrill would run through me as if someone had said my beloved's name or something.

I was beginning to see my manifest destiny and it had four thick strings on it and made the most incredible sound in the whole world.

The teachers at high school were much cooler than Fergo-fart and Slagger Slade: we had Miss Alexander, who was about twenty and wore floral and paisley miniskirts looking like she'd just rolled in from Chelsea. She had one of those Mary Quant hairdos, and eye make-up that made her look like Cleopatra only with ginger hair. I had a massive crush on her. There was Miss Liepins, the art teacher, who had BO and was from some European country; she too was some kind of bohemian I'd never encountered before. The school was awash in groovy characters; you didn't have to look far. I fell in love with one girl after another. And one by one most of the bullies gave me a thump or three, which I guess I usually deserved.

And guess what? At Lyneham High School we again encounter this Nigel Murray character whose propensity to bully was really coming on nicely. I mean he was a really good bully: he was awfully good at inciting the big bullies to pick on other people. I always picture him as the jackal that runs around after the lions – after the big tough bully had thumped you one Nigel would sneer and say all the stuff he was good at saying. One day a bully punched me down at the tennis courts, after Nigel had incited him to clout me. Well it really hurt and I started to cry so Nigel said, 'Aw, look he's crying ... Bless you child!' Yes, he had a good line in patter; he was the nastiest, sneeriest little bully offsider you could ever meet. (And I, some thirteen years later, let this rascal into my first-ever successful band, despite knowing in my heart of hearts that guys like him never change.)

One day in the middle of the year as I was walking down a corridor after school some absolutely fantastically intriguing sound wafted towards me. I stood outside a classroom in awe. What the hell was this music that was emanating from the room?! Eventually I opened the door and went in. There was Miss Alexander and a bunch of kids sitting around a little portable record player. 'What's this?' I asked.

'This is *Sgt Pepper's Lonely Hearts Club Band,* The Beatles' new album,' Miss Alexander answered.

And after that the world began to rapidly change. Suddenly we were in the middle of 'The Summer of Love', even though it was actually winter in Australia. Everywhere there were flowers in hair and psychedelic paisley, and the hippies seemed to come out of nowhere and suddenly be everywhere at once. My dad grew a walrus moustache and had sideburns! That's how far-reaching *Sgt Pepper*'s influence was, though he didn't like the new psychedelic side of the music, it left him cold. The first time 'Strawberry Fields' came on the radio I was stunned, but my dad simply said 'I don't like The Beatles anymore if they're gonna do stuff like that!' and I realised that the older generation couldn't possibly grok what The Beatles were achieving. They were transcending the limits of what pop music thought it could be, and they took everyone with them for a few brief months there back in 1967.

3
THAT AWKWARD AGE

Sometime in 1968 my voice broke and puberty reared its ugly, pimply head. It was a strange time all round; kids would go away for the holidays and come back as muscled-up brutes. My life was a whirl of lessons and fashion, and falling in love with girls and getting thumped by bullies – and plenty of rock music of course, the great constant, flowing through my life like a river.

IN 1968 WE could choose two elective subjects and I chose French and Latin from the rather dismal choices available – I mean, commerce and metalwork weren't really that appealing to a renaissance boy in the spring of things. But French did not reveal itself to me: it spat me out and had a good fucking laugh at my dire pronunciations. It was like maths: after a while a voice in my head said 'boy, why are we even bothering with this malarkey?' I always know it's bad when that voice says stuff like that, it means it's gonna switch my brain off to that particular thing. It'd already done it with maths and science and next French was getting the chop.

But the voice said good things too, like when I came across my first Latin lesson and it said 'OK ... this we can really handle ... Go!' It was like I wasn't learning Latin but remembering it, similar to my ancient Greek recollections. I had such a hunger that I devoured it declension by conjugation. For two years under the wonderful Mrs McGlynn's tutelage I raced ahead of the class and was deep into the textbook in no time. Sitting around at home doing Latin exercises because I loved it! Finally, after those bloody French lessons – going on about Monsieur Dubois eating a breadstick down at Pont Neuf, we were invading Gaul and laying waste to the cities and our centurions were hailing 'Mighty Caesar' fresh from victories in Britannia! I loved Latin, and it came so easily I must've spoken it in some past life; I have no doubt about that now. But no Frenchmen in the woodpile – I ditched that as soon as I could. Anyway, as I always say, you can't be good at everything.

Strange characters ebbed and flowed through my life. I became really good friends with a Swedish misfit called Stefan Strom. When he arrived at our school with his long blond hair and his accent and the prescription sunglasses he was allowed to wear in class, the girls flocked to him. All six feet three inches of him – he was like a Scandinavian Peter Fonda. But after a short time he proved too offbeat a character for the straight lassies of Lyneham and was marginalised with the other weirdos like, um, me. Stefan had already had sex with girls, had already smoked dope and inhaled a packet of Benson and Hedges a day. Nothing was a big deal to him. He was a true bohemian and didn't give a damn what the kids at school thought. He was a lunatic: one day he pulled up out the front of my place in a car that had no seats. First of all, at fifteen we were far too young to have licences ... and a car with no seats? So Stefan had stuck two deck chairs in there, one for him and one for me. Every time we went around a corner or he accelerated or braked the deck chairs slid all over the place. Stefan held onto the steering wheel for grim death as our seats went sideways and up'n'down.

Or he'd come and drink all my father's Advocaat and wobble home on his 'borrowed' bike. Stefan also used to wag classes and kids would convene at his house and listen to records – he was way ahead of his time when it came to music and was listening to whole albums when we were just listening to singles. 'Teenyboppers,' he sneered.

As I got closer and closer to sixteen my need for my own bass guitar became a real gnawing longing. I was walking along a school corridor one time when I heard some familiar chords being strummed and looking through the window in the door I saw this kid called Don Robinson, three years younger than me, strumming 'Atlantis' by Donovan on a nylon-string guitar while a bunch of appreciative girls sat around him oohing and cooing. 'Atlantis' was one of my favourite songs then – it still is – and to hear some kid playing it kind of incensed me, reminding me that I still hadn't gotten anything musical together. (Don Miller-Robinson, as he's now known, is musical director and guitarist for Shania Twain and I'm not surprised: that kid had loads of music in him, and was very handsome to boot!)

My music dreams were temporarily shelved, though, when I went through a period of wanting to make it as a footy star – I gradually got sucked into watching and talking about and then actually playing Aussie Rules football. I randomly picked Essendon to barrack for because they had the best jerseys, black with a red hoop; nobody else I knew followed them so that appealed to me too. I joined the Turner Footy Club and started practising every Tuesday afternoon.

Again, Nigel Murray hove into view because he was in the team too and cried much derision when I joined and went out of his way to mock and deride my admitted hopelessness. My dad bought me my own expensive football, a Sherrin, and the second day I had it I kicked it to Nigel and one of his big mates, who simply walked off with it. I never saw it again. (And I let that villain into my bloody band!) I had one good thing going for me in that I could jump very high: I was a skinny kid and could leap up in the air without much trouble. In school I'd always been pretty good at high jump and long jump and Aussie Rules is all about players jumping in the air, sometimes on top of each other, to catch the ball on the full. It's very spectacular and exciting to watch – the high mark is an incredible thing that Aussie Rules has that all the other codes don't. Crowds go apeshit when someone 'pulls down a screamer'. (Astute readers may recognise the phrase from 'Outbound' on my *Painkiller* album.)

But the trouble was I was bad at all the other stuff: the tackling, the shepherding, the handballing. I was scrawny and I was a coward. I didn't care enough about the fucking football to get hurt over it; nothing could turn off my self-preservation mechanism, which just wouldn't send me into the thick of things for a football. Plus, at fifteen, some of the other kids were already built like grown men, and had moustaches and stuff. I wasn't gonna go up against that rabble! I was relegated to the B team, and then to be a bench warmer who was sometimes allowed to run around the field for five minutes when it didn't matter anymore because our side was being so easily thrashed.

So I consoled myself by coaching an Under 7 side, and then I actually became an umpire. At 7am on freezing winter Saturdays you'd find me with my whistle, running around applying the rules to a bunch of weeny kids who were only just playing Aussie Rules at all ... Until one morning at an oval in Reid – you read about this kind of thing all the time nowadays but back then it shocked me deeply – a bunch of parents on the sideline started getting nasty with me and the kids and each other. Soon I was presiding over a free-for-all with parents coming on the field disputing my decision, and eventually every bitch and bastard there was angry with me and screaming for my blood.

The umpires were issued with this little card so they could comment on the matches and report the scores. So I reported back what had happened, and got a call a few days later that a car would be coming around to take me to a tribunal! Sure enough a big black car rolled up with a driver in a cap and everything and drove me to an office somewhere where three important-looking geezers sitting behind a long table questioned me over and over about this stupid fucking Under 7s football match. They brought in witnesses and everything to make sure justice prevailed! And there was one of the dads carrying on as if he were in the High Court or something, saying I'd deliberately rigged the match. And this from one of the ringleaders of all the trouble, who said *I* was bringing our great game into disrepute! That evening Aussie Rules and I parted company permanently: this was not the kind of caper I was enjoying anymore. Me? A tribunal? You gotta be joking!

So my sixteenth birthday was approaching and I began to seriously ask my folks for a bass guitar. I wanted a violin bass, the same as Paul McCartney's, because that was the first bass guitar I'd ever really noticed or thought about. In all truth I wouldn't have known a decent bass from a plank of wood; I'd never even picked one up or handled one. I was an absolute beginner. My dad had his reservations and listed off a few things I'd taken up and spent money on and then quit – piano lessons, Navy Cadets (I kid you not!), football, and the Bullworker I'd gotten him to get me at some stage, hoping to give my scrawny self the muscles this contraption guaranteed so some bully wouldn't kick sand in my face if I ever made it to the beach. It wasn't that my dad was stingy; he just thought I seemed like what you might call a flake. That I was 'gormless', as my Aunty Lou Lou would've put it. No one thought I had the gumption to pull anything off, but the voice in my head was going crazy telling me to get the old man to get me a bass guitar. I knew the likelihood of my sticking with anything didn't look good on paper, but something told me I'd stick to this. Jesus, I wish my dad could be at my 60th birthday party; I'd pick up my bass and say, 'How's that? Forty-four years and still pluckin'!'

So eventually September rolled around and my dad agreed to buy me a bass. He always had mates who had businesses who owed him a favour, and would do him a good deal because he'd gotten them a cheap fridge or something, so on Friday late-night shopping we drove across Canberra to the neighbouring town of Queanbeyan where Dad knew some geezer in a music shop. We walked in and I looked around. There wasn't a single bass guitar in the shop, just a few acoustic nylon strings and one cheap semi-acoustic red thing up on the wall.

'Hello Les, what can I do for you? Need a new piano?' said the geezer.

'No,' said Dad, 'I've come in to buy my boy a bass guitar. Do you have any?'

The guy looked at my dad and shook his head: 'Nah ...' he scoffed, 'No one's playing 'em anymore, there's not much call for 'em. They've gone outta fashion. Everyone's playing rhythm guitars now.' And he gestured to the red cheapie on the wall. 'That's a good rhythm guitar, that is. You can have it with a case for 40 bucks.'

'That's a good deal Slim!' said my dad to me.

'But Dad ...!' I said sullenly. 'I want a bass guitar!'

'You heard what he said, no one's playing bass anymore!' The guy looked at me and shrugged like he was saying 'that's the truth'. Dad was starting to get the $40 out of his wallet and everything.

'Please Dad, can we go and try somewhere else?' I begged.

As we left the shop the guy was shaking his head and looking at me as if I'd soon find out he was right, but I directed Dad to Tuffin's Music House where I knew there was something exactly right – but would he come at the price? It was $80! Well, luckily he did and we arrived home that night, on the eve of my sixteenth birthday, with a brand new Aria violin bass – which was a fairly decent copy of Sir Paul's old axe … if you didn't know anything about bass guitar that was. But I was in love, and that bass rarely left my side.

At first I didn't know what to do with my new bass; I didn't have a clue. I bought a book on playing and learned how to tune it and the names of all the notes. But when the musical fly-shit dots began appearing a few pages in I chucked the book in the wardrobe of unwanted things (along with my footy boots, Navy Cadet get-up and the tattered remains of the music to 'Marche Militaire') and carried on regardless. One useful thing I did do was put on my favourite records and pretend I was playing the bloody thing while watching myself in the mirror. I looked pretty good with my violin bass and preposterous pageboy hairdo. Skinnier than skinny. (Actually, this exercise was just a small step up from the tennis racquet and 'Please Please Me' days: miming along and singing and plucking my bass and pretending.) It was within me, now I just had the tedious job of figuring the whole 'music' thing out!

It was like learning how to speak another language or something; there were general overall rules you had to get your head around before you could start getting specific things down. It was hard at first. I had to learn, or relearn, a load of things and understand certain concepts – about tuning-up, octaves and flats and sharps and all that stuff. Then there were the chords of songs and how they related to bass guitar …

For a while there I was amp-less; luckily my bass had a hollow body so it made a bit of a tonal sound – that is, you could hear the different notes in a quietish room. (Unlike my Fender jazz bass, which has almost no sound if played without an amp.) I also discovered that if I held my bass against the wardrobe of unwanted things it was amplified acoustically and I could get a bit of a *bassy* feeling. Then Dad came to my rescue again, procuring an old disused school PA system from somewhere. It had a one-column speaker and the amplifier, which he'd mucked about with so I could wire my bass straight in, seeing there was no jack plug.

I was very grateful, though it was possibly the worst bass sound anyone had ever heard! The thing crackled, and dropped in and out, and the bass sounded like a chainsaw going through a fuzz-pedal with a flat battery. Talk about a duck farting on a muggy day! It was a diabolically ugly and feeble sound. I probably blew the speakers in the first minute when I turned the volume and bass knobs up to full and strummed all four strings at once. (That's an awful fucking racket let me tell you!) And then, after tooling around on it obsessively for a few weeks, and getting blistered fingers all over the place, I began to figure out simple bass riffs.

The very first one I ever figured out was 'Little Green Bag' by the George Baker Selection. Then Chicago's '25 or 6 to 4', which I hammered away at for hours until my mum or dad threatened violence if I didn't desist! Then they all started to come out of the fret board: the Black Sabbath and Deep Purple and Led Zeppelin riffs. The blues riffs and the rest. I persevered and was rewarded. People would come over, relatives and stuff, and ask to hear Steven playing his electric guitar ... but they wished they hadn't after I'd given them a sample of my riff menu. Nobody really knew what a bass guitar on its own was supposed to really be; I guess it didn't sound so good in the living room at 7 Baines Place, Lyneham, in 1970!

At the same time I bought a ten-dollar nylon-string guitar and got a book of chords and figured them out too, but I was never as comfortable playing the guitar as the bass. The bass is like my native language and with any other instrument I'm translating it in my head. It's like my guitar and keyboard playing is broken and stilted and my bass is fluent.

After a while Dad bought me a very nice Maton amplifier; it was actually a Maton stack with four inputs, meaning other instruments could get in as well as the bass. I took up with a bunch of catholic kids from Daramalan College – there was a drummer called Mark Tolley and a guy named Fernando O'Reilly who played guitar. They probably liked me more for my amp than my bass playing, which was blah: we were all just figuring it out. Sometimes we went to Mark's place in Dickson and practised in his garage. When I say 'practised' I'm using the term pretty loosely! We figured if Fernando played his E7 chord and I played a bass riff starting on the E string, and the drummer went boom, boom, boom, crash, wallop, we were roughly approaching some boogie number that those guys liked. They liked Savoy Brown and Foghat and bluesy boogie twelve-bar stuff. Which really wasn't my cup of tea, but things aren't always perfect and sometimes we all have to make do.

So Fernando and I became friends. We used to smoke Galaxy cigarettes (the shortest and cheapest on the market), and we'd gatecrash parties trying to pick up young ladies with questionable morals, whom Fernando termed 'slackies'. One night we ended up at a party and a slackie sat on my lap and starting tongue kissing me like a machine. As Fernando would've said, 'she pashed me off.' Wow, cigarettes and guitars and kisses, I was really apprehending the adult world here!

Eventually there were a load of guitar players and me, the lone bass, hanging out of my Maton guitar amp stack on any given afternoon – in either our garage or Mark Tolley's. Did I mention Mark had a good-looking older sister who dated Tony Hayes, one of Canberra's most famous local bassists? He had a Burns Bison bass with the 'horns' and two big Lenard speakers. Along with his long blond hair and good looks 'Hayesy' also had his own powerful bass sound that I really admired. He had it all down. I wanted to be like him. So practising at Mark's gave everything a slightly cooler feel; he even had this little pad out the back of the garage, with pop magazines and his sister's old fashion mags, where we'd hang out and smoke ciggies ten to the dozen. We'd sit there playing 'Rock Around the Clock' or something like that for hour upon hour upon hour – this was what all the Daramalan catholic boys were into. All afternoon I'd play along to these incredibly boring, lacklustre, noisy twelve-bar jams that were going nowhere fast.

Between sessions Fernando and I would go into Tuffin's Music House and, while I distracted Mr Tuffin, Fernando would hastily scribble down chords from the music books that were for sale up the back. Copying the chords to all these old-time blues and rock'n'roll numbers, oblivious to the fact that basically they're all the same! Sure the keys might change but the progression always does the same thing. We were so naive we hadn't quite cottoned on; besides, I'd resigned myself to playing this dull meat'n'potatoes stuff. Still, it was good to play with the drummer and the other guys and so we played the chords to 'Rock Around the Fucking Clock' all afternoon ... or any other song like that you can think of – and there are thousands!

During all this there was no singing, no microphones or anything. I was gathering from the boys that the idea of singing was kind of pretentious, so no one even mentioned it. We had an unspoken uniform too, which no one dared transgress, though I don't know where this uniform came from. My father used to always ask me,

'Yes, but who decided that all this stuff was the fashion, that's what I want to know.' I still ask my kids that same old question and no one has ever found out. It's hilarious, isn't it? I guess most of it came from surfies or someone who knew a kid who went to school in Sydney; maybe someone a year older who went to a cool high school in Sydney, who was probably a surfie and had his own little pad where he played some electric guitar, smoked loads of cigarettes and had sex with his gorgeous surfie girlfriend. This guy had determined our uniform as thus: footwear had to be thongs or Ugg Boots or possibly desert boots. The thongs had to be white or at least black – white thongs showed off your suntanned feet. Thongs showed the white pattern left on your suntanned foot when you slipped them off after a long day of surfing, drinking milkshakes, eating hamburgers and hot chips and rooting attractive catholic girls.

Pants had to be jeans or cords. Now the jeans had a hierarchy in themselves, which varied from school to school. This was my school's jeans hierarchy: first of all the basic 'cool' jeans were Levi's. This was the base level of jeans. You couldn't wear Amco or Leisuremaster or any other corny, cheap or no-name jeans – it just wasn't on and almost everybody understood that. To be out in something less than Levi's was social suicide; I never tried it after I twigged what was happening. There was an underground word-of-mouth: someone would say, 'I saw Geoff Bancroft in a pair of light green Levi's cords and he looked tough!' Tough was what you wanted to be. Tough meant cool. Paradoxically if you said 'cool' that wouldn't have been cool or tough at all! Wanting to be described as tough, I'd hasten along to a jeans store in town trying to locate the pale green Levi's cords that Geoff Bancroft had looked so tough in. Though none of these fucking jeans ever really looked good on me either: they all had a bit of a jodhpurs look to them, which was vaguely disconcerting but it was the uniform. I'd always say to the guys in the shops, 'Will these shrink?' And if they were already a bit big the guy would say, 'Oh yeah!' But they never did! And if the guy could see they were already a bit tight he'd say, 'Nah, they might even stretch a little,' and they'd always shrink.

If you wanted something slightly cooler than Levi's but a few dollars more you could go Lee – Levi's were ten bucks a pair and Lee were twelve. Lee Cooper were next at thirteen bucks and Wranglers were fifteen bucks a pair, which seemed a fortune. Then one day someone spotted Geoff Bancroft in a pair of (imported from America) Bear-cat jeans, which were pronounced the coolest jeans of all. Somehow I found out there was one shop in all of Australia that stocked Bear-cat jeans, and so I talked my dad into driving to Melbourne to visit our rellies and friends just so I could get to the Bear-cats in some mall there!

We had a great drive down listening to the radio and discussing music; I was beginning to like my dad more and more. He was a truly reasonable bloke. Once in the shop in Melbourne I found my Holy Grail at twenty dollars a pair but the bad news was they had them either in the size above or size below my regular size. I asked the guy if they would shrink. 'No way!' he said with much authority. There I am thinking this guy is incredible just because he works in a groovy Melbourne jeans shop and I'm a squirt from Canberra, so I buy the too-small pair. They're a bit small but I can get away with it. A school social is coming up where I plan to unveil the Bear-cats. The kids are all kinda miffed and envious, just as I'd hoped, but my mum washes 'em, doesn't she? And did they shrink? Oh boy, yes indeedy! The night of the social they've climbed right up my calves until they're only half an inch below being knickerbockers or something. And the famous label is covered up anyway because I've had to drag them halfway down my waist and my shirt is out to cover that up. (Unlike today!)

Some kid came up and sneered: 'Love yer Bear-cats, Kilbey!' This is the kind of thing that's shaped me into the flaky fool I am today!

4
A SUMMER HOLIDAY

Ah, a quiet dreamy moment ... I wonder where the old rocker doth roam in his head's heart? You'd imagine the concerts, the travel, the greasepaint and crowds. No, it's not so. In my mind today I relive a summer holiday. That's where my errant thoughts wander; back to those days of my most callow youth and a series of many first times for me and the things that influence my life to this very day.

IN NOVEMBER 1970 I was under many spells. The spell of music was taking hold of me for a start – I needed to become a rock musician the way other blokes needed to be priests and missionaries (I imagine). And as well as being infatuated with my new bass and my urgent desire for rock stardom, I was in love with love itself. Oh yes, there was a girl attached to this love of love and she was the enabler of my dependence upon love, which began about then. You see, I fancied myself a lover, a player and a romantic; I wanted 'the real thing', which I'd glimpsed in rock'n'roll clips and foreign films and books I'd borrowed from the Dickson library. When I fell in love with love itself, via this girl, I was swept up in a powerful haze of chemical bliss that must've been the equivalent of shooting a speedball every half-hour.

At sixteen, I'd never felt this before. Just kissing the girl gave me almost out-of-body sensations. I guess she was more experienced than me – when she let her fingers roam randomly over my back or kissed my neck I indeed heard music. Songs by Bread, actually: 'Make It with You', 'Baby I'm-a Want You', 'It Don't Matter to Me', are now inextricably bound up with one night when we sat outside the assembly hall at Lyneham High School and kissed. She talked about how often she shampooed her long black hair and I listened and each word vibrated in the air, transformed by love's incredible power – more powerful to me at sixteen than any drug I've taken since. No drug could've improved that warm, dry Canberra night, smelling of the pine trees that grew all around. She said her hair looked better on the third day after a shampoo. Did she realise her words would echo forever in my head, along with all the other stuff that's whirling around in there? A tornado, flinging out random memories that sometimes land in my songs? That's a good reason why it's pointless me analysing all my lyrics. They're not about anything; they're an abstract canvas. My songs are a portal to your own mind where I give you a guided meditation. Chaos just blew through the junkyard of my memories and reassembled all those songs!

Of course extreme youth itself is a formidable drug, according to various newfangled takes on adolescence that argue teenagers aren't quite like the rest of us. That they're temporarily but seriously out of it on some weird teenage hormone that drives even the best of them loony. Well, I reckon I had it in spades: I was tripping on youth itself, if you like. I was a skinny, sulky, pretty boy with a

Prince Valiant hairdo, carefully dressed in whatever the very latest mode was – according to the kids at school who were in the know, or had big brothers or sisters who knew a 'zigger' jacket from a pair of 'Anti-lopes'. Pictures of me at the time reveal a poncy, slightly girly-looking type, posing languidly on our settee for my dad's new Polaroid camera. Love, music and youth all had me by the balls, and one night a few weeks later they collided spectacularly at my first real party.

My new girlfriend had many brothers and sisters, who all had boyfriends and girlfriends, and they threw a party one night when their parents were out. I was wearing a double-breasted suit that'd been bought for me to wear at my Uncle Ken's wedding: it was powder blue and I was wearing the kind of see-through turquoise blousy-looking shirt that was fashionable in London in the summer of 1970 (my mother had brought me one back from a holiday). As I walked along the alleyways between houses that Saturday night I felt rather pleased with myself; I was no longer that awkward gawky kid I'd been only the day before. There I was quietly padding through the backstreets of Lyneham to my first real party.

And that party was about as good as it could possibly get for sixteen-year-old me. A hot night ... the kids (all aged between fifteen and twenty) laughed good-naturedly at my suit. It didn't faze me; they were all dressed in T-shirts, jeans and thongs. My suit represented my ardent ardour. I was in love with love and it all seemed like a scene from an incredible movie. I liked her brothers and sisters; they were slightly amused by me. They were all catholics and moved in different circles from me – I didn't know any of them at all. My girlfriend's sister, who was one year younger, had a boyfriend called Claudio. Boy, he really seemed to know his music! We stood outside on the porch and listened to what was playing; he scoffed at my lack of knowledge about 'album' music as opposed to 'singles' music. Claudio went in and commandeered the record player and stuck on a record he'd brought to the party himself: Chicago Transit Authority. As the record played Claudio raved to me about the music I was hearing. He explained how cool this and that was, and we opened up the double-album package and looked at all the pictures of the band. I found myself loving Claudio's take on all this stuff – even though he was a year younger than me, I listened to him as though he was an oracle. In a flash I knew I had to get into album music myself.

Claudio played me much of his collection that night, including Flaming Youth, featuring Phil Collins before he was in Genesis. I particularly remember him endorsing a really bombastic, hopelessly romantic song called 'Guide Me, Orion': I still think of that song and Claudio whenever I hear anything about Orion. But it's Chicago Transit Authority that I most associate with that halcyon night; it was their music that set me free from the immature pursuit of singles. From there on in it was only the odd single for me – the ones that weren't available on an album.

Meanwhile, the party was a blast. I went to the bedroom my girlfriend shared with about four sisters and we kissed. We smoked cigarettes and we talked. And other kids came in and kissed and we giggled as we watched. People all over the house were kissing and smoking cigarettes and listening to the latest selections from Claudio's collection.

When I eventually went home I was elated. This was the adult world I was in, and there was much grooviness to be had! It was certainly abundant in Goodwin Street, Lyneham, that warm November night in 1970.

That Christmas, Dad decided our whole extended family should have a get-together up on Queensland's Gold Coast. A proper family holiday, involving lots of driving and staying in motels.

I loved staying in motels and in Surfers Paradise we'd be staying in the best, most-famous joint – Ten, The Esplanade. At ten storeys it was the highest building on the Gold Coast at the time. Dad had a brochure and it made my heart skip a beat just looking at that place and imagining staying there.

In the meantime I'd been getting into Chicago Transit Authority, and their second album, more-succinctly entitled *Chicago II*. Over and over and over I took those records in. There were three singers, as far as I could tell: Terry Kath with the deeper gruff voice, Robert Lamm with the smoother mid voice and Peter Cetera (who years later I saw lying on a beach in Malibu) with the high voice that sounded like a male Supreme or something. I kept on playing that bass riff from '25 or 6 to 4' for hours on end till one or other of my parents told me to pack it in again. I stood in front of the mirror and mimed along to Chicago on my bass – all their love songs became *my* love songs. Those Chicago songs instantly transported me back to that perfect party night where there were no children or adults, just teenagers, an abundance of music and passionate kisses in noisy, smoky, dark rooms.

I felt like the band was singing for me and my girl, and my love of being in love. I was walking on air … but it was becoming obvious that she didn't feel that way about me. Perhaps my *idiot savant* ways didn't please a sixteen-year-old girl from a catholic school: I was just another boy she'd gone out with. And I guess after me she tried another one – and good luck to her, I can now comfortably say with cozy hindsight … But back then, as I sensed her slip away ever so slightly, it felt like life and death to me. I loved her and I loved being in love and I tried to project every great female lover of all time onto a very unwilling and plain sixteen-year-old from 1970 who really wasn't looking for anything like *Romeo and Juliet*. Just someone to play Housie Housie with at the O'Connor church hall on Thursday nights. Someone to walk to the Dickson library with, and maybe hold hands.

After the party the slow slipping away began as she went through a boyfriend-cooling-off period. So Chicago's music represented the whole history of my love and all of love itself with their various songs about the ups and downs of romantic life. And then my dad brought home Joe Cocker's *Mad Dogs and Englishmen*, and when I was occasionally sick of Chicago I'd play Joe Cocker. There were some great love songs there too, particularly the gorgeous 'Superstar' by Leon Russell. So that's really all I was listening to: those three double albums. And I knew 'em all off by heart.

Naturally it wasn't easy to be apart from my girlfriend for three weeks, however much I was looking forward to our motel holiday, but I optimistically imagined my absence would make her heart grow fonder ... Though she received the little black and white Mary Quant make-up bag I bought her for an early Christmas present in a neutral way. Her parting kiss was vapid, tepid and insipid. Still, I was under love's first spell; I dismissed her distant demeanour as a temporary thing. My oh my, I just couldn't read those signs!

My dad had bought a new car not long before the much-vaunted summer holiday – a Holden Premier – but it blew up outside a town called Gosford on our way to the Gold Coast. About five hours into the journey something gave out and the car stopped dead. We waited out the days it took to be fixed at a motel with a swimming pool; it seemed like no one else was staying there and my brothers (brother John arrived in 1967) and I had the blue pool to ourselves. I'd dive in even after dark on long hot evenings. Coming from dry old inland Canberra, Gosford seemed subtropical with its ferns and palms and what have you. Deep in the quiet pool, the lights above dazzling through the lens of water, I contemplated love, music and youth.

At the motel, isolated and frustrated by the breakdown, for the first time I became the only other English bloke my dad had around to confide in. We walked around Gosford smoking these mini-cigars with white plastic tips that had a sweet winey taste (he was trying to give up cigarettes, or 'fags' as he called them). My dad spoke frankly in his jokey, cockney-slang way about women and music and bloody bastard Australian cars. He liked a good chinwag, and he often approached philosophical questions with a healthy English disregard for toffee-nosed pretentious types. (Ironically, kind of what I am now!)

One day there was a radio show on playing all the hits in England at the time. Two songs I heard then for the first time were 'My Sweet Lord' and 'Ride a White Swan' by T. Rex. These were portentous times indeed – the music seemed broadcast from another sphere entirely. The implications of these songs gave me much to think about. They implied endless new possibilities I had never even dreamed of before. I still love both of those songs to this very day.

Eventually our car was fixed and we continued northwards toward Christmas and Ten, The Esplanade. I was experiencing sweet separation from the object of my fevered affections: everything I saw or heard made me think of her, and in her absence I began to imagine we had an incredible deep love affair going on and that this girl was 'the one' for me. She lived straight across from my high school ... It was meant to be! I wrote her some letters and sent postcards too. I wonder now what they said (how did I forget that?) – something extremely corny and awkward for sure, quoting somebody else's line and pretending it was my own no doubt ... well that's sixteen and love, isn't it?

Eventually we arrived at Ten, The frickin' Esplanade, Surfers Paradise ... albeit a few days late. And there to greet us was my Aunty Lou Lou. Now some of you readers will know that my eldest twin daughters have a very successful band called Say Lou Lou, named after this legendary power-wielding matriarch of our family, but they never really met her. Here was the lady in question: my dad's big sister – she was ten years older than him. And she was the bane of my existence. She didn't like me much and she never had. (I heard that after I got vaguely famous she decided she'd liked me all along, but I never saw her then so I wouldn't know. It would've been pitiful if my celebrity had changed her opinion of me: we were diametrically opposed.) Lou Lou thought my dad should discipline me more. She didn't dig my groovy trip one bit!

I'd spent a bit of time with Aunty Lou Lou as a kid and she could be quite disparaging. She was good at coming out with random dismaying comments accompanied by a monosyllabic snort or mirthless laugh. She was so unlike my kind-hearted and generous dad I wondered how they could possibly be related. She was a woman of extremes. To the few people she liked she was a fountain of syrupy goodwill, but to a proto-fop like me – and her children's partners – she could be blunt and demanding. My collection of girly magazines confirmed her opinion of me as a complete ne'er-do-well (thanks for sharing, Russell!). 'That's disgusting!' She thought a good spell in the military would 'smarten up my footwork'. She figured I was a lazy, effeminate, rude and ungrateful so-and-so, who'd never amount to anything, and she told me so at any opportunity ... Though you have to admit now she was kind of right! Then, I thought she was a nasty, smelly old lady who I wished would bugger off and leave me alone. So I was hardly thrilled to see her waiting for us with her dour husband Uncle Ern; she'd recently retired up there and was living just up the road in Mermaid Beach. We were going to spend Christmas Day there: Oh Jesus, that didn't sound like a fun time at all! There'd be no youth or music or love at Aunty Lou Lou's ...

Ten, The Esplanade, sure was the swankiest hotel I'd ever stayed in. I think we were on the eighth floor. The sea was directly opposite, but I spent most of my time in the pool; I just loved swimming pools that much. That whole holiday I didn't go on the beach once in daylight hours. I just hung around – and in – the pool. It seemed as glamorous as one could possibly ask for. And I never liked to ask for too much. Surfers Paradise in 1970 was impossibly groovy: it was sleazy, quaint, cheesy, tropical and fantastically bohemian. It had Meter Maids dressed in bikinis putting money in the meters to encourage people to go shopping there. Most buildings were only two storeys high, and there was lots of foliage. Lots of chlorine. Lots of darkened doorways leading to ... I wondered where.

It was a few days before Christmas and people were already celebrating. For the first time I wandered through a strange city on my own, half boy and half man. No one was keeping a watch on me. I had a little money and could come and go as I pleased. I went into the shopping strip and bought a green grandpa T-shirt with buttons. (I still had it years and years later.) I went into an arcade below street level, and there was a jukebox. It had 'Make Me Smile' by Chicago and the B-side too, a ballad called 'Colour My World' with a classic piano line. I stuck ten cents in and played those two songs. A kid playing pool asked me why I'd picked them and said it was a good choice. I played them again and we both enjoyed them even more the second time. We started playing pool. He was really good and much better than me at first, but some strange luck came into play and for absolutely no reason I started to beat him a bit. I also saw that if you put twenty cents in the machine you got six plays so I played those two Chicago songs over and over. No one in the arcade seemed to mind; they all seemed to like my choice of music.

There I was, playing pool with some real cool kid my own age, listening to my favourite band, and then I started to win. It was my first-ever winning streak – I mean I could not put a cue wrong. We argued over the rules a bit: I said if you hit one of my balls first I get two shots. The kid said it wasn't so. No penalties said the kid, that's real pool. There was an older guy behind the counter in his 40s who was watching us play with interest. Commenting on the good shots, commiserating with the kid on his near misses. The kid seemed to be the older guy's pool protégé. Real pool doesn't have penalty shots, the older guy agreed. Nonetheless, just by willing it and being completely detached, I manage to sink a load of tricky shots.

Eventually I ran out of money for the jukebox and went back to our apartment at Ten, The Esplanade. My mum was making toasted baked-bean sandwiches because my parents were going out to dinner. My brothers had returned from the beach and the pool and had had a bath and were wearing their pyjamas. The smell of chlorine lingered in their blond hair ... We were on holidays!

The next day I again walked around Surfers Paradise on my own. Man, I was sixteen, and I had a bass guitar and a girlfriend waiting for me at home. I was dressed in cool threads. I mean people checked me out when I slunk along with my bad posture and my white skin! (The next day it was bad posture and red skin because I always got sunburnt.) I went down to the arcade and, as I'd hoped, there was the kid and there was the older guy. Fifty-cent coins got you a whole heap of jukebox plays and I just kept playing 'Make Me Smile' and 'Colour My World'.

Now the kid and me began playing in earnest; and the loser paid for the table. The kid was humiliated to be beaten at his table, in his arcade, in front of his pool mentor – who told me he had high hopes for the kid. High on love, music and youth – fuelled by the endless mantra of Chicago on the jukebox – I beat that local kid over and over. As if by magic, you might've thought. After dark the thought of another toasted baked-bean sandwich pulled me home and I made to leave that green felted den of leisure and wasted youth.

'Will you be back tomorrow?' asked the kid.

'But tomorrow's Christmas,' I said.

'We'll be open though,' said the guy behind the counter, where you could buy a cold bottle of Fanta or a packet of Smith's crisps or get the blue square chalk to use on the cues.

'I'll be here then I s'pose,' I said.

The next day my mum and dad tried to get me to go to Aunty Lou Lou's, whom Dad called Zulu. They warned me she'd be furious, but I was too old now for them to be able to make me go.

'You'll be in trouble Steven John,' my mother said with a shrug. My dad just shook his head. Eventually they drove off without me.

So imagine me wandering through this beach-shack town on Christmas Day on my own. Man, the implications of just about everything were astounding! At the pool parlour the usual crew was waiting around. I stuck in my money and Chicago started up. 'Make me smile!' exhorted the singer in some hoarse ecstasy. The song bounced along so marvellously loud, seeming much louder than the other songs on the jukebox. It was so cool to be down there playing pool on Christmas Day and not at my Aunty Lou's – across town in Mermaid Beach I knew she'd be chucking a serious wobbler about my absence.

Eventually me and the local kid decided to have a best of three to see who qualified as the true champ. When I won the first two he asked for best of five. When I won the next one he asked for best out of seven. It was just like in that famous comedy sketch, except this was 1970 and that sketch hadn't been written yet. I said it was ridiculous: I said I should be declared the champ now. The older guy said if I was a fair bloke I'd play the kid again or I should get the fuck out. Everyone watching agreed. I didn't like to keep asking too much from my luck so I left my pool hall haven dejectedly amid whispers and some under-the-breath jeering. It'd be the last time I was ever that good at pool again.

The next day was marred not only by my being told off by Uncle Ern and Aunty Lou, but by my father making a rare and unintentional comic slip. He was a real jack-the-lad cockney geezer and had a standard line of patter: a bunch of jokes that got applied to different situations, which usually made all the punters laugh. Real Benny Hill stuff involving all the usual tits and bums – I'd heard most of his gags before but was always amazed by his timing and how he'd modify a joke on the fly to suit a particular occasion. But that day he got it wrong, which I guess is the risk you take out there in the no-man's-land between cheeky and offensive. My mother's brother's wife's sister had come out from England with her new man to meet everyone. It was a bright, warm, clear Boxing Day on the eighth floor of Ten, The Esplanade. My telling-off still hung in the air but we were all trying to just get on with it. There were relatives galore plus loads of kids running round when my mother's brother's wife's sister turned up. Boy, she was a good-looking type too. Kind of buxom and curvy and really pretty. Her husband was a quiet, clipped, muscly little type – looking like you wouldn't want to get on the wrong side of him. They were introduced around the room and I guess my dad was trying to break the tension and also get a laugh when he said, 'Didn't I see your show at Last Card Louie's?'

Well instead of laughing the woman started to blush and look nervous. Her husband said something like 'What the fuck?!' and stormed off into that good day. It turned out his wife had once been a bit of a stripper in England and that rankled with her new hubby. It was a very sore point, in fact. Nice work, Dad!

I needed to get away from these angry bickering adults with all their baggage, and all the bloody kids running around just tempting me to trip one up or something. No longer welcome at my pool hall I drifted round Surfers disconsolately; I would've taken anyone as a friend. Then somehow I was talking to these two guys – a little fat geeky type and a tall skinny geeky type, who immediately didn't like me one bit. He kept trying to get his mate to move on but the short guy had found out I had Chicago and Joe Cocker records and told me to go with them to a block of holiday flats where someone was having a party.

We walked along, me and the short guy bragging about ourselves I suppose. He said he had a beautiful girlfriend in Melbourne whom he was 'on' with. I lied I was on with my girlfriend in Canberra. (It was a pitiful fib and sadly not the last time I said such things, but I think the rottenness I felt when I said it was ample punishment for the stupid lie itself … or maybe not.) This guy talked fast and big: his dad was a millionaire in the rag trade; his dad drove a Mercedes-Benz, which was rare in Australia in those days; his brother rode a Harley. I was quickly impressed.

There was something different about these two kids that I couldn't put my finger on. I hadn't met many exotic people in my short life, but when we got to the party at the flat the tall guy told me to wait outside until they said it was all right for me to come in.

'OK,' I said – but why wouldn't it be all right?

'Because you're a gentile,' he said. Jesus! Suddenly I hated being a gentile even though I wasn't exactly sure what it was. Something biblical, something wicked, something unclean and outcast.

'OK,' the short guy came out. 'You can come in.'

Inside were a bunch of crazy rich kids aged between sixteen and eighteen drinking booze. They all stared at me in my green grandpa shirt and cut-off white Leisuremasters as if I were a curiosity in an exhibit. I was feeling very, well … gentile. And it was weird, suddenly being this outsider in this place and feeling a bit ungodly or something. I was totally confused. Eventually a dark-haired dusky-skinned girl started to look at me and roll her eyes around a bit. She was definitely making it clear she didn't mind my gentile-ness up to a point!

After kissing me for a while in a bedroom she put her hand down into my Leisuremasters, then withdrew it as though she'd been bitten by a snake – very Benny Hill-esque! I realise now there was (ahem!) more to me than she'd perhaps been used to handling. As I sat there looking at this girl, who was looking back at me in shock, I felt so incredibly gentile that I took my leave of the lot of them and slunk back to Ten, The Esplanade, where Mum was cooking egg'n'chips for dinner.

'How was your day?' she asked.

'Mum, are we gentiles?' I asked.

'Of course we are, you silly devil!' she said.

I spent a few more days just hanging around the pool at Ten, The Esplanade. Trying to drown my brothers and cousins, you know: all the things bored, lonely, lovesick sixteen-year-olds do. Then fate rolled a really cool new person into the equation in the form of a blond-haired surfer kid whose mother worked at the motel. He was raving on about Johnny Winter and *Led Zeppelin III* and Jimi Hendrix. We went next door, where he lived with his mother, and he had an actual Farfisa organ with the different coloured bass notes! He could play the riff from Vanilla Fudge's 'You Keep Me Hangin' On' and everything.

'OK,' he said. 'I got something for you now.'

And he started up his record player and queued a strange song that took up one whole side! It was 'In-A-Gadda-Da-Vida' by Iron Butterfly, complete with bass solo and all. And the lead guitarist was only sixteen. Sixteen! I was sixteen and would've given everything to be in an amazing group like Iron Butterfly. We hung around a bit and I probably told all the usual fibs about being 'on' with beautiful girls. He knew a lot about music and surfing. And then it was New Years Eve and I was going out with him and his friends. Little did I know I was about to go to a proto-Schoolies-type bash, a precursor for the herds of wild teenagers who'd later create drunken havoc in the very same place ... Always ahead of my time.

At about eight o'clock we congregated with a whole bunch of mostly blond-haired surfer kids outside a bottle shop where the boys managed to talk someone into buying a king-size bottle of tequila. Then we headed down to the beach, where we all took gigantic swigs of it. Except me; I only pretended to – it tasted vile! Soon enough kids were throwing up and staggering around disoriented and clutching at each other. A third of our original company elected to see in 1971 facedown in sand and vomit. I just couldn't see the appeal. We lurched wildly around the streets. I had a total contact high: not one drop of booze had gone down my gullet. It was the lights, the strangers and the insanity of the times. We tried to get into nightclubs and got thrown out and the boys got in fights with bouncers. We gatecrashed parties and got kissed and thumped for our troubles.

Eventually there was no one left but me, and I went home to bed as the first rays crept over the beach at a very dishevelled Surfers Paradise.

Of course I couldn't wait to get back to see my girlfriend and the journey home seemed to take forever. When we got back to Canberra I went straight around to her house. I remember it was a very hot, dry day; I wore my new green grandpa T-shirt – would she like it? Her sister told me she was working in the drycleaners in Dickson, and gave me a look that probably should have warned me something was badly amiss. I rushed to the Dickson shops and found the drycleaners, and there she was standing behind the counter looking so lovely.

But my love fix was about to be badly disrupted: she wasn't pleased to see me at all! In fact, she hardly said a word. When she did, it was in a high-pitched weak voice as though I were a stranger on a bus. Accompanied by a sad smile such as a vet might give before putting down a guinea pig. A vacancy in her eyes where I was sure love had been ... just three weeks ago! I was trying to talk to her while people were coming in to pick up their dry-cleaning. But I didn't know what to say. So I said, 'Do you want me to go?' Another sad smile and a half shrug.

Miserably, I left. I wandered home with that punched-in-the-guts feeling. An ache began to grow in my young heart, replacing all the feel-good pheromones with feel-bad ones. I was already jonesing for love by the time I got home. The world seemed hot and desolate and empty. It took me a long time to fall out of love with that girl – but she'd be a granny now!

5

BECOMING A GROAN-UP

The years sailed past so quickly, like a very warm dream.
One day my father gestured to our family and our house.
And he said, 'I wish things could just stay like this forever.'
But things never do Dad, and so the story moves on;
eventually it leaves everybody behind.

IN 1971 A lot of the idiots were gone from our school because it wasn't compulsory to stay past Fourth Form, which is now called Year Ten. This meant the violence was much diminished and a lot of the bullies went off to jobs as labourers, and I heard some were even already doing time. Do not pass Go! Eliminate the middle-man and go straight to jail instead!

Anyway, I'm sure you'll be pleased to know I was plugging away on my bass night and day. And I had fallen in love with Marc Bolan from T. Rex, who was my first real idol. Man, I lay on my bed and I listened to the album *T. Rex* and the album *A Beard of Stars* over and over and over. I guess I was formulating my songwriting plans and Bolan could certainly show me how to do it. He was reconciling all these contradictions in his rock'n'roll. He was a walking contradiction. A fey stud! A sexy classicist! On the album covers Bolan looks like a Greek tragedian with his white make-up and his absurd Pre-Raphaelite looks. My addiction to Bolan has been amply documented elsewhere and so it bores me a little to go on about it too much now. But suffice to say Bolan slew me more than The Beatles and the Stones and Dylan all put together. He just turned me on. But not sexually, even though my mother had her doubts about the huge poster of his face that hung over my bed. 'I could understand it if it was a naked girl, Son … but another man's face … I don't understand it!' My father's opinion was disdainful – after I protested to him that I thought Bolan was a genius my father retorted, 'The only clever thing about that bastard is he can spell tyrannosaurus!'

It was around this time I also got quite involved with debating. I'd already been doing it for a few years and eventually got picked to represent the school along with two friends, Bronwyn and Joanna. Bronwyn and I are still friends to this day; she's a professor at some university in Queensland. We made a good team. Joanna was very good looking and had a forthright manner and she was our first speaker. She also had a big pair of breasts, usually uncaged; I felt this somehow gave her authority. I was the second speaker: the long-haired kid with the smart mouth. Bronwyn was third, and she waded in with devastating precision. Eventually the three of us became the ACT team and we went to a big debating play-off. We were representing our state, only our state was a territory … oh never mind! We went to Adelaide and Sydney and stayed in hotels and everything. At night I'd roam through the halls changing all the orders people had left on their doors, ordering ten plates of eggs and fifteen bowls of Corn Flakes and things like that. What an anarchist!

Doing the debating thing gave me a taste for being on tour and staying in hotels; it was really exciting. The second year we did pretty well and knocked our first two opponents out of the ring. But for the final we came up against New South Wales who had this geezer who was already a legend in high-school debating circles: one Malcolm Turnbull. Malcolm was third speaker for NSW and he demolished our flimsy arguments, and us, as if we never existed. And put paid to our chance of being the Australian champions. He wasn't like a teenager; he was already like some young lawyer. It was as though the 60s had never happened for Malcolm – no long hair, no swearing and no hint of a fashionable item of clothing. He meant business. He had a sneering, arrogant, know-it-all manner that was dynamite on the debating scene. Even as he sat there watching me speak I could feel him shaking his head and writing a thousand notes to himself on how he could rip apart our case. He was the Muhammad Ali of high-school debating. The total heavyweight champ. It almost wasn't fair! He was like some big kid of fourteen playing football with the Under 7s. He had more intellectual firepower than any other kid I'd ever seen debate, and I'd seen a few intimidating speakers. I love to come upon freak excellence of this kind; it fascinated me, although Malcolm himself was so fucking square.

As luck would have it Malcolm and the rest of the NSW team came down to Canberra to give us another thrashing, and Malcolm got billeted to stay at my humble abode in sunny, treeless Lyneham. Well NSW gave us another good hiding: it was like a bunch of knights in chainmail going up against a bazooka! Afterwards we went to a pub in Kingston and Malcolm tried to chat up Joanna. You remember she was very forthright and that night she was quite to the point. Malcolm chatted and chatted. Joanna wasn't interested. I wonder if she would've been had she foreseen his future? But she rejected him rather rudely and colourfully with something like 'fuck off', I imagine, though her exact words have flown from my mind over the intervening years.

Soon we were in my little Mazda driving back to Lyneham. Malcolm stamped so hard on the floor – he was that pissed off with Joanna – that I feared for my rusty chariot's wellbeing. He was muttering something like 'Who the fuck does she think she is rejecting a big cheese like moi?!' Of course those weren't his exact words because he didn't ever swear.

Now strangely enough back then Malcolm was a huge, huge Labor man. I mean he was a staunch lefty. So we were driving along and I thought I'd get his attention because he was pretty much totally ignoring me; like an adult might ignore some kid he'd been forced to spend time with. And both he and the kid thought the other was a total turkey! So I said something provocative and somewhat silly and boastful and untrue – the stupidest thing I could think of.

'Oh, Malcolm, I've been, um, asked to join the Country Party,' I said.

I looked over at him slumped in my tiny tinny bomby car, wondering if I'd impressed him. His look was withering. He snorted in derision and then chuckled to himself in a very off-putting way.

'As what?' he asked. And I didn't have an answer. We didn't speak for the rest of the trip.

The next morning Malcolm was hanging around in the kitchen dressed in a kind of expensive smoking jacket and – was it a cravat? He and my mother were talking about grown-up matters (she in her Queen Elizabeth II accent). Malcolm was telling her all about the bad scene between his mother and father.

Then they discussed the politics of the day, and of course Malcolm was a know-it-all and a mum-charmer at the same time. When he'd gone my mother declared that one day he'd be the prime minister of Australia. And my mother was always right and she's still waiting to see her prediction fulfilled – strange to see a problem as banal as 'ute-gate' bring a complex and together guy like our Malcolm undone. But you never know what fate will roll into your life, and politics is just like rock'n'roll, I guess, with its winning and losing streaks.

As my seventeenth birthday loomed things got better at school. We used the senior common room at breaks and it was rather like being in a club. I really dug it. People smoked cigarettes and there was coffee too. There was a record player and guess who seemed to dominate the other kids in that department? We played records all the time and smoked ciggies and drank coffee. All the kids would bring in their records but I usually managed to adjudicate what actually got played and what didn't. We all liked the band Free in those days, so there was a lot of Free. The Moody Blues got a lot of play and the various Beatles solo albums of course. King Crimson's *In the Court of the Crimson King* was another much played.

Towards the end of high school I saw an ad in a paper looking for a bass guitarist to join a 50/50 band called Saga. (A 50/50 band meant you played half Top 40 and half standard numbers, so you were a good all-round band to have at a function.) They auditioned me at the Methodist Hall in Lyneham and lo, I was pretty bloody shaky! But they gave me all these songs to learn and I went away and learnt them diligently. The next week I came back and played and I got the job.

By the end of my stint in Saga we could play nearly a thousand songs, some of which we might read from chord charts, but we could play them nevertheless. 'Little Old Wine Drinker Me',

'Wichita Lineman', 'Morning Dew', 'Hold On, I'm Comin', 'Ghost Riders in the Sky', 'Running Bear', 'A Little Ray of Sunshine', 'Kansas City', 'Imagine', 'Delilah', 'Amarillo' and 'Black Magic Woman'. Even today I can still remember them … and in a way am still churning them over in my mind.

Saga was made up of Ron on lead vocals, who was actually quite a good singer; then there was Howard on the organ, who really wasn't too bad; and Dave, a Scottish guy, on the drums. He hated me immediately and grumbled and complained about everything I ever did or said. These three guys were all about 23 and seemed such old seasoned pros of the Canberra cabaret circuit to me when I joined at the tender age of seventeen. They all had jobs and wives and even kids. They'd traded in any dream of playing their own music long ago, and were just happy to be part of the 50/50 world. For one thing it paid very nicely! The bookings poured in – mainly because of Ron's silky-smooth voice. He could really sing, and was quite a joker and all round jack-the-lad. By day he was an insurance sales clerk, I think. His wife Wendy was very nice – sometimes we went to their house in a new part of Canberra and picked out new songs for our act.

The first gig we ever played was at the university, in a bar. I was so incredibly nervous – not in a bad way but in an anticipatory way. I didn't make too many mistakes and I got through OK, though the others probably disagreed. Dave the drummer thought I was the worst bass player and stupidest little fuck-knuckle he'd ever met. That I was a totally inexperienced and naive ninny who shot his big mouth off often. It's true: I must've been quite insufferable to these serious big-time pros! I wonder why they let me in at all; Dave made it quite clear that he'd never voted for me in their selection process. I think Ron wanted me because I was very young and quite good looking. Oh yes, there was a guy called Hugh too;

he played guitar and was about the same age as me. But he was a very Canberra sort of guy: kind of straight and prissy and prim. Ron was the only one who really liked me – he could sense that within me I had some good music. I guess the others put up with me because of him.

I must've been in Saga for about eighteen months: we played and we played and we played. I got to see some weird and wonderful places, and I got to glean something about music and songs and bass playing. We played restaurants, pubs, clubs, bars, weddings, birthdays, staff Christmas dos, and even in barns. We had a residency at Wests Rugby Club every Sunday night for ages – the place erupted as we played our amazing finale of 'Ghost Riders in the Sky' and the drunken footy crowd would conga round the room egged on by Ron's antics. The crowd would be cheering and laughing and Ron appeared to be enjoying himself, but sometimes he'd turn around and look at me briefly and roll his eyes and look at his watch to indicate this was all just a load of palaver. Finish the gig, pack up the PA, get paid and go home, that was the agenda; the turkeys in the audience were just part of the job. He had no ambitions beyond that.

Well we were making 200 bucks a week out of this caper – I was almost making as much as my father! It was a lot back then, believe me. My mum asked me to pay board and I happily did. (When I left home in 1974 she gave it all back to me. What a top lady my mother is!)

Sometimes we had a real adventure. Once on our way to a gig on the south coast we got caught up in a tropical storm erupting on Clyde Mountain. We were driving in Hugh's tiny Ford Anglia and its one windscreen wiper stopped working. But Hugh was across this possible malfunction and he came armed with a potato cut in half. So he and I would simply jump out and rub the potato all over the windscreen, which would repel the water for about a minute of driving before we'd stop and do it all over again.

Hugh always sternly reminded me how much money we were earning as teenagers and advising that I should behave myself more and not be a nuisance to the older guys in the band. The band had big plans to make the jump from being a mere cabaret band to being a show band, which was like the difference between a Ford Falcon and a Ford Fairmont. We'd be a superior cabaret band on a slightly more deluxe level ... and would be paid a fair bit more to do it.

But what did Saga need to do first? Well we needed a uniform for a start. So we all trucked on down to Garema Place in Civic, where Ron knew a guy in the suit trade. There we got fitted out in five identical lavender safari suits with white skin-tight body shirts and crimson velvet ties and a hanky for the top pocket. We would wear this fine outfit to every gig, this would be our look, and we'd learn even more songs and work harder by having routines and dance moves and stuff like that. There was a band on the scene from Sydney called Chalice; Saga envied the safaried pants off 'em. What with their gags, and the way the guitarists walked forward and kicked to the side together ... Saga wanted some of that action! Every guy in Chalice had his part: the shy one, the stupid one, the handsome one, the funny one. Their show was a fucking *show* not five oiks dressed in different clothes playing some songs.

But at the same time that Saga was trying to evolve into a show band I was evolving into a serious Pink Floyd and Hawkwind devotee, and boy was it hard to reconcile the difference between mincing around to 'Crocodile Rock' and the wild space frontier that was out there calling my name.

Oh yeah, I also had a girlfriend during this period. It's that same damn girl from the other chapter – the one who brushed me off at the drycleaners. Not one to learn my lesson easily, I'd been picked up and dropped by her three times by now. And I'd eventually even return for a brief fourth time in the future! I'm not so sure what it was about her; she didn't particularly care for me. I was just someone she drifted back to when other things fell through. What did we do together? Well, we drove around in my car, and sometimes we parked and engaged in what might be called heavy petting. But my girlfriend was always slightly reluctant in these matters, which I realise now was because she didn't really like me that much. I was certainly good looking but my erratic, idiosyncratic behaviour turned ordinary people off.

The fact that she was always slightly removed also made her more desirable, I see that now. In between my bouts with her I'd see other girls and they were all jumping my bones and it would turn me off a bit. Never really being able to *get* this girl just kept me hanging on and hanging in there, I suppose. So my life was centring on the girl and the band but I was too blind to see that it was all going awry: I was completely out of step with Saga by this stage. I guess they all hated me and my negativity towards the show band concept but I just didn't feel my future was being the opening band for female impersonators or playing stupid medleys at rugby clubs. Although, by fuck, it paid well!

Then one night the girl dropped me, and couple of hours later so did the band!

The next morning I walked into my parents' room stifling a tear and announced, 'You're gonna be seeing a lot more of me round here from now on.' At nineteen I'd been cast away and used up by everyone I hung out with.

By this time I'd left high school and had a job in the public service. I never got into university because I completely failed maths – I bet I didn't even get one question right on the whole paper! But the public service took me in, although I was unemployable really. They soon found that out and I made myself a nuisance I was so unhappy there. I was assigned to a computing division with the Department of Agriculture, processing forms and putting data in columns. After about three weeks it quickly got old, and I'd determined that the work and all the other 'shiny bums' (a Canberran nickname for public servants) were a thorough waste of my time. I felt so thwarted ... so I became a nasty little lazy public so-and-so doing absolutely nothing with the most vicious contempt for my fellow public servants.

Actually a lot of things were happening in my life at this time. It was at this point I became a vegetarian because a voice in my head said, 'You must become a vegetarian.' It was the same voice that'd told me to play bass and would later guide me and still, in fact, does. So all the meat was gone from my diet – usually replaced by my mother with two eggs, fried. Bless her. I don't eat eggs now though, vile little things.

I really don't know what actually made me become a vegetarian: I didn't know one vegetarian, had never even met one. There were no vegetarian restaurants in Canberra, or even vegetarian options. Being a vegetarian was a hard austere slog in 1973! You couldn't go anywhere without some kind of fuss being made. But I was looking at everyone around me turning into blobs, and I wondered why that was. I began to realise that meat and alcohol were ruining people's looks: you see it wasn't health or animal rights, it was because I perceived meat as bad for your appearance. I looked at the geezers around me wolfing down steak and booze and they were all characteristically stuffed. Bloated, red-faced, big-bellied oafs.

So I became a vegetarian. I did collapse a few times, but I haven't eaten the disgusting stuff for 30-odd years now. And am feeling much better for it! And still looking like the me I used to know, albeit with more wrinkles. But I haven't disappeared into a puddle of splodge cheering on a footy game on TV – I was desperate to avoid that scene and being a vegetarian was a step in that direction. It also allowed me to be holier than thou, which is an opportunity I never walk away from. It must be my Virgo nature.

Meanwhile I was meeting a couple of interesting musical types; sadly both of them have now exited this world. The first was Paul Culnane. Paul was a strikingly handsome bloke a year older than me. I met him one day at the record shop in David Jones – I was looking for a Hawkwind record and he overheard me. Next thing I know, there's Paul in my face rabbiting on about every band that I knew and loved. And Marc Bolan ... Paul *loved* Marc Bolan. We became fast friends.

Being a rather naive kind of boy I couldn't quite put my finger on what it was about Paul, though, that was so different: it was like we were in love. We'd spend hours dissecting records and haircuts and anything to do with pop. Paul knew more than I did about everything I was interested in. Hell, Paul knew more than anyone I'd ever met! The guy dripped facts and quotes and opinions about rock. And he introduced me properly to David Bowie: I said I could never accept Bowie over Bolan, but Paul assured me I soon would. He was right. Bowie became absolutely everything to me and Paul for a while. We wanted to do this for ourselves. For the first time I started writing proper songs: I wrote 'em on the bass guitar. I wrote my first wave of glam rock songs like 'Jetfin Rock', 'You're Starting to Make Me Ill', 'Zsa Zsa's Place', 'Igloo Blues' and 'Mascara O'Hara'. I could hear if the chords needed to be minor or major so I just wrote on the bass.

It was at roughly the same time that I bumped into a kid called Dave Young. He was a year younger than me and a great guitarist. We got together and started writing songs like 'Twenty Buck

Passion'. We decided to form a band with me on bass, Dave on guitar, Paul as singer, and a very pretty boy called Peter Hansen on drums. At first we were called Ramp Speed 25 but we changed our name to Beyond Beavers in some ridiculous failed attempt to cash in on the burgeoning Bowie bisexuality thing.

Here portrayed bisexuality rears its head for the first and last time in my life – I was dyeing my hair and wearing blouses and stuff onstage. When I say 'onstage' I mean at school socials and parties and things. I was so into Bowie I wished I could be bisexual just like him ... just like I wished I could take all of Keith Richards' drugs. But bisexuality was not forthcoming for me. I wasn't remotely curious about other men: I was fixated on girls even while I mimicked a lot of the androgynous hoo-ha of the times. Paul told me all these things about queens and bitches – the entire lingo – which I didn't think was so strange because, after all, our great idol across the waters was bisexual himself. It was like a sacrament in the house of Ziggy to be bisexual.

Of course I never realised that Paul was actually bisexual and struggled with his feelings. My girlfriend didn't like him one bit; neither did my dad, who was always uncharacteristically rude to him. Paul and I were certainly raising some questions as to where our true loyalties lay and I'm almost certain now that he was sort of in love with me. He'd ring me up just to chat about Marc Bolan's garden or something and we would talk for hours. He was the best friend I had never really had ...

But when it came to the crunch and our band was going to do our first gig, Paul crumbled. I was scared to play at the O'Donnell Youth Centre in Braddon too, but damn it I was going to do it! When the night came we turned up at the gig and it was packed. We were one of about five or six bands on and when Paul went and looked around the curtains he spied some bullies from his schooldays and refused to go on. I went and looked and saw four bullies from Lyneham High, who I was sure would've loved to thump me upside my dyed-red Bowie do. 'Fuck it Paul, I'm scared too. Can't we both go on and be scared?' But Paul still refused. And he walked out the back way and into the night.

Dave and Peter said, 'You sing!' So I went out there and I played bass and I sang all those (mostly stupid) glam songs I'd written. We got through it with no disgrace, a real power trio, ha ha! And from that moment on I played bass and I sang and I wrote the songs.

And while all this was going on, I had a bizarre other life on the side. I was playing bass for the Stirling Primmer Trio. Stirling was a marvellous old-school electric piano player, with a drummer called Dave who went on to be a famous author who wrote a prize-winning book called *The Glade within the Grove*, or is it the other way around?

Reading from chord charts meant I had to be quick. Playing golf clubs and weddings and the like with Stirling was great practice – we even played the music for *You're a Good Man, Charlie Brown*, at the Canberra Theatre. I sat in the pit and played bass. And when one of the characters did something unusual I had a little selection of whistles and pipes, and I made noises to illustrate it. Like balls being hit in games and people flying a kite. But glam rock was beckoning and just when I was getting good at walking bass lines and 'Days of Wine and Roses' I quit.

Soon I was to meet a very pivotal character in my life. Remember the Methodist Church Hall where I auditioned for Saga? Well the now Paul-less three-piece Beyond Beavers was practising there as much as we could. Dave and I were churning out songs together and alone. One Saturday afternoon we turned up to find there'd been a double booking. Another group called Timelord were there unloading their gear. They were a fairly ordinary rock band playing covers. So they set up at one end and we set up down the other and when one band played the other watched.

When Timelord started to play the main guy immediately caught my attention. He was tall and slim and had ultra-long hair. He was very good looking too, in a European kind of way. Yes it was Peter Koppes. Born in Australia to a Dutch–Portuguese dad and a German mum he was a year younger than me but was already a consummate guitarist. He reeled off Santana licks like I'd never heard. I couldn't understand Peter's deep careful craft in music then and I still can't now.

So imagine, there's Peter down one end of the Methodist Church Hall playing these clichéd cover songs … only his calibre of musicianship shines like a beacon above the rest of the band. As they go through boring old rock numbers, me and Dave Young snigger and whisper to each other. Dave and I thought Bowie and glam was the be-all and end-all of music. Full stop! It was an intolerance that punk was to cultivate a few years later to great effect: to automatically disdain everything, unless it was of your genre and time. So fully justified and glutted with our own glam we perceived them as no threat. Yeah Santana and Deep Purple or whatever it was they were playing … but it was so yesterday. Still I couldn't help but gawk at the tall guy's guitar prowess. He had flair, style and individuality!

Then we started up. And they sat and watched us, probably full of contempt. I'm sure it was an awful racket. But strange as it was, at least we played our own songs. I had that audacity. I remember saying to the Saga boys 'I'm gonna write songs!' They just laughed and said, 'better learn to play other people's properly first.' But a songwriter doesn't dwell on other people's songs too long because what use is that? Jump in and go for it. It's like painting: a lot of people are so intimidated by a blank canvas that they can't even make the first move. Their progress is doomed if they can't muster that mojo to have a go. So we were probably a rotten band but everyone who came across us was amazed that we were churning out our own glam anthems. In truth, we were more like The Sweet than David Bowie but that was more than almost any Canberra band had ever done. The Canberra music scene had sentenced itself to eternal covers long before, but I wasn't having any of it.

Then Peter's band had another bash and Peter dismissed the drummer for one song to show him some drum part. And proceeded to play one of the best drum solos I've ever heard in my life. Totally out of the blue. Wow! He was equally as proficient on the drums as guitar. So afterwards Peter and I started talking and I guess we were impressed by each other. With all his prowess, had he written one song? Nope. With all my songs did I have any prowess? Not a shred. But even in these early days we sensed that we could definitely use what the other could bring to the table. And even though he was skeptical of glam rock we stayed in touch from then on.

Peter was unsure of this glam rock bullshit and he had every right to be. Apart from Bowie almost anything else that was glam rock was just shallow pop with a sissy wardrobe. Bands full of formerly masculine beefy guys were putting on eyeliner and eye shadow, and coming on with the forced 'bi' bit. I think he was willing to overlook the musical shortcomings and see how this 'original' song thing was done. I think maybe he was impressed with my ultra-confident bravado about my own abilities.

Soon enough Peter joined us as a second drummer and then Peter Hansen left and Ken Wylie joined. And we had two drummers ... just like Gary Glitter! We did some gigs but not many. For the two drummers I did two Roy Lichtenstein–like cartoons of a girl's face on round cardboard to go over their bass drums. The first caption said 'I couldn't believe it when he told me he was …' and the section caption read 'Beyond Beavers' under a picture of the girl with tears in her eyes. Jesus, imagine the awful muffling effect of that cardboard on the drums?!

Eventually Beyond Beavers split up. And from the ashes rose Baby Grande. Peter switched to guitar – it was a bit of a waste having him on drums, and the two-drummer thing hadn't worked all that well; they were both just going for it and it was cluttering and obfuscating the beat rather than strengthening it. So Ken became the sole drummer.

About this time Peter and I saw a newish Australian band at the Canberra Theatre called Hush. Hush had two Chinese guys in the band, and Peter and I were both very impressed by their flashy attitude and looks. Peter knew a Chinese guy who played bass called Joe Lee. So hoping to get some of Hush's glam clout I relinquished the bass guitar and Joe joined. He was a year younger than me, and the son of a diplomat. He was the first oriental guy I'd ever known, a nice bloke and a proficient bass player.

The final member of Baby Grande was a guy called Dave Scotland. He was good looking and could play guitar as well as Peter. But he had a beard. Envoys were sent and it was mentioned to him that he could join our band if he'd shave the beard. You couldn't have a fucking beard if you wanted to be a glam rocker – that was obvious. So after a while Dave joined but he was always the most reticent member. Not that any of the others really 'understood' glam rock. I was the ideas man and I foisted (or tried to foist) all my ideas on them. We sort of mutated a bit – taking in influences from the New York Dolls and Iggy Pop and all of that scene. A writer at the time described us as 'screaming gutter rock'.

And I hooked up with my first real manager about then too. She was a woman of about 40 called Barbara Kimmins who'd been around the biz doing this and that. For the first time ever someone looked at me and could see I was gonna make it someday. I almost lived at her place day and night tossing ideas about and planning our assault on the scene.

Baby Grande stayed together for two years or so. Peter left to go overseas and we became a four piece, with me playing rhythm guitar, but nothing ever worked out for us. The crowd never liked us. No one in Canberra wanted to see a Canberra band playing original music. To a city as unhip as Canberra in 1974–75, the New York Dolls and Iggy Pop were still completely unknown. No one played music like that. It was all still Free and Deep Purple and Black Sabbath. And so it's probably more surprising that we got signed by EMI than that they dropped us after the first recording when they heard the lacklustre rubbish we had come up with!

We made other recordings too but there was something awful about all of them. I just couldn't get the sound I had in my head onto tape. My recording ambitions were way beyond my skills. The idiot engineers at the time had really bad attitudes too, especially if you were some unknown kid who didn't understand recording studios and were very ambitious. So I always fought a fruitless war against technical boffins telling me that what I wanted to do was not gonna happen for a list of incomprehensible reasons that stymied me.

Peter was overseas when I started hanging around with a former girlfriend of his, Michele Parker. She was three years younger than me. She was small, skinny and angular and looked like David Bowie with long blonde hair. She had a big mouth just like me and could piss people off real easy. We got on like a house on fire ... for a while. My dad thought she was the loveliest girl he'd ever seen and was very perked up when we came around to visit. He'd always wanted a daughter called Michele and now it seemed his dream had sort of come true.

Meanwhile Baby Grande got a PA and roadies even. Stefan Strom – my old mate from high school – was one of them, and he added to the general mayhem. We played loads of gigs opening for AC/DC and Andy Gibb, and anyone else visiting Canberra. We even played in Sydney a few times. There was just one small snag: nobody liked us.

One night in December 1976 we were playing a gig at the Deakin Inn, and I looked up and saw my parents' neighbour, Rudy Kohlhaze, in the audience. He beckoned to me and I got a very sick feeling in my stomach as I took off my guitar and announced we would be having a short break.

'Your father has had a heart attack and has died,' he said. My heart broke. Dad had been down the coast at a little house he'd bought a few months earlier. He'd already been diagnosed with angina and I'd seen him have some nasty turns a few times when his face would go grey and he'd clutch his shoulder. Anyway, apparently he'd eaten a big lunch and climbed up a ladder to do some ceiling painting. He'd had a massive coronary and was dead by the time my mother and the others there got down the stairs. Which all makes me very sad ... so I won't dwell on it any longer. My dad was one of the nicest, kindest and most generous and tolerant blokes you could ever meet. I was blessed to have a father like that. It's a pity he never got to see me crack the music biz! I still miss him almost 40 years later.

It wasn't that long after that that Dave, Joe and Ken kicked me out of Baby Grande and tried to shaft me on a PA we'd bought together – for which my father had gone guarantor on the loan. They tried to take the PA and leave me paying the bills for it! We got lawyers and everything. Joe kept saying, 'I have no respect for this person!' (meaning me), as if that would get them out of giving me the PA back. Well I got it back and I sold it. I was done with bands. I'd spent so much time and money on this damn rock'n'roll thing for no perceptible rewards whatsoever. Here I was getting kicked out of my own band! And no one had ever seemed to like the stuff I was coming up with; hell, *I* didn't even like the stupid songs I was writing. They were a hodgepodge of all my influences and Baby Grande was a ham-fisted plodding racket. If you don't believe me have a listen to the Baby Grande tracks I stuck on *Addendatwo*. There they are in all their badly recorded ordinariness. There had to be a better way.

6
THE FOUR TRACK, LONDON AND SYDNEY

Even today I know guys who've been playing instruments for years who've never written one song. I guess it came naturally to me. Sure my first songs were pretty corny and unoriginal, but I had the audacity to impose my own ideas on four minutes of silence.

MY DARLING DAD had left me some money and I bought a brand new townhouse in the Canberra suburb of Rivett. Michele picked out all the carpets and colours and tiles and accessories. It was actually a lovely home though I never felt at home there. It was split-level, three bedrooms, two bathrooms and a lovely courtyard garden. We had bright red carpet and stark pure white walls (not the slightly off-white the painter recommended) and black velvet furniture.

Michele was working in a bank and I was doing the public service thing – a complete fucking waste of my time and theirs. A bunch of boring empire-building guys in bad suits being little cogs in some great stupid machine. Fortunately for me there were a bunch of misfits there so I had company. I thought the public service was the most boring, pointless, phoney malarkey ever. And I was a thorn in their sides. They moved me around all over the place but everywhere I went I was a nuisance and I never did any work. I played cards, drove around in a government car, drank coffees at Gus' cafe down the road (Canberra's first sidewalk cafe) and snuck off to Impact Records where I was mates with the owners and got first pick of all the imported vinyl coming in.

You see Australians were slow to release overseas records, and many obscure and arty records were never released here at all. All my records were imports. They were better quality, better vinyl, had better covers with fold-out sleeves and included lyrics, which the Australian versions didn't always have. I sought out records after having seen them reviewed or mentioned in the imported English and American papers and mags, like *CREEM*, *NME*, *Melody Maker*, *Sounds* and *Rock Scene*. When I read about someone that sounded like my cup of tea, I would get down to the record store and order it in. So I'd be sitting at work and the guys at Impact would give me a call and I'd be down there like a shot to grab the stuff I wanted. As they opened their big box of records I would be diving in grabbing stuff that I wanted.

One day, not too long after I moved into the townhouse, I saw an ad for one of the first domestic four-track tape recorders ever released onto the Australian market – the TEAC 2240S, I think it was called. I arranged a loan with the bank for about $1500 and ordered one from a hi-fi store in Phillip just near where I lived. I can still remember getting the call that it'd come in. I remember the weather, and the shop, and going in there and picking up this wonderful machine. I also bought the little Model 2 TEAC mixing desk to go with it.

Over the next few weeks I figured the whole thing out. I stuck it in one of the spare bedrooms with the rest of my instruments and equipment: I had an Ibanez Les Paul bass, black with bright red strings; a gold Emperador Les Paul guitar I'd bought off Dave Scotland when I became the rhythm guitarist in Baby Grande; a cheap Aria 12-string guitar; a Roland drum machine, the second earliest one; a Roland 'domestic' synthesiser, which my dad had bought me to muck around with but I hadn't liked; and a couple of pedals, fuzz and flange – but they were noisy primitive things and greedy battery suckers. I also had a Shure microphone I'd salvaged from Baby Grande and a mike stand and a few leads and cables. I was set to go. This new machine would enable me to overdub. It would allow me to jam with myself as I listened to the tracks I'd just laid down. I could record on track one and then play along to it on tracks two and three and then 'bounce' them all onto track four and start all over again. Sure there was loads of tape hiss and stuff but I could overdub with myself. I was in business!

This is where I really learnt how to write songs and where I began to turn into myself for the first time ever. For a long time before this I'd been writing the lyrics first and then trying to fit the music against them, which always felt like an arse-about way of doing things. So I started doing it the other way around. I'd write or create music and then I'd set the words to that after it became apparent to me what the music was suggesting. I virtually retired upstairs to that little spare room and I wrote and I wrote and I wrote.

Since Baby Grande had broken up I had no social life. I'd drop Michele off at work in the morning, then I'd go into my job, and at night I'd come home and just head straight into the music making. I must've written hundreds of songs in that room. It was my obsession and it was my one joy … other than collecting records from Impact Records.

What was I listening to in 1977–78? David Bowie, of course, always David Bowie. I was also digging a very obscure band called Metro whose single 'Criminal World' was covered by Bowie on *Let's Dance*. I was listening to Patti and Television and all the good, bad and stupid new wave and punk records. I was listening to Steve Harley and the Doctors of Madness and Be Bop Deluxe. I was listening to Eno and taking note of everything he did. I was listening to Dylan and the Stones and The Who. And Big Star and the Raspberries. And anything experimental, weird or foreign.

Michele wasn't really into any of this. She came home and made dinner and when I played her some music she stood in the doorway in case something came on TV that she didn't want to miss. 'Oh, that's nice Dear,' she'd say or something. I must admit I'd hoped she'd be a bit more interested in what I was doing but it didn't really matter – I was obsessed and carried on regardless. At least my brother Russell was interested in listening to what I came up with. By then Russell was fifteen and growing into a real cool cat.

After a while, as I paid more attention to things, I started to get somewhere at last. My method was to put the drum machine on and jam with that even if it was something simple. I'd start on bass or a 12-string or synth (which was a monophonic; it could only play one note at a time) or electric guitar. It didn't matter how I started, I always finished up with some good result. And from this I learnt to persevere with music and not give up on something immediately.

Of the hundreds of songs I recorded, only a fragment remain. Every song was 'mastered' onto a cassette and the cassettes broke and accumulated mould and they warped and all that. You can hear some of them on various bootlegs and on my own *Addendaone*. I had no reverb but I got a slap-back echo by putting the machine out of synch with itself. I learnt how to double track my voice and all about octave harmonies. I learnt about the pointillist method of making music – just one small thing at a time … and making use of every available minute in that spare room.

Eventually I wrote a song called 'Chrome Injury', which bears some resemblance to the 'Chrome Injury' on The Church's first album. Even Michele came by my room and said, 'That's good!' So I was making all this groovy music and I was convinced only the English press would like me and understand how tricky I was and lo, I decided I had to go to England. So I got three months off work with no pay (the bastards!) and me and Michele went off to England. We got married first, and when we arrived in London I thought this was truly where I wanted to be. I was thinking, why did my parents move me away from here? I immediately had my old childhood cockney accent back overnight (once again, check *Addendaone* for confirmation of said accent at age five!), and I lapped up the fashion and haircuts and the incredible feeling of being where the action was.

Michele and I stayed in London for a few weeks in some low-rent Australia Club place but I didn't want to hang around with Aussies. We hired a tiny gutless Renault and drove around Britain all the way up to Scotland, which was forlorn and bleak in some parts and filled me with some gloomy thoughts. We drove through Wales and Devon and Cornwall and went to all the big cities and saw castles and cathedrals and all that sort of thing. Michele was a good companion, cheerful with a good sense of humour. She was looking at the fashion and thinking about doing it back in Australia. We had a good time mostly, but sometimes I was sad to note that two could feel more lonely than one.

Eventually we rented a horrible bedsit in a run-down big old house in some crumbling bit of Kensington; I've forgotten the name of the street now. It was a dark, damp, dank, squalid, unappealing hole that cost a small fortune. Every night this woman would vacuum upstairs at 3am and it sounded like a construction site. She'd wash up and argue with her husband in screeching Spanish while he cursed and bullied her, all in the wee small hours. His name was Tony del Toro, and when we complained he said 'I am the bull!'

In London we went to see gigs and we saw some great ones: Japan at the Music Machine were brilliant. I learnt something that night listening to 'Obscure Alternatives', something about the chords all changing around the bass. They had some truly transcendent moments. We went to the Marquee Club and saw an amazingly good band called Dead Fingers Talk (a William Burroughs title). The lead guy Bobo Phoenix was a real star in a Lou Reed kind of way. I already had their album *Storm the Reality Studios*, produced by former Spider from Mars Mick Ronson.

Bobo was a great performer too and even dressed up for a song I think was called 'Harry' – strange it never got released because it was the band's most popular tune. We also saw Brian James from The Damned in a band called Tanz der Youth. We saw Cabaret Voltaire and the Doctors of Madness's last ever gig, again at the Music Machine. They had a great tape too of Kid Strange introducing them – that really impressed me. TV Smith from the Adverts came out and sung some numbers. Boy it was exciting! The Doctors blew me away, and left me elevated like Japan had. I focused on what it was that I liked about their music and what methods they used to achieve that effect on me.

I was really beginning to turn into a little song-computing machine. Going over and over songs in my mind, picking them apart aspect by aspect, I began to see the mechanics of songs: strengths, weaknesses and sometimes the paradox of the weakness transmuted to strength. I listened in on the inner workings, the small sounds of tambourines and whispers. I took apart all the things that held it together, and I marvelled at the way small things could mean so much in music – like a little violin or a distant guitar or some hazy voices drifting over a lazy song.

One night we went to see a band called The Only Ones at some big gig in London. The place was packed to the rafters. I really loved The Only Ones' first two records and their indie single with Vengeance Records called 'Lovers of Today'. We grabbed a table and sat down early. A couple in their 70s asked if they could sit with us. The man was English with a really nice posh accent and the woman was Austrian or something. It turned out they were the parents of the lead singer and songwriter, Peter Perrett. We became very chatty with them and they told us all about Peter. After the gig they drove us back to our flat in their white Jaguar, or maybe it was a Daimler. They even gave us their phone number and I had visions of me and PP meeting up and writing songs together and stuff. I held on to the phone number for a month but was too nervous to call and try to set up a meeting. Eventually Michele rang 'em up, but we'd left it too long and the conversation fizzled out and we didn't get invited around to PP's parents' house where he still lived apparently. The Only Ones were extremely disappointing live; I was far more interested in chatting to the old mum and dad. But we got some great Only Ones merch with the rose and the barbed-wire T-shirts!

While I was in London I bought a book that contained the names and addresses of every record company in England. So I had brought like 50 cassettes of songs with me and I sent them all out. And they all came back with the usual letter: 'Sorry we do not feel this type of music suits our roster but thank you for sending it.' Not one encouraging word from one person! My illusion of the English accepting me was well and truly shattered. I was a no one in London, hanging around in a pigsty bedsit in Kensington, trying to get involved in something, anything. London was a great big uncaring, dirty, tatty place with a few glamorous bits and a load of sordid rotten ugly bits. It was laughably expensive and I couldn't find a way in. I had a nice house back in Australia and winter was coming on. The bedsit was shabby and threadbare and worse than all that it was *cold.* Even as you were having a bath or shower in the communal bathroom you had to feed the meter with ten-pence pieces! It was truly bullshit.

So we flew back to Canberra where we tried to big-note ourselves with all our London punk fashion. But still no one was interested! We marched around Garema Place in our zip-up shirts and snakeskin print Mod-Z Art pants, tottering about on our brothel creepers, me with dyed jet-black hair – which looked stupid and all fell out leaving me fearing I'd gone prematurely bald. But no one looked let alone understood what we were supposed to be.

I joined a band in Canberra called Tactics for five minutes until they kicked me back out. They were an awful racket with a guy called Dave with a squeaky voice who was trying to sing like Neil Young, but it was truly fingernails on the blackboard stuff. I was a total jumped-up turkey and Dave was a hopelessly untalented singer and writer with big pretensions to something … but what that was eluded me entirely. After they kicked me out Tactics moved to Sydney where they achieved some notoriety and even got played on the radio a bit. As soon as I got slightly famous Dave of the screechy voice was all over everything saying how he'd kicked me out of his hipper-than-thou band. He must've been fucking writhing in paroxysms of envy! It warmed the very cockles of my heart.

Stuck in Canberra, in the public service and with zero admirers of my music, I was in a really bad place. But there was a faint light up ahead. Michele had been thinking about clothes and fashion and printing and stuff. So she bought a sewing machine and I bought some silk-screening things and we set off to do our own line of clothes. Everyone said it couldn't be done, but while I mucked around in my studio getting it together Michele mucked around on her sewing machine. And we figured out simple silk-screening together. We made about a hundred T-shirts printed with all the hip punk stuff we'd seen or bought in London – like Andy Warhol's *Marilyn* prints, pictures of Keith with 'junkie' written in lurid green paint, album covers and stuff like that. We went to a big market stall in Canberra and sold a big fat nothing! No one even looked at our hip punk T-shirts. No one! It was as if we were invisible. What the fuck were we supposed to do? London had rejected us, Canberra had rejected us. Michele had one last suggestion: Sydney.

I'd always had a very funny relationship with Sydney. Melbourne I'd always liked but Sydney seemed like the biggest, hardest, fastest city I could imagine. It frightened me. The few times I'd been there I felt dwarfed. I wasn't optimistic that Sydney would take us in but Michele knew of the Paddington Markets, which were situated around a church in Sydney's eastern suburbs. So one night after work we chucked all our T-shirts and the clothes she was making in our car, and did the five-hour drive to Sydney, stopping only for cheese and asparagus toasted sandwiches in Mittagong on the way. We arrived at Michele's grandmother's house late that night and rose very, very early the next day to drive to the Uniting Church in Paddington. We got in a queue for 'casuals' and waited to be allotted a stall. How we envied the 'permanents' who were already setting up out there assured of their places! Luckily we got a spot ... and by the end of the day we'd sold twelve T-shirts and made a bunch of friends. Which was weird because we didn't have any friends in Canberra. We drove back thoughtfully that afternoon, knowing we'd have to leave our spacious townhouse in Canberra for Sydney's grimier ambience.

My final year in Canberra was a strange time. I'd put on some weight in England so I began to jog around Lake Burley Griffin every lunchtime. Every day a Japanese guy came running the other way. And he'd communicate with me as he ran past, letting me know how his run was going. A shrug or a smile a grunt or a grim stare would be enough and would speak volumes to me. I felt like I had known this guy all my life.

After the run I'd have a shower and note the wonderful effect of those bloody endorphins kicking in as I sat back down in the office. Having demonstrated my disdain for the public service I was pretty much left alone and got away with doing hardly any work. Instead I read the *Illuminatus! Trilogy* and wrote song lyrics and even phoned some of my new pals in Sydney to talk. I ran around the lake every day and on Friday nights we'd drive up to Sydney, where we stayed with the grandmother and got up early to go to the Paddington Markets.

We started to get an identity there. We were 'that young couple from Canberra'. I was 23 and Michele just twenty. 'Those kids', some fashionista at the markets once called us. People were buying our T-shirts and talking about the big Sloppy Joes Michele was making. We had friends and a reason to exist. People in Sydney rated us! They liked our clothes and also the cassettes I began to make. Finally we put our spacious red-and-white Canberra townhouse on the market and gave notice at our jobs.

At the same time, marijuana began to rear its trippy head. Quite formidably too. Soon it would become a permanent habit. I'd been smoking weed on and off for a few years but I'd never completely cottoned on to what was so damn great about it. Then I got into smoking pot and listening to *Dark Side of the Moon* stuff, listening to records, going 'whoa, trippy man!' and having these almost acid-like trips.

It was around 1978 that I began to realise that me and weed had a truly special relationship. It's a delusion that many poor druggies fall under and, no doubt, many of my readers will shake their heads and tut tut tut and all that. But me and weed go back a long way now and the stuff rarely lets me down. I remember so clearly the night I realised how weed could be the answer to every question I asked. We'd just gotten back to Canberra after the long, arduous drive from Sydney. I was wired and nauseous and anxious about everything in my life. Could I really leave my safe little townhouse for the sordid streets of Sydney? I got into bed but I could feel something like a panic attack coming on. I went and sat in our living room and a voice told me to roll a joint. As the first sweet hit entered my lungs a feeling of wellbeing swept over me: my troubles melted away. I'd found a haven within my own mind. I picked up a guitar and strummed a boring old C chord. Suddenly, a world of sonic possibilities opened up. The panic and anxiety slipped away so I went up to my studio and knocked out a few songs on the spot, even more effortlessly than before. The pot was rewiring my brain and I was coming up with all kinds of new things.

I was mightily impressed with pot's ability to amplify my creativity. It did it then and it still does it now. I don't care about the law or the morals or what anyone thinks about it; I've written over a thousand songs on pot. It's working for me, I tell you that. If I wanna paint a picture or even write my frickin' memoirs, I smoke a joint. I don't sit around watching TV, eating toast and guzzling sodas. I don't play video games and I don't go crazy on the weed either. I work. Hard. Pot is my companion: the joker in the pack.

Could I have done all this without pot? Sure, but pot made it a lot easier and a lot more fun. I can't see that changing either. I'll be smoking as long as I'm creating. It's worked pretty well so far – I knocked out every one of those songs you like!

But kids, don't do this at home! I don't believe pot is good for young minds. I was lucky that I was about 22 when I seriously started smoking weed every day. I even smoked it at work ... and then wrote a computer program to write poetry. Unfortunately the big boss caught me and closed it down before I got too many poems done. And so I finished out my 'daze' in the public service stoned out on endorphins from running and from visits to my car for a quick puff! What a caper!

After we sold our place in Canberra, Michele and I got a place in Rozelle in Sydney's inner west. It was a bleak industrial landscape of disused power stations and little terraced houses all blackened in soot and other nasty stuff. I felt this would give me some grimy authenticity. Here I magically changed from pudgy public servant to skinny urban poet and fixer of coolness. Our place was a dark and dingy two-storey house with a tiny back garden, a filthy old blackened fireplace and an even filthier basement that flooded in the rain. It smelt of mould, and there were cockroaches, mosquitoes and flies and fleas. It was a long way from our roomy split-level in Canberra.

I silk-screened under the house while Michele sewed like the clappers upstairs. In some ways we were already drifting apart; I really admired her 'savage' work ethic but she was very bossy and hardline. She didn't really care about my music: she was focused on sewing and designing and paying the bills.

One day we went out to a material shop and Michele bought up cheap all these little offcuts of this terry towelling material and asked me to silk-screen something different on each bit. Then she took those bits and sewed 'em up into these new Sloppy Joes. Each one was totally unique. And bang! They sold like hot cakes. We were even selling to big fashion shops in Sydney like Black Vanity.

Life began to get faster and stranger for me in Sydney. We'd take LSD and roam through the Callan Park loony bin, which was still operating back then. We'd work on our clothes and drive around Sydney buying material and delivering the clothes. I snorted coke and tried pills. I made lots of new friends who'd all pile over to my house every Saturday night after the markets. We'd smoke dope, and I'd play my new friends the music I was working on. And for the first time ever people were beginning to see that maybe I was on the right track after all.

I covered the walls of my front room studio with pictures from magazines: a wallpaper of weird scenes. And with and without an audience I banged out even more songs that were steadily improving all the time. Many of the songs on the first Church album were written there in a mad prolific rush. But what could I do with all that on my own?

And then one afternoon Peter Koppes walked by our stall at Paddington Markets. He had another guy with him who turned out to be Nigel Murray, who was now calling himself Nick Ward. Remember the bully-kid from my school? He'd taken the name of one of his main victims (a big, strange-looking kid with a weird head). That was the real Nick Ward. Anyway, Nigel/Nick wandered off contemptuously when he realised who I was.

It turned out Peter was in a band called Limazine and Nick was their drummer. They were based in Sydney but included a bunch of old Canberra boys, like Mike Hamer, who was actually a very good singer. Limazine were doing OK; they had gigs and had even been to Melbourne and Adelaide. I admit I was envious. Melbourne and Adelaide? Wow! What lucky devils. I talked Peter into coming over to check out my new recordings and very soon we started re-recording some of them with Peter playing guitar. Man, that cat could reinterpret my songs and have 'em come out all improved. This time we knew we were onto something; we could hear it in the songs. This was the true genesis of all the ideas that would become The Church as you know and hopefully love it. It sounded good!

7
THE CHURCH OF MAN, LOVE

Sydney, 1980. Such a long way from the sterility of Canberra. Suddenly I felt like I was finally part of something. Live music was exploding; there were gigs left, right and centre every night of the week. The pubs and clubs had flung open their doors and the place was rocking! I had popped up at the right time.

I DECIDED TO CALL the band The Church for a load of reasons. We picked the name from a long list of names, including Nylon Choir and The Satin Odyssey – imagine that?! But mainly I think that I really wanted to create a feeling of spirit, although I wouldn't have put it in those terms in those days. And of course there was the David Bowie reference from Ziggy Stardust.

The Church's first rehearsal was pretty damn good. I loved hearing the songs out loud with a drummer and another guitarist playing along. Nick's drumming wasn't bad and Peter was already playing the way he plays now. He had his sound and his style and his schtick. We didn't sound a hundred miles away from what would become the Church sound of today. For the first time I could see the possibility of something eventuating from all this.

After a few more rehearsals we did our first few gigs. Nick hadn't changed – he was still Nigel! He could vaguely see I was a good songwriter but he couldn't get over the fact that he was 'taking orders' from a guy he could easily beat in a fight with one hand tied behind his back. I mean I'd ask him to play something and he'd kind of snarl at me like he was only just controlling his urge to give me a good smack around the head like in the old days at Lyneham High. His agenda was still intimidation. And it still worked.

Even though I'd started the band, Nick's behaviour made me dread rehearsals. He made my life miserable. He nagged me, bullied me and sneered at me. It was like fucking Groundhog Day and I was carting this permanent high-school melodrama around with me. He was a truly rude and obnoxious sod. Still, we managed to do gigs. Someone mentioned Cream so I got a frilly shirt. I think Peter did too. Not Nick though. He had his cut-off black T-shirt so the world could see his tattoo of the axe man lifting his bloody axe and saying 'Next?'

How were we as a three piece? Not that bad! We were playing in some club one night and a load of Peter's friends came down to see us. Among them was Lucy and her young husband Marty fresh off the plane from England. We were all sitting backstage when they walked in – Marty was about 22 and had a tiger-skin jacket, tight black jeans, gym boots and long crimped hair. He looked like a missing member of Def Leppard. We chatted for about half an hour and then I asked him to join the band. He said yes.

Peter was bemused I'd asked a guy to join the band without hearing him play, but Nick was absolutely incensed. How dare I fuckin' ask some unknown, untested wimp into our band because I liked his fuckin' looks?! But I'd seen into the future and I knew Marty would help get this thing off the ground. Even if he couldn't play the guitar … he looked like he could! Anyway, fortunately he could play the guitar. He wasn't amazing but we already had Peter to play amazing stuff.

Peter was neither thrilled nor unhappy about Marty. He just got on with it. Peter and Marty famously have different styles and parts because Peter never interfered or gave advice on what Marty should play. When Marty asked him what the chords and parts were apparently Peter responded, 'I had to work all this out for myself, so why don't you work it all out for yourself too?' From that day on Marty sorted himself out for parts and things to play. And up sprang The Church's marvellous two-pronged guitar attack. Peter and Marty never wondered what the other was doing, they just fell in together, naturally.

Another good thing about Marty was Nick couldn't stand him, so it took the heat off me a bit. From the first day Marty showed up Nick made his life a bloody misery. Funnily enough we both just accepted this behaviour; as though always being nervous and flinching and on the defensive was just how it was in a band.

Still, we carried on. Nick had a four-track machine the same as mine. We all figured we could do some fancy overdubbing with the two machines together. We recorded some backing tracks at a four-track studio in town and fled with the tapes to Nick's garage where he lived on Forest Knoll Avenue in Bondi (which is just down from where I am writing at this very moment).

The songs we demoed included a couple that would end up on our first record: 'Chrome Injury' was on there I remember. They were pretty good; I felt sure that whoever heard this stuff would like it – it was new wave and old school at the same time. Peter was already doing his echoey chorus thang. Marty was jingle-jangling a bit. I was doing sing speak and playing a fretless bass for some stupid reason. I mean, the fretless looked good and sometimes sounded good but my singing must've been out of tune a lot playing that thing. I must have been always a little bit sharp or flat. But people were impressed and that was the main objective, in my books at least, in those days.

Peter wasted no time in taking the tape to a guy called Chris Gilbey who'd starting managing the record company ATV/Northern Songs in Australia. Chris'd had a bit of a colourful career and had managed The Saints for a while. Now he had these nice offices in North Sydney and his brother-in-law working for him. Legend has it that Peter took the tape to the office but Chris was too busy to listen to it so Don Bruner, the brother-in-law, piped up and said, 'Come into my office, I'll listen to it.' After a few minutes Gilbey asked what the music was coming through the wall. It was The Church.

The next day I went in to see Chris and walked out of there with my head swirling around. I had no idea songwriters got their own payments or did their own separate deals – I hadn't been writing songs for money; I'd had no idea that's where all the money was!

Gilbey was a great motivational music-biz guy. He had a great sense of humour and was fun to be with most of the time. And he could see I had the potential to write a good tune so he nurtured my talent and gave me some guidance. But my initial deal with him was totally fucked up and set the precedent for most of the rest of the deals I ever did. I got a $500 advance and we shared the songwriting split 50/50. It'd be hard to find a worse deal unless you go back to the Tin Pan Alley days – not that I knew that at the time. Anyway, I spent my advance on a garbage bag full of marijuana I bought from a horticulturist called Rod from Hurstville.

For those oblivious to the music-biz economy this is how it works. For each record released in whatever format the songwriter(s) make a certain fixed percentage. Say, I dunno, ten per cent of the record? (Don't quote me!) The songwriter usually also does a deal with a publisher, whose job it is to collect money and also hawk the writer's songs around. For this service the songwriter gives the publisher a split of the take. The law had been changed in the 70s so publishers couldn't take more than 50 per cent, so Gilbey had given me the most basic deal there was. Eventually he signed the other geezers in the band up to the same lousy deal: the usual split in those days was 75/25. He sure wasn't doing us any favours.

Gilbey had also recently done a deal with EMI to reactivate the Parlophone label in Australia, and so we were signed to The Beatles' record label and their publishing company. It was an auspicious start! We were gonna make an album in a big studio and Gilbey was gonna give us another advance to buy some new gear. We also got a road manager … but he immediately formed an alliance with Nick because they both thought AC/DC were the best band in the world. I never really cared for them, especially not after Bon died.

So this new road manager and Nick decided the band would be better off without me because I couldn't really sing or play bass properly. They complained I had no microphone technique. They were, however, going to allow me to remain as the songwriter because I could, after all, write songs. How decent of them! Peter was bemused by their attempted coup. Marty came to me and told me what they were planning. I complained to Gilbey, who immediately put the conspirators back in their place but it was a never-ending battle. The way they spoke to me and Marty was just fucking unbelievable! Rudeness and threats. And the road manager and our wives immediately hated each other; he even forbade them from coming into our dressing rooms, citing some half-baked idea about girls being turned off if they knew we were married.

By this stage we'd been jump-started on the circuit because we had a record deal. There was an old adage in Sydney that you couldn't get a gig without a record deal and you couldn't get a record deal without gigs. So it was like a Buddhist puzzle to penetrate and reconcile the paradox. But we had gone another route: we'd made a very good demo. I'd written some articulate, modern, classic songs and we had Peter's brilliant guitar work. Oh and we were all OK looking.

So we were on the circuit, the famous Aussie pub circuit. In mid 1980 we were the opening act for just about everyone you can think of. Then one night it finally happened. We were at the Rydalmere Family Inn opening for a band called Mi-Sex. I'd written a song called 'Is This Where You Live', which had a long slow beginning and went on for about eight minutes before a frantic guitar-heavy ending. I was singing when I realised that the audience were actually listening to my song. They weren't impatient for the next band to come on. They were rapt in my song and our band and our music. Peter picked up on it and was even more flashy and illustrative with his huge chorus echo sound. Marty opened up his playing too. And I began to be that character that I'd always wanted to be.

I turned a corner. I was no longer the pudgy public servant slobbering over some other group's records, nor the stoned screen-printer from Paddo market. I was becoming the aloof, disdainful pop star as epitomised by Peter Cook in *Bedazzled*. The distant, cold star in a bubble of narcissism that is fascinating as all get out. Here is the point where I started to become the angular fey ninny that would slay Australia for four minutes.

But I had problems too. It wasn't working out with Michele. We had to split up. She was bossing me around and always cross-examining me about everything. The final blow came one night when I'd just gotten in from an exhausting day of rehearsing and bumping in. As I was eating my dinner she was coaching me on how I was gonna go in and demand this and that from Gilbey.

'What are you gonna say, Steven, when you see him tomorrow?' she demanded. I repeated whatever it was she told me to say. 'Yes but let me hear the way you're gonna say it!' Michele demanded.

So there I was rehearsing how I'm gonna tell Gilbey off when a voice in my head says, 'Fuck this, you gotta split up with her!' And that voice was always right. From then on in I was just waiting for the right time to leave her.

We threw ourselves into recording and opening gigs for anyone who'd have us. We opened for INXS – I've still got a letter from their manager Chris Murphy castigating us for not hanging around for a load-out one night in Avalon. Hutch was already a star, even then. It was only a matter of time ... though personally I thought their music was a bit rinky-dink, a bit nursery rhyme or something. Michael was one of the only guys I ever met who had real charisma. Even up close in a dressing room or in a car park he had that indefinable thing.

We also opened for Cold Chisel. I remember it was a fucking excruciatingly hot afternoon gig and in frustration Barnsey chucked a full can of beer at the windows that wouldn't open. We opened for Midnight Oil and Men at Work.

And we were in the studio recording at every opportunity. Our first album. It's hard to listen to now actually; I had some serious vocal posturing going on there and it all sounds pretty out of tune. The guitars are too heavy and too rock'n'roll for me. And the drumming is plodding and boring, which is kind of ironic given Nick was constantly rubbishing Marty and me and bragging about how he could do it better!

Here's an amusing anecdote: Nick was left-handed and couldn't play our instruments, which (understandably) frustrated him. One day I was doing a bass overdub and Nick was in the control room going 'no no no no!' But he couldn't show me what the 'right' thing was because he didn't have a left-handed bass to play, did he? So he said, 'Fuck it, I'm going home to get my own bass!' But by the time he arrived back I'd gotten lucky and nailed the bass part by myself. Then a little later on Marty is doing a guitar part. Nick is bitching from the moment Marty starts tuning up. It's an intense and manic tirade of abuse loaded with words like 'fuckin' and 'mongrel' and 'hopeless'. But he can't show Marty how to do it properly because 'fuckin', fuck it!' Marty's guitar is the wrong way around for him, isn't it? So off he goes home to get his own guitar! Again, by the time he gets back we've laid the guitar part down on tape without his help. Then a few hours later I get on the piano and he starts up again about my (admittedly) mediocre playing. Only Nick didn't phrase it that way. It was still 1968 in his mind, and he still thought bullying was everything. Anyway he's ranting on about my piano playing and Chris Gilbey says, 'I think Nick's gonna go home and get his own piano,' and the whole place burst into laughter – all except me and Marty who were the objects of Nick's intimidation.

Why do I dwell on this? Because I'd worked hard at being a musician for ten years and just when I should have been having some fun I had this macho, pathetic, childish goose ruining every single occasion. Whether it was having our photo taken or at a gig the guy was a relentless bad-vibe merchant. I loathed him so much and I was so frightened of him.

It was awkward one day when we both turned up to rehearsal and no one else was there. He was so in contempt of my hopelessness he could barely talk to me. Eventually I started tooling around on a little riff and song I'd made up that morning – strangely enough it'd been helped along just a little by Michele, who 'd been anxious to go out and see to her rag trade stuff and needed me to drive her. I was sitting there saying 'not yet, I'm working on a song.' So she sat down and helped me put it all together. Anyway, I'm mucking around on the bass and singing the song and Nick jumped on the drums in a rare spirit of co-operation and actually said he thought the song was good.

By the time Marty and Peter arrived we had a good version all worked out. The two guitarists figured it all out pretty quickly and when our new road manager Kent Gorell strolled into our rehearsal space he declared the song a hit! Chris Gilbey came on down and instantly agreed: 'It's a fucking hit!' He was delighted. Everyone was. But I didn't see what was so special about 'The Unguarded Moment'.

(I forgot to mention – because it wasn't worth remembering – that sometime during this period EMI released 'She Never Said' as a single and it pretty well disappeared without a trace, except for one or two lukewarm reviews. It was all my worst dreams come true.)

We stuck 'The Unguarded Moment' on our album pretty much at the last minute. Chris Gilbey then did two things: one of which was brilliant and the other stupid. The brilliant thing was he got Bob Clearmountain to mix our record. The stupid thing is he got a friend of his called Christopher French to make a video for us. French thought making a video would be easy seeing as he was a director of commercials for perfume and soap. Surely it wasn't such a big jump?

But it would turn out to be one of the worst experiences I've ever had in show biz. French had seen this whizz-bang new film gimmick that made everything blurry. The concept of our video was that we were four colours joining up walking along like blobs. My colour was grey. Peter's was Lincoln green, head to toe. Marty's was pale blue. And Nick's was errr ... black cut-off T-shirt, as usual.

So French marched us around Kings Cross on a blazing hot day as we colours searched for each other. I got incredibly sunburnt. My nose looked like a red traffic light. Then we went into a studio and he applied every rock video cliché that he could think of only more clumsily and awkwardly than they had ever been applied before. Think of a Queen tribute band in your dad's garage shot with an iPhone that has fogged with mediocrity and you've some idea of what it was like.

After we watched it at EMI I was so incensed that I told Gilbey and all the horrified EMI staff to bin the video forever. I ranted and raved and threatened to break my contract with all of them if that bilge ever saw airtime. Despite all that eventually a moron at EMI leaked it out, apparently thinking he was doing us a favour. So that awful video with Nick in it is still actually extant. You can find it on YouTube to this day, and I still hate its clichéd amateur-hour guts!

After that experience it was with some trepidation that we attempted our first tour of anywhere other than Sydney, and it just happened to be Melbourne. I drove down in the big truck full of gear with Kent Gorell, who was also our sound guy. We had a bag full of the worst weed in the world but we kept on smoking away at it. It was the middle of summer and it was hot and dry. Nick had been telling Marty and me how we wouldn't survive being on tour because we didn't have the right stuff. Things were rapidly reaching a head and he really was ruining it for all of us with his constant jeers and intimidation.

But when we got to Melbourne it was Nick who had the week-long panic attack and locked himself in his room. Only Spot the roadie could coax him out of there to play the gigs each night. (Spot, of course, eventually had an album named after him: *A Quick Smoke at Spot's*). We impressed a few punters in Melbourne but quickly learnt it was gonna be a long hard slog to the top.

It was an eventful trip: I met a load of the old guard of Aussie rockers in the hotel where we stayed, called Macy's. There were the guys going up and the guys coming down the ladder, and they all stayed at this hotel in Melbourne. We smoked our bag of tepid weed and strummed guitars and jammed with the people roaming the halls at 4am. There was speed being snorted by roadies and many bleeding nostrils. There was Nick springing his girlfriend with another man *in flagrante delicto*. 'He jumped up and I saw his bar and everything!' he told us sadly.

A few weeks later we were doing a gig in some little town south of Sydney when Nick called in to pick up Marty to take him to the gig. Nick refused to bring Lucy, Marty's wife, along in his car so Marty refused to go to the gig. We did the gig as a three piece, which didn't please Peter or me at all. But Nick was thrilled and used it as an opportunity to agitate against Marty and try to have him booted out. He couldn't see that it was him who had to go. We'd all had a gutful.

The next gig we did was at the Governor's Pleasure in Sydney, where Marty and Nick argued about the incident. Nick got physical and starting kneeing Marty, and then Lucy jumped on his back screaming and flailing. We did one more gig with him before we told him to get out. After the gig Nick and I drove back together and he was so sad and dejected he almost talked me into having him back in the group. What can I say, I'm a big softy! I was prepared to give him once last chance. But at the after-gig get-together at Peter's flat in Bondi Nick was bullying people and being aggressive and even I could see he was never going to change. He was only in the group for a year but, boy, he made a massively negative impression on us. He became part of our in-band folklore and we all did impressions of him – even people who joined the band much, much later were doing impressions of our impressions of him. But by Christ it was a huge relief when he was finally gone.

Though then we needed a new drummer. Marty had a friend who was about 27 at the time, which was one year older than me. He was an amiable guy, not bad looking, and he'd played drums in a few bands. He was a sweet guy with a nice wife and everyone liked him so he seemed a shoo-in. I just wanted to give him the gig and be done with it.

Someone, however, wisely insisted we advertise for the job. So we stuck a few ads in the paper and one day Marty got a call. The guy asked our ages and when Marty said I was 26, the guy on the other end exclaimed, '26! Whatever happened to teenage rock?!' That hurt me a little I must admit. Just how old was this guy then? It turned out he was eighteen and he was coming to the audition. I was determined to hate him.

We held the audition at a big rehearsal complex in Paddington. I can still see the room and I remember the names of the other bands rehearsing there that day. All drummers were instructed to bring their own gear. There was our mate, the nice guy who was the shoo-in: he was tall and had long dark hair and looked a bit like us already, I thought. There were a few nondescript blokes and there was this kid dressed like a skinhead – with the boots and braces and the whole lot. What a total turkey! It was very uncool, in my considered opinion. Yes, it was the teenager. He looked about fourteen and had a big head, although he was undoubtedly handsome. When he introduced himself as President Camembert I fucking wanted to throttle him. There was no way he was going to join this band.

Eventually our mate with the dark hair has his turn on the drums. We're playing songs like 'The Unguarded Moment' and 'For a Moment We're Strangers'. You know, early Church power-pop numbers. I'm a bit disappointed in the guy even though I want to give him the job anyway. I've never really known a lot about drumming but I could tell he was tired and rusty and uninspiring – he seemed worn out just playing a couple of songs.

The cocky kid had somehow gotten into the other guy's audition and was mocking him and giggling at his ineptitude. He was a complete little loudmouth nuisance. When our friend got off the kit after his underwhelming performance the kid jumped on his kit.

'You were supposed to bring your own kit!' I snapped.

The kid shrugged. Whatever. OK, for the first song I pulled out a brand new song I'd written called 'Too Fast for You'. It was a tricky little number with stops and starts and places for Keith Moon–type drumming. The kid nailed the song and then some! With effortless aplomb and a weird, fascinating way of playing, the kid brought my song to life in a way I'd never heard. Way beyond Nick's plodding old-school drumming. We played a few more songs and the kid demolished every one in an explosion of boundless energy and enthusiasm. Still, I hated the little bastard for being so clever ... and I didn't want him in the group.

Outside the room Peter said, 'I'm voting for the president!' And we all laughed. I couldn't deny he was the most brilliant drummer I'd ever seen. I didn't know how the fuck we'd ever get on, but I knew he couldn't be any worse than Nigel Fuckin' Nick Bloody Murray Ward.

'What's his real name, anyway?' I asked. It was Richard Ploog.

8
THE FIRST BLUSH OF SUCCESS

I had finally fully morphed into the guy I'd always wanted to be: some skinny dandy with eyeliner and a bunch of stupid kids screaming at me. I already looked world-weary – suffering from some fragility caused by ennui and too much stimulation. I'd waited a long time for this moment and fortunately I didn't blow it. The Church played it up to the hilt, grabbed our 4 minutes and 13 seconds of fame and held on for grim death.

RICHARD WAS A lot of fun and had heaps of energy. Gigs became exciting. We were free to have some fucking fun at last! We did gigs, smoked dope and even started work on a new record, which was to be a double single. Chris Gilbey and I had dreamed up this idea that we'd get two singles in the charts at once. Wouldn't that be a coup!

Then EMI, who were getting ready to release 'The Unguarded Moment', gave us the good news that we were to appear on *Countdown*, which could make and break acts in 1981. We flew down to Melbourne and entered those hallowed halls of the ABC. We'd all been watching *Countdown* for years; it was an institution.

For our set they gave us this stained-glass thing that looked like an aura. We mimed along to our song – me pouting like a fey little fop. (Kids at my youngest brother John's school wanted to beat him up because they thought I looked like such a bloody poofter on the TV.) Someone wrote an article the next day about me pulling David Bowie faces. The other guys looked pretty good too: there's Marty looking like Prince Valiant, the perfect pop star; Peter, tall and thin and handsome with his mane of hair; and Richard so young and cool as he mimed along to Nick Ward's drumming.

Our gig the next night was sold out beyond belief. They were turning people away. We made so much at the door that someone gave me a wad of cash and told me to just spend it and shut up about it. Suddenly I had a bunch of friends everywhere I went; I was seeing about five women at once and definitely breaking up with Michele once and for all. We got ourselves a proper big old manager in the legendary Michael Chugg who, instead of sticking a cigar in my mouth when I agreed to have him manage us, stuck a joint in my mouth and lit it. Wow! This was what I always wanted ... wasn't it?

Two weeks later I hosted *Countdown* and made a complete turkey of myself. My narrow perception of who I thought I could be turned me into a bit of a simpering buffoon, which wasn't really me at all. I had some good raw material but I blew it. I should've trotted out my inner cockney charmer just like my dad used to do. Because if my dad had ever got a chance to be on telly he wouldn't have come across like a ning-nong! But I was suddenly bereft of any personality to speak of and I failed the test.

Another dismal time after that I had my arse hauled onto a fledgling quiz show somewhere in Melbourne in 1981. They plied me with a huge joint and a line of charlie and then a couple of shots of Johnnie Walker Black Label. By the time I got out there I would've made Percy Bysshe Shelley seem like Chuck Norris, I was so fragile and longingly reticent. I was so embarrassed by the host and his questions and the audience and just about everything else. Of course the most embarrassing thing was me: this jumped-up silly sod sitting there being so bloody embarrassed! Talk about the blush of success!

Once on a Saturday morning show I was sitting there stoned, smug and silent when in a commercial break the host Donnie Sutherland got right in my face and hissed, 'If you're not gonna talk ... why did you fucking come on here then?!'

Meanwhile back in the studio it was a real joy to be working with Richard. He was so full of energy and explosive vitality and he had the drums totally sorted. His bright, jokey personality brought a much-needed breath of fresh air to The Church: we finally found our sound and realised what we could be.

My singing and voice had dropped a lot of the pretension; not all of it by a long shot, but a lot of those awkward mannerisms disappeared as Richard energised the band with his teenage enthusiasm. You just couldn't tire that guy out. He was everywhere at once. He had everyone in stitches. He could smoke as much weed as anybody, and then he'd sit down and play the songs perfectly and differently every time.

Sex and drugs were becoming ever more prevalent at this time, and I got the opportunity to, ahem, sleep with a lot of women. I didn't need to do much chatting up after I'd been on *Countdown* a few times, but it wasn't exactly how I'd pictured it. My new fame was a double-edged sword. I'd go to a party, the ladies would crowd around but the men would be real angry with me and I'd slip off quick.

Just because I had the opportunity to sleep with a lot of women doesn't mean I took the opportunity every time it presented itself, but sometimes I did dally with the young ladies I met backstage after a gig. Fame is intoxicating like that: you get near to it once and you wanna chase it forever and ever. Girls were almost throwing themselves at me, writing me love letters and propositions; our roadies had girls perform sexual tricks in the hotel rooms, but I never saw that myself. Marty did once accidentally and was quite appalled.

Soon enough I *really* fell in love for the first time in my life. I'd been doing an interview at radio station 3XY in Melbourne and I locked eyes with a young woman named Jennifer who was reading the news. I loved her immediately. I wrote 'Electric Lash' about meeting her, and then many other songs too. But first I had to pursue her a bit, which as you know I wasn't averse to. I jumped ship from The Church and stayed behind in Melbourne, got her number from a friend at 3XY and called her up. I'd never done that before. I'd been with Michele for a while, and then there was just a few months of naughtiness before I met Jennifer. So I rang her up and asked if I could see her. She said sure. We spent a lovely evening together but I didn't try any funny business. We saw each other a few more times and eventually it was apparent that she felt the same about me so we were quite inseparable for a while. I pretty much moved into her flat in South Melbourne for weeks on end. She was a truly fine woman: stylish, cultured and a real Australian aristocrat or something. She was very kind and warm, and we got on so well. When I left Melbourne I got very sad, which usually resulted in a song as I tapped into the sweet pain of separation for a young man of 26 who'd just fallen in love.

To me, Jennifer was a goddess and she made me want to write songs to impress her. We were young and affluent, and both of us a bit famous after she got a job reading the news on TV. She showed me her Melbourne and on cold winter days we'd drive to lonely spots by the sea and talk and kiss a bit too. It was a totally romantic love affair – after the regimented drudgery of my brief marriage I was, for a while, really happy.

Those were halcyon days. I spent Christmas 1981 with Jennifer's lovely family in Essendon, in some gorgeous stately house there. It was the sort of place where the gentlemen took brandy after dinner and played billiards. Man I'd come a long way! My band was pretty popular, I was making a good bit of money, and I was in love with my famous and good-looking girlfriend. I couldn't have hoped for a better result. One night on tour in Surfers Paradise I remember Richard putting on a cassette of the Beach Boys album *Pet Sounds* and me sitting there and wondering at the loveliness of my brand new life. I took in every detail of Brian Wilson's masterpiece, which I'd never listened to before in its entirety. Here I was in a big apartment, enjoying a few joints after a gig, finally having broken into the inner sanctum of the music biz. We were on telly, we had a big-shot manager, we sold out gigs, and we had a recording contract and everything!

Some biggish cheques began rolling into my letterbox, so I bought Michele out of my Rozelle house, and in came Russell who lent me some money he'd inherited from Dad to cover part of her share. Russell was about nineteen and he brought with him a lot of friends as well as his girlfriend at the time, Kim Sandeman, who had moved with him from Canberra to enrol in a nearby school of fashion and design while Russell started up a band. My house was flooded with loads of kids all younger than me hanging around and smoking bongs.

But Kim and I were often at odds. One day I came back from being on tour and saw a guy in the street wearing a paisley shirt that looked just like one of mine. A really rare one actually: an unmistakable one that I'd worn in a video once. And I said to the guy naively, 'Oh wow I have a shirt like that!' And the guy kind of nodded like he wanted to get out of there. Inside there's another guy wearing a paisley shirt just like one of mine, only this couldn't be one of mine because the sleeves had been roughly cut off. And then Kim hove into view ... wearing what looked like one of my skivvies cut up into weird geometric shapes.

'What the fuck is going on here?' I asked, not unreasonably I thought, considering the circumstances.

Kim just shrugged and said, 'Well I thought when you moved into a place you got to share everything with everyone ... so, you know, we're wearing your clothes.'

She'd also spilt something black and thick all over my red carpet and then put something else on top of it to hide it. My house was full of people wearing my clothes and acting like I was so uncool to be angry. Still Kim remained in my house for about three more years: we loved to fight with each other – I was her oldie to rebel against and she was my wayward kid to chastise and catch out! This was so not how I pictured things would be.

Now I realise it's about time I explain the paisley shirts once and for all. So here's my version, though the other guys would probably tell it differently. In fact, for almost every memory I have Peter Koppes will contradict me with a different version! So with that general caveat applied to everything I say, I'll tell you *my* version of how we came to wear the paisley shirts.

Back in 1981 the guys in The Church wore tight black jeans and some of us wore black suede boots; we tended towards either mild glam or mod or psychedelic even. I'd always loved paisley and floral since the days of Lyneham High School socials, but in 1981 there wasn't a single paisley shirt in a high-street shop anywhere in

Australia. They were still around, though ... flooding into op shops along with the rest of Australia's unwanted clothes.

So The Church were touring, touring, touring around Australia and every town on and off the beaten track had at least one or two op shops: St Vincent de Paul, the Salvos, Lions Club, Rotary – they all meant rare shirts and pants. So we started hitting the op shops hard. We used to race each other inside to find the best clothes first. As usual I was the worst offender. One day we hit a garbage bin as Peter was backing into a parking spot, but I still jumped out and ran into the fucking shop and scored some shirts ahead of him! The nastiness increased when we'd advise each other against buying shirts only to grab them for ourselves. I definitely wrestled Richard for shirts, which became torn as we fought over them, but honestly there was a superabundance of paisley shirts. We were inventing what would later be called the Paisley Underground. We might not have been the very first to wear paisley, but it'd been sixteen years since The Beatles had done it so we claimed the title anyway!

After a while the ladies in the op shops began to remember us and put stuff aside. One day a lady in Kempsey in northeastern New South Wales took me into a back room and showed me box upon box of unopened paisley shirts from the 60s! Some of them even came with medallions. It was like bloody Christmas. And the most amazing thing was that I owned literally hundreds of paisley shirts but only ever paid five dollars max for any of them.

So the more we wore paisley the more we seemed to be ... wearing paisley. After a while it became a uniform for me and Richard, though Marty and Peter only wore it occasionally.

We'd kind of worn out the paisley by 1983, but other bands all over the place had picked up on it and were keen to be identified as psychedelic. Which accounts for certain sneering comments I used to make about all the bands that paid $120 for their paisley shirts.

I was talking about the Johnny-come-lately types that'd adapted the fashion and look and even the sound but hadn't grokked that psychedelic music was supposed to be trippy and surrealistic.

Back then, when we started out, there were no other psychedelic bands on this planet that I knew of. It was almost a dirty word. The Church pioneered Psychedelia Mark II, though my pride in this fact is tempered by the knowledge that much of what we did was enormously influenced by The Beatles and The Byrds and Dylan. What we did had already been pioneered before in the 60s, from whence all modern music still seems to spring. Originality seemed to have vanished from rock music by 1980, but we were as original as we could possibly be and still 'make it'. So for a while it was paisley and Beatlesy things galore as we got everything lined up to go into the recording studio to make our second album.

Life in those days was pretty idyllic. I lived in Mansfield Street, Rozelle, in a house teeming with cool young arty people. My brother's friends were all musicians, and new instruments and new gadgets would come in and out of my studio. I'd get up in the morning and smoke dope and sit around listening to music blasting in my lounge room. I had a skylight put in the roof. There was forest wallpaper and black and red walls and red carpet with black stuff spilt on it. There was always some dress design pattern or photos or dummies or something lying around. And loads of people smoking bongs day and night and sometimes taking acid.

I remember the time I met these three air hostesses and they had a house in the hinterlands. We went there and they had a pool and everything. We all ate these magic mushrooms and I was swimming in that blue pool surrounded by the laughter on the gentlest evening imaginable. It was one of those rare moments where everything was how I wanted it to be. This incredible night in the tropics, I sat with my legs dangling in the pool drinking champagne and I could see the faint distant glow of Southport where we'd just played a sold-out gig *and* done an interview with the English music mag *Sounds*. Maybe there was room for me in England after all. The future seemed full of promise. I was so high that my jaw was aching from smiling. I was ecstatic. I was young and successful and having a good and trippy time.

Things were going so well for a while there. Once on tour we arrived late at the Gold Coast airport and our plane was beginning to taxi away from the gate. Unchecked, we ran out the door carrying our luggage and waved to the plane. Legend has it that some hostie looked out and said, 'Stop! It's The Church!' And the plane stopped and they put a staircase there for us and we climbed on *and* got bumped up to business class. Ah, those were certainly the days for both The Church and civil aviation!

At home I was spending my evenings and nights recording incessantly. Often I had a little audience of a few other muso types offering their suggestions and generally geeing me on as I created song after song after song in preparation for entering Studio 301 in the middle of Sydney to make the first really good Church album. After the stodge and bluster of the first record The Church were finally ready to be *The Church*. Our second album was going to be a beautiful-sounding record thanks to our producer, engineer and mixer, Bob Clearmountain, who Chris Gilbey had wangled out of the universe for us. Bob had already produced or mixed a load of top albums, including for the Stones and Roxy Music; getting him to work on our album was a real coup.

Bob was a quiet and modest kind of guy. He was no studio tyrant, although he was Number One at the time. He never liked the music loud in the studio. He was very focused on work and had his own idiosyncratic way of doing things. For instance, he recorded the kick drum at the end of a long tube of special carpet he brought with him from New York. Bob was also the guy who brought about the popularity of those famous Yamaha NS10 speakers, and had been the one to come up with the idea of the tissue paper that hung over the front of them because they were supposedly too 'toppy'. After Bob gave them his blessing every studio in the world had a set of those speakers. One day a guy rang Bob up to ask him what brand of tissue he recommended for them! Bob's influence at the time cannot be overestimated.

I enjoyed making the album with him, even though he later allegedly said I was one of the most stubborn people he'd ever worked with. Then again, he also said *The Blurred Crusade* was one of his favourite albums he had ever made.

The Blurred Crusade was so much more accomplished than the first album. I was free to follow after the sounds I heard in my head – like how I wanted a harpsichord on one track, so one day a guy turned up and assembled a complete harpsichord for me to play around on. Bob was very encouraging and nurturing and all that stuff. Really that album was an almost unimaginable leap forward for us.

After we finished recording it I dropped into EMI to pick up my mastered cassette and then walked on down to Paddington Markets where I bumped into a friend of mine who had a brand new invention, the Sony Walkman. I smoked a joint and sat in the shade and listened to the album from beginning to end. I was quite shocked at how luxurious and lush it all sounded: Bob had done an amazing job and I was gobsmacked. Our difficult second album was nailed! I felt sure people would like it.

Oh what a carefree time in my life that was! The Church flew and drove around Australia playing gigs and it was all fun and games for a while. Ploogy got better and better on the drums, especially if he had a new girlfriend at the gig and then he was just unstoppable. On the rare days we had off I hung out in Melbourne at Jennifer's flat and we always had a good time.

In early 1982 *The Blurred Crusade* came out to pretty good reviews. The single 'Almost with You' was a moderate hit too, although the second single 'When You Were Mine' pretty much sank without a trace. The record ended up selling over 40,000 copies in Australia, which was double gold at the time. I think it still sounds fairly fresh and vibrant. Peter plays some very lyrical and very melodic guitar. I played all the keyboards and all of them were real: real piano, real Hammond, even a real Celeste at the end of 'Field of Mars', which I thought would be a good song for Marty to sing. I wrote that song about a graveyard in Sydney called the Field of Mars, which was where my neighbour was buried. His name was Ron Wiseman and he died of emphysema, which must be a terrible way to go. He'd been a good friend to me in the few years I knew him until one night an ambulance took him away and he never came back.

At this time Ploogy and I had become friends with a journalist called Stuart Coupe, and we used to go over to his house some nights to play records and things like that. When Coupe asked me to do a big interview with him for *RAM* magazine I thought I was in safe hands. Ah but I was about to learn the hard way about the duplicity of the press! Coupe came over to my hotel room at the Diplomat one evening while we were on tour; Jennifer was there but she fell asleep listening to me rabbiting on.

We smoked some grass and drank some booze and Coupe pulled out a packet of speed and I stupidly snorted some, which made me rave on more and more stupidly, like a real braggart. I thought we were sort of friends but I guess we weren't. I thought Coupe would temper my ranting; I took it for granted that all the silly stuff I was saying wouldn't be used against me. Boy was I ever wrong. The article came out and I looked like the biggest wanker you'd ever seen. It upset a lot of people, including Molly Meldrum, who I had to go around and apologise to. Coupe had asked me why I'd got to host *Countdown* so quickly and me, being facetious, said, 'Well it wasn't because I had any talent, it was obviously because Molly fancied me.' And Molly had not in any way done or said anything that indicated that. It was unfair of me to say it even as a joke. I also said I was the best songwriter in Australia, which upset all of other best songwriters in Australia, and I insulted the band in an arrogant and high-handed way. I didn't think Coupe would've put it all in but he did. It was too good a story to let any notion of friendship get in the way.

I was shocked and unprepared for the wave of sheer hatred and outrage that followed, even though my mother had always said that my big mouth was going to get me into trouble. I officially became the most unpopular man in the music biz. Only Michael Chugg had a good laugh. He was the only one who found my jumped-up arrogant pop star act vaguely amusing. I was jolted badly though. I didn't have the resolve or strength to play Public Enemy Number One. The other guys in the band were miffed and it drove a wedge between them and me. I don't blame Coupe or even care about that anymore, he was just doing his job. Fast-forward to 2014 and we're friends again now.

Meanwhile, overseas was beckoning. In Sweden 'The Unguarded Moment' had made its way into the charts. It also became a hit in Canada. In England, while not a hit, the new and cool version of 'Unguarded' had been played on *The Old Grey Whistle Test* and people were digging it. *The Blurred Crusade* received rave reviews. It wasn't easy to get good reviews in the English press back then and we were greatly heartened. So when the news of a long overseas tour in September, October and November came through I was incredibly anxious and excited. We were doing Sweden, Denmark, France, Holland, Germany, Scotland and England. We were going over there to crack it!

PART II

I SING THE INFERNAL ETERNAL TOUR

i sing the madness and the light,
the evangelist gone off the rails

in the back of a tour bus in the
sanctum now silent i ride down
the road

the rain rushes over the black
glass of the window as a night
rushes by

ordinary people in their homes
all asleep but i hurtle along in the
wake of a storm

music that rings on in my ears
won't let me sleep i am exhausted
but wired ever so tired

the bus sloshes through the rain
somewhere a million miles away
past factory past field

the others are all asleep in their
bunks dreaming of god knows
what in the close dark

but sleep is elusive so i sit
here alone as the outside
goes by

last night we hit some town whose
name has already escaped my
memory

my memory has somehow become
full ... events queue up to be
admitted

things go in one eye and out
the other

we check into some motel or is
it a hotel or a motor inn or a
travelodge ... ?

yes that was us a rowdy crowd
at three in the morning walking
through the door

arguing over this and that like
incidentals and credit cards and
queen-size beds

i take my key and drag my
suitcase up to my room and kick
open the door

the room is nondescript functional
neutral neither welcoming or ugly

inside over a desk is a full length
mirror and i catch sight of myself

crumpled tired stoned stupid
dishevelled barbarian minstrel
idiot

i stand for a long time just gazing
at myself and what has become
of me

i fuck around for ages with the air
conditioner and its remote control

it's pumping out cold air and
i'm freezing from the inside out
anyway

i can't make it stop so i stuff a
pillow into its vent in frustration

i crawl into the bed and i dream
that same old nightmare where
everything is going wrong

i'm standing onstage and it's all a
mess, i can't remember the words
or the music

even in sleep i am pursued by
myself

some part of my mind can't leave
itself alone and it invents another
thing to worry about

in the morning i wake up sick and
cold and feeling lonely like the sky

i ring home and a woman's voice
answers

oh it's you ... says the voice
and i sit there in my motor inn
somewhere wondering what to say

we had a great gig the other night
... i hear my voice as though from
a great distance

there is a silence on the line for a
while and in that time the miles
crackle and the satellites roar

great ... says the woman's voice
and again i wonder if that's it or
should i say something more

well ... i say ... i was just checking
in i guess ...

ok ... says the voice half
disappointed half glad that our
conversation has ended

i love you ... i say but i realise
i am talking to a dead line that
leads to nowhere

i go downstairs for breakfast
standing in a bit of a line with
businessmen i presume

a slice of toast goes round on a
machine while a yellow liquid
labelled orange juice drips from
a spout

i sit down with a couple of the
road crew and one of the band

they're arguing over some stupid
football result and i move away
again before i go outside

outside it's like there is no
weather at all ... no heat no cold
no rain no shine no anything

i light up a smoke and i verily go
into a dream standing there on
that street in the non weather

we were doing sound check and
i was waiting around in the
vestibule

i was so fucking tired and stoned
and hungry and had filled up on
smarties from a machine

three cappuccinos had given me
the shakes and the screaming
wee wees

i am an astronaut cut off from
earth and i have entered some
other space

i go on unthinking through my
ritual and some automatic part of
me takes over

i climb onstage at the sound
check and the guy hands me
my guitar

i walk up to a microphone and out
comes that familiar voice

the fingers on my hands seem to
know what to do and they wander
over the strings and frets

the words come out of storage and
the voice sings them out

and the real me is standing back
thinking about something else

every now and then the process
is disrupted by a vile stab of
feedback piercing my ears

or i stop to fiddle around with the
settings on my guitar

people wander into the room to
watch us sound check and they
stand there gawking

the band have a little argument
about what we will play and i feel
embarrassed and frustrated

everyone in the band is tired of
everyone else ... our betrayals and
alliances are a tangled web no one
can sort out

every word is loaded and every
gesture symbolic and this tour has
been volatile

an ongoing collision of ambitions
and agendas with brutal clashes
and long cold silences

jesus christ everything in my life
is some kind of battle or some
kind of prolonged negotiation

it's hard to remember why
everyone is angry with each other
and the chronology of trespasses

we stumble through a few
numbers and suddenly the sound
check ends when we run out
of time

outside it's cold and the band
run into some people we know
and we go off for dinner

even at dinner we compete for
attention as we do on the stage

private and financial grievances
are aired while unpleasant looks
are exchanged

after dinner i go back to my
room and watch some doco and
end up asleep

i wake up groggy and disoriented
when someone bangs on my door

the bus is leaving for the gig
in five minutes i run around
ineffectually getting my
stuff together

i try ironing a shirt but i just put
more wrinkles into it

i go out on the balcony and have
yet another smoke and i fall
deeper within my haze

at the gig our dressing room is
full of people i don't know if
i know

i nibble on the chocolates and
chips at hand and i feel nervous
and a little unsure

i hear the sound of the audience
coming from the other side of the
curtains chatting and laughing

i get into my outfit for the night
and i go and look in the mirror ...
fuck knows what i'm s'posed
to be ...

the others in the group look
similarly shoddy but the word
we use is bohemian ...

the people in the dressing room
make themselves at home with
the food and the drink

there is some woman from our
record company there and she's
kind of frowning at me

she comes over and talks to me
eventually … apparently i'm
s'posed to remember her from
somewhere …

i'm trying to think of something
encouraging to say to her when
the tour manager kicks 'em all out

fifteen minutes till you go on,
gentlemen …

he wryly smirks … we are not
gentlemen at all … at least not
towards each other …

this town we are playing tonight
needs to be reconquered says
some napoleonic twit from the
record company

they see it like that i guess
and i feel some pressure on my
shoulders to be good

actually i don't feel good at all or
even ok or even just middling

i am in some kind of conflict with
everyone in my tiny world and
everything has become complex

the more complex the more i drift
away and then it all becomes even
more complex

once when i was a kid i thought
touring in a band would be a lot of
fun and i was not wrong

there certainly is fun fun fun
of all and every description to
be had

but there's a lot of waiting around
while other people obliviously fuck
about with stuff

listening to the same old stories
over'n'over as you come to each
new place

and we big note ourselves all
over again

the familiarity sure breeds
contempt in spades and the
backstabbing of everybody
is endemic

we whinge and whine about
each other incessantly moaning
and banging on about our many
personality flaws

actually all members of the group
are quite nutty only each believes
he is the sane one

we are like europe at the outbreak
of world war one constantly
plotting against itself

we are jealous we are childish we
are nasty we are stupid

we also happen to be an incredible band which is due to luck and talent only

the members indulge in continual acts of brinkmanship threatening to quit the band and fuck it all up

certain friends of certain members stir up trouble and try to foment revolt

each friend whispers to his band member that he is truly the indispensable one

tensions swirl around me as i am the most brooding and seemingly sarcastic member

people either love me or hate me but i seem to meet far more of the latter variety

of course many of the ones who start out loving me end up hating me too

though rarely the other way around strangely enough ha ha

someone hands me another smoke and we fire it up in the toilet

i'm seriously off my trolley now plus my first and only drink of the day has kicked in

a big shot of mescal ... everything is moving in pulsating rhythm just out of eyeshot

the intro music comes on and i feel like i wish i was anywhere else

i just wanna crawl into a bed somewhere and hide from the world but this is the exact opposite

i have yet another nervous piss and even then someone knocking at the door telling me to bloody hurry up

we go onstage and there is a bit of a roar a bit of a cheer then it goes all quiet

our first song building in momentum slowly and lifting off from the ground

my fingers work the guitar and my voice works the words

it all goes off fairly smoothly and a lot of my early discomfort is now gone

as we play song after song i begin to lose myself in it all

i start to drown in the sound we are creating succumbing to my own spell

the crowd have ceased to exist for me oh i s'pose i can see them beyond the dazzling lights

they sway and clap or just stand there listening with their eyes closed

i am lost to myself as i move
about the stage bobbing and
weaving to the beat

i break out in sweat and soon i
am drenched as i pump away at
my guitar and sing out hoarsely

it's so easy i just switch off
and stand back and watch it
all happen

the music has become effortless
and it flows away from us like a
river of sound

i turn around and lock eyes with
our drummer and we start to
hammer down together

some strange thing has happened
i have become weightless painless
the worries of the day all gone

the whole band has synched up
to something bigger than itself
and we are off on a cloud

oh how to describe that place
that music can take you to when
you're having an 'on' night

my body on complete automatic
now my mind vacated by my soul
which detaches its self

in some non-verbal place a realm
of ineffable sound as me 'n' the
drummer pound down and down

it seems that life must change
after something this profound but
no eventually we touch the ground

i reach for my towel the sweat is
gushing from my skull

we start another song this one is
quietly insistent and i lose myself
within it all again

eventually with a load of
commotion and carrying on the
gig ends and spits me out

i have a long shower and change
back into my street clothes and i
try to redo my hair

the dressing room has filled up
with people by now and some of
them make a bee-line for me

too late to get away i am
surrounded by people demanding
some kind of response

so i go into my head but there are
no responses to be found

the volume the heat the lights the
travel the crowd

the two hours running around
with a guitar and yelling out have
all rendered me null and void

ooh he's a rude bastard ... says a
disgruntled customer pushing his
way out of the room

some pretty woman is smiling
at me as some incomprehensible
wanker rambles on in my ear

some big geezer next to the pretty
woman is frowning at the same
time in my direction

some other wanker is interrupting
the first wanker to disagree with
his analysis of the uh situation

they both look up to me for some
kind of explanation but i am
shell shocked

a jet-lagged doped-up insomniac
rascal i just couldn't give a
fuck about my lyrics or their
interpretations of 'em

others break through the queue
formed around me while others
stand back and watch my
social ineptitudes

oh boy i say as the room whirls
round and round and all the faces
get closer and closer

a woman is squeezing my thigh
while a guy tries to stick a tape
of his group in my pocket

the other guys in the group are
all laughing or arguing or deep in
conversation with someone

someone chops out some white
powder and i snort up a big line
which burns and freezes my nose

a serious out of body experience
as i float over myself as i stand
there with all these people
talking at me

i see myself pale and still
sweaty my empty aching head
and my singing ringing ears

i see the room from inside and
out and upside and down and
then nothing ...

the next thing i know i'm riding
in a car and i sit up suddenly
against the seat belt

a soft female voice assures
me everything is ok and we're
going back to my motel

who are you? ... i ask as we
whizz past unfamiliar suburbs
and strange dark gardens

oh you know who i am ... silly ...
the female voice giggles and
purrs ... as we zip along

oh gee my aching eyes even
when we stop i can't really get
a good look at her

soon enough we're inside my
room and her hands are inside
my shirt

wait a minute i'm trying to say
but she's strong and persuasive

we fall on the bed and she's
whispering something i can't
understand

wait she says i gotta put some
music on and oh no it's your band's
music some old single you hate

insistent kisses quell your
resistance as she pushes you down
into the valley of night

whatever happens so long gone
from all memory now it's all hard
to believe and then

she gets up and dresses and
quietly leaves you see her face
in the mirror briefly she is
not beautiful

you toss and turn looking for sleep
and then it finally arrives and it is
sweet and black

oh it envelopes your aches and
your pains and it takes every
question from your lips with a
gentle sshh

and you're standing there with
sleep on the edge of its narcotic
nothingness and with one last
lingering gaze ...

and then the telephone ring
ring ring hey man sorry were
you sleeping oh yeah look i'm
sorry ok ...

you dive back under the blankets
but a noisy party has started up in
a room somewhere fathoms below

and you lie there groaning there is
no escape from whatever it is that
whips you forwards and goads
you on

have another smoke on the
balcony it's getting light in the
eastern sky and the motel has
grown quiet

you lie down in the bed in this
room you will never see again and
sleep arrives once more

and this time you depart and you
disappear into that wonderful
healing realm if only for an hour
or two

for soon the heavy hand of a tour
manager will bang on your door

and you wake up to find you are
doing it all over again ... i sing the
infernal eternal tour ...

9
THE CHURCH INVADES THE NORTHERN HEMISPHERE

The Church really is like a traffic accident that all the onlookers remember differently. And Peter's perspective often varies wildly from mine – so if I'm half-right half the time you can disregard almost three-quarters of this book for a start! A PK-annotated version of this humble book you hold in your hands would surely induce me to laughter and tears and sharp denials and embarrassed admissions …

JUST BEFORE WE left for Europe The Church nipped into Studio 301 for a few days. Capitol Records, our American record label, were looking for more 'hits' and they didn't think *The Blurred Crusade* had any hits on it.

To tell you the truth, the people who were working in most American record companies wouldn't have known a hit from a bar of soap even if it'd bitten their arse. I knew in my heart of hearts that we didn't have any more hits, but I'd written a few interesting

Top left: Our last Christmas in England, 1956.

Above: My first press appearance in *New Australia* ship newspaper, for chucking Mum's watch overboard. Check out the fancy footwear.

Me in Canberra, 1971. I only ever got one pimple at a time but it was always a whopper!

Me rocking the loungeroom in Lyneham, 1970, with my first bass.

Me and Fernando, 1971. We're in the garage going through 'Rock Around The Clock' for the one millionth time.

Saga in a Canberra newspaper, 1972. Far right is the singer Ron. He had a really great voice.

Me and Dad. He hated that I had grown taller than him, and I took every opportunity to stand up straighter around him to get that extra inch.

Above: Me in 1972, figuring out the mysteries of a C chord ... looks like I got it wrong!

Right: Baby Grande in 1975 in a Canberra newspaper. The article said we played 'screaming gutter rock'. And I've got my Mum's blouse on back to front!

Above: Me and Ken from Baby Grande, 1975. Perhaps we were attempting to embrace bisexuality.

Left: Me in London, 1978. The English music industry did not take me to its bosom.

Below: The Church's first ever band photo shoot, 1980. The look on my face says it all.

Above left: At the very first Church gig as a three piece, a homemade banner and me attempting some rococo malarkey, 1980.

Above right: Playing fretless bass, 1981. I had finally achieved the angularity and the aloofness.

Right: Me at the Diplomat Hotel in Melbourne, 1981. Enough eye makeup to make a panda laugh.

Below: The Church photo shoot, at Richard's house in Balmain, 1981. Ploogy ever the snappy dresser.

Woolloomooloo, 1981. One of my first big photo shoots on my own.
I thought life was a bowl of cherries.

Above: Melbourne gig in 1982. Fans took so many pictures of us, we must have kept Kodak in business for a year.

Below: Stockholm, 1983. This was from a Swedish newspaper, and the headline was 'Never a dull moment'. This was taken in Karin's incredible apartment.

Above: The Church goofing off in Bondi, 1986.

Left: Dinner in Paris. By the looks of me and Ploogy there were no vegetarian options, 1986.

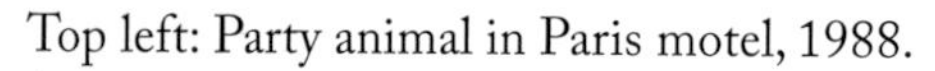

Top left: Party animal in Paris motel, 1988.

Top right: Me, Ploogy and a German record company guy at the Berlin Wall, 1988.

Right: Me and Ploogy clowning around in the clouds in Europe, 1988.

Below: Me getting interviewed on Dutch television, 1988. We loved Holland for obvious reasons.

Left: Karin and I with one of our twins, 1994.

Below: Me, the twins, and my good friend Dr James Blogg, 1994.

Above: Me and my second set of twins, Aurora and Eve, on Bondi Beach, 2002.

Above: Junky daze, London, 1998.

Right: Me in Prague, 2007. At least I'm not in a fucking Kafka tshirt.

Ooooh, the modern era, baby. Kilbey, 2014. Photograph courtesy of Mal Viles.

Black Madonna by Steve Kilbey.

Mary was a little lamb by Steve Kilbey.

WHEN THE FIRST SHOCK
HIT IT LIT UP LIKE DAY

Renaissance man searching for a renaissance … a self portrait.

new songs that I wanted to record; would they be the hits they were looking for? Fat chance!

The resulting record was *Sing-Songs*, an EP of mismatched bits and pieces. We had the archetypal Church number 'A Different Man', which is such a Church-by-numbers piece of mediocrity I can't bear to listen to it. We did two versions of 'A Different Man' – one with real backing vocals and one with vocoder backing vocals. I don't know which is worse. We also did a video for this track in a forest on a misty morning, where we all looked wholesome and psychedelic, which is no mean feat. There's an outtake from *The Blurred Crusade*, 'I Am a Rock' by Paul Simon, which sits on the end of this record verily like the spare prick at a prostitute's wedding. And then there are the three other songs with a more modern sound – I really thought that 'The Night Is Very Soft' was cool and mean and sexy in a way that The Church had never been before.

But hardly anyone else anywhere agreed, and *Sing-Songs* went quietly into that bad night with barely a whimper. Capitol Records – full of philistines who'd succumbed to the 80s zeitgeist and were falling over themselves to sign up the next Thompson Twins – dropped us cold after doing nothing but releasing our first record with a stupid cover and butchering our single. *The Blurred Crusade*? Nah, no thanks, too classic, too intelligent, too sensitive, too subtle. Capitol were looking for something with a handclap machine and a quirky sing-along chorus.

Peter and I flew to the US and met them in the famous Capitol Building. They were fuck-knuckles to a man. I'm not surprised they couldn't find something to like on *The Blurred Crusade*; it was way too high-brow for them. It was almost a compliment that those guys hated the record. Well, I hated *them*. What did they know about music? They were just selling black plastic with tunes on it.

So we hit the UK, where we were signed to Carerre and we had some things lined up. Unfortunately one of which was opening for Duran Duran – a band I hated then and still hate now. Yes, hate is a strong word but their new romantic twaddle and their silly videos were anathema to me. Our record company had paid something like thirty thousand fucking pounds to be on their crumby tour playing to eleven-year-old girls in tears. Now maybe I would've been happy with that if only we hadn't hit The Venue first. After an OK warm-up gig opening for a band called The Truth somewhere in suburban London, we'd booked a gig at The Venue, which could hold more than 2000 people. And we sold it out and got rave reviews. Our tour had somehow coincided with a small psychedelic revival in England, and we were seen as godfathers of the whole movement – the audience went bananas when we walked onstage. When I sang the line 'Who you trying to get in touch with?' during 'Almost with You' the whole place was pointing at me and shouting 'YOU! YOU!' I kept thinking there must be something else happening because surely they weren't all screaming for us!

Backstage people treated us like royalty. I heard one guy repeating to his wife over and over in disbelief: 'Look, Darlin', IT'S PETER KOPPES. IT'S PETER KOPPES!' Something you still might hear me repeat at a gig, much to PK's bemusement. We later found out that Dave Gilmour from Pink Floyd had been at that gig, and he'd said he thought I looked like Syd Barrett. Wow!

Michael Chugg rented us a huge house in Kensington with a spiral staircase and a rooftop view over London. We hit the continent and played a bunch of shows in different cities. We'd been bequeathed Slade's road crew – now they were a whacky bunch of characters. Slade were a huge British band during the 70s, and although their star had waned a little by 1982 they could still fill arenas. The road crew was made up of Chas on front of house, who had all these little rude sayings like 'Wrap your lips around Kilbey's pips! Ooh ooh!' and 'For a crunchy lunch try Kilbey's bunch! Ooh ooh!' Chas also mixed for Slade, who were one of the most heavyweight loud bands known to mankind, but he maintained that The Church was so fucking loud he couldn't get the guitarists in the PA. That is to say the two guitar players' amps were already exceeding the combined volume of the rest of the stuff in the PA. One gig he warned Marty and Peter that if they didn't turn it down they'd see him down the front drinking a pint of Guinness. Sure enough the boys didn't turn down and there was Chas in the front row, a big smile on his face and a Guinness in his hand.

Then there was Leggy the guitar tech and general lugger, who was no spring chicken even in those days. He reminded me of one of Robin Hood's merry men: he was a big man, with long grey hair and a big grey beard. He had as much sex as he could with whomever he could get it with. One night on the tour bus, with a young lady in his bunk, Leggy called out dejectedly to the tour manager, 'Dennis, she's got a fucking dick!'

An answer came from the darkness: 'You've paid for it Leggy, you might as well suck it!'

Dennis himself was a shrewd little cocaine-addicted English geezer with a rodent-like tenacity and an outrageously good way of talking himself out of bad situations. When our passports were stolen, Dennis talked us in and out of Sweden and Denmark just by showing the customs guys our album covers! He did a whole tour on white chocolate, milk and cocaine. But where the money came from nobody ever knew or asked, at least for a while – we were at large in Europe with an incredibly bizarre cast of characters; nothing made sense!

Now people saw The Church as this mysterious group but in fact most of our adventures turned into fiascos and our continental tour was no exception. The ferry ride there was not a good omen. Ploogy filled up on baked beans and eggs and chips and hash joints and then decided he loved the taste of the ferry's lager so he washed all of it down with a few foaming pints. About an hour later the boat began to go up and down and back and forth in the sea. One minute Ploogy was standing there talking to me and then suddenly he turned and explosively vomited over the side of the boat. Only it wasn't exactly the side – it was over onto the next level down, and he drenched one of the officers in vomit.

Later on, all four of us were in the same cabin. It was totally black inside and three of us were tired and anxious to go to sleep but Richard, now re-energised after his enormous puke, was crawling around on the floor and grabbing each of us, making us scream out or roar. Then Ploog would stop and wait and do it all again. I was absolutely furious with the little bastard. It was terrifyingly silly and I was giggling hysterically and warning the darkness, 'PLOOG!'

We hit Sweden first and played a gig in Stockholm. I guess we were quite mediocre and maybe they were a bit disappointed in us. It certainly wasn't like the rapturous response we had in London. Then we went to Gothenburg and our bus broke down. But after the gig I met Karin Jansson, who was the guitar player in an all-female Swedish group called Pink Champagne. The moment I saw her I felt like I was being harnessed to a greater cause. I looked into her eyes and I just knew …

Then fate played a strange hand. Peter and I caught up with Stefan Strom – remember him from my schooldays? Well Stefan was living in Stockholm and so we got him to drive the tour bus, which he subsequently crashed so we had to spend an extra night in Stockholm waiting for something or other. Lucky he wasn't hurt! That night I met Karin again in some bar and we spent the night together, although there was nothing physical yet.

I was head over heels in love with her from that point on. Jennifer, back in Melbourne, was still my girlfriend, but the conflict of the situation was doing my head in and I became quite oblivious to a lot of the gigs. To top it all off someone nicked our clothes so we had to wear and play in the same clothes for days. Thankfully a groovy English guy in a Stockholm mod shop gave us some white turtleneck shirts to wear.

We hit Denmark and Germany and Holland; the tour was a fucking weird little tour I can tell you that. We had long days off in strange places. In Munich we enjoyed the massages of a groovy old lady as we listened to ambient music. We strolled around the city and did a TV show there with a band called Talk Talk, who were angry at having to go on before us. In Amsterdam Ploog and I went nuts smoking the legal weed and choosing it from menus and eating the space-cakes on offer. We sampled some unbelievably good cocaine one night and, having nothing else to do, Marty and I wrote '10,000 Miles', which would appear on the *Remote Luxury* EP and album.

In France we ate a huge meal and some elaborate desserts less than half an hour before the gig. Five minutes to go and the band was feeling frumpish and sleepy so Dennis chopped out a big line of cocaine for each member and we ran on stage energised and pumping. But the cocaine wore off after fifteen minutes and slowly we turned into stodgy sludge before the French crowd. A night to forget, that's for sure.

We didn't get the same great reaction that we'd had in London until we hit Madrid, where we sold out two nights at a huge club. And the owner was some old aristocratic Spanish guy and was so pleased with us he gave Richard a huge chunk of hash that we almost couldn't finish ... The Spanish crowd went pretty nuts over us; it was rather heartwarming. Everywhere we went in Europe people thought maybe we could really crack it big. Early indications in Spain were good but we never sold as many records as they hoped. But every country abounded with enthusiastic fans waiting around to get something signed and they really helped keep our spirits up during some bleakish times.

Eventually we wound up back in England getting ready to open up for Duran Duran at the Hammersmith Odeon. But again the audience of girlie teenyboppers did not dig us one single little bit. Andy, Duran Duran's guitarist, came into our dressing room and was very gracious but we rudely gave him a frosty, muted reception. So both bands ignored each other after that. To their credit, Duran Duran live were just like their records – if you like that kind of thing, which I really didn't at all. They also needed elaborate strategies to escape from theatres because of all the girls chasing them.

Duran Duran's audience would've hated anyone who was on before their idols; they weren't an audience you could win over with clever lyrics or tricky guitar parts. They couldn't dig a bunch of Aussie hippies wearing paisley shirts and playing jingle-jangle rock. We were in Perth, Scotland, one night and drove up to the gig and a bunch of screaming girls ran to the car but they stopped in disgust when they saw we weren't Duran Duran. 'It's not THEM!' sneered one angry twelve-year-old to all the other kiddies who'd rushed the car.

That night Marty broke a string and angrily left the stage and a whole load of the kids cheered delightedly. It was like one down, three to go. We couldn't operate under such unfavourable conditions so I pulled the plug. It was meant to be a 25-gig tour or something but The Church jumped off after about five or six gigs. It cost our record company dearly but it was the right decision. The whole thing would've been a demoralising waste of our time.

Having quit the Duran Duran tour we suddenly had a lot of time to kill before our next gig at The Venue in December. Peter had just had his first daughter, Neige, so he went back to Belgium to spend time with his Belgian in-laws. Marty was originally from London so he disappeared back into the suburbs, which left me and Richard and Dennis living in that opulent flat with the spiral staircase.

One day Karin came over to London and stayed with me for a few days and that was when I really fell for her. I was amazed with everything about her: her accent, her wild ways – she smoked and drank and swore like a trooper! She was a punk-rock girl of 23 wearing cut-off black jean jackets and hennaed vivid red hair. We had some magical days in London together and I was gone hook, line and sinker. The sense of destiny I felt with her was quite overwhelming. She wasn't that easy to get on with, and she wasn't bowled over by me or the band, but that just made her seem so much more elusive and attractive.

Meanwhile we went to Scotland and played in a legendary town called Bannockburn. The locals came out in force and The Church and Bannockburn discovered they loved each other. We got a riotous reception. The next day I got a phone call from the mayor of Bannockburn asking if we'd play again that night – he personally guaranteed another sellout, but alas we couldn't do it.

Back in London we didn't have much to do. Richard and I went on expeditions to find hash and vegetarian food. Richard loved all things Jamaican and we used to always go into dodgy parts of London (and LA for that matter, too) chasing down Jamaican food. Richard was crazy about it. We'd pop up in some heavy-duty places and Richard would breeze in and everything would always be cool. Richard had a strange affinity with all kinds of people: we'd just walk into these totally Brixton Rasta cafes, both of us in paisley shirts and Levi's, corduroy jackets and tight black pants and suede boots. But Richard never felt out of his depth and I walked along, fearful, but trusting in his affability to get us through. One night we got tickets to see Neil Young at Wembley. The tickets got us in but there was nowhere to sit so we left and got chased by skinheads howling for our pansy blood. Richard and I hid in the darkness as they ran by searching for us in the shadows of some dismal suburb. Obviously we survived.

Eventually the time came to play our final gig at The Venue. It was sold out again and people went nuts. Jesus the famous hippy attended the gig, which was a good sign for our kinda psychedelic music. Jesus came down the front beaming and banging his tambourine out of time, causing us to lose our rhythm so I had to ask Jesus to put his tambourine away! Talk about feeling like a killjoy. Towards the end of the tour some big shot from Carrere took us out to dinner. I told him I was a vegetarian so he took us to a seafood restaurant. I had chips for every course and didn't say one word during dinner as everyone munched away on sea creatures – eating crustaceans turns my stomach; they just don't look edible to me. Anyway within a few years Carrere went belly-up and they didn't bother to pay us any royalties either. The scoundrels! And at the same time Stunn Records in New Zealand, who'd released our first lot of records, went broke too – again without paying a cent in royalties. Nice work. We've had a load of them do it to us: most recently, Thirsty Ear Recordings in America did the same thing *again* without paying any dough. Yawn.

Back in Australia, Jennifer met me at the airport but things changed a lot between us after I told her about Karin. Our relationship struggled on for a while but it would never be the same.

The Church then played some big shows – we had some big bands opening for us – but the public reaction was lukewarm.

We just weren't always so amazing live I guess. And our star had faded while we'd been overseas trying to crack the big time, just like every other Australian band was doing at the time. Then our manager told us to our great shock that we'd run out of money! So we embarked on another tour around Australia and New Zealand. Dennis came with us, freshly imported to be our tour manager. The fact that he snorted 1200 bucks worth of blow every day should have alerted us but we just naively accepted him as our tour manager. There was an awful lot of cocaine being snorted everywhere in those days by all the guys making money off musicians – they could afford 200 or 300 bucks a gram. Not me, I didn't think I could afford that ... until heroin came along, but that was much later.

On that tour we played just about everywhere there was a gig to be played. The reaction was lukewarm in New Zealand, which made the halcyon days of London seem far behind us. We were on our first little dip and we could feel it. Stuart Coupe came over to my house to do another interview and more or less pronounced us washed up and finished. People still came to our shows but a noticeable shift had occurred.

Still, we had loads of fun and games with Dennis, who could still talk his way out of anything. One night we had two pounds of marijuana in the boot of the car as we were driving through Adelaide after a gig. Ploogy called Dennis our lackey and Dennis warned Ploogy to never call him a lackey again. Immediately Ploogy said, 'Lackey, lackey, lackey, lackey!' So Dennis just slammed on the brakes in the middle of a big four-way intersection. He jumped out of the car and tried to get at Ploogy but Ploogy locked the door. So Dennis forced the window down to get in and get the lock up. And they were both screaming and shouting at each other, Ploogy almost mad with fear and giggling like a fiend trapped in the back seat next to me. Suddenly Dennis made a breakthrough and opened the door and got hold of Ploogy, and started dragging him out of the car. But Ploogy was holding onto the door columns for dear life. Dennis had gone absolutely crazy! Then in the middle of all this the South Australian police bowled up.

Dennis said, 'Evening Officer (in fact, he probably pronounced it *ossifer*), it's just the boys letting off a bit of steam after a gig, that's all.' The cops took him round the back and looked in the boot but somehow his constant jabber distracted them from noticing the two garbage bags of dope in the boot. He blinded them with his banter, and they let us go scot-free. More such zany times ensued.

There were many amusing conflicts between Ploog and Dennis – Ploog was like some kind of proto-situationist. He liked to push the boundaries and explore the edges of social norms. One day Dennis was checking us in to a rather posh hotel and encountered a bit of difficulty. He was talking on the phone to someone at the management office as well as the staff on the front desk as he tried to sort out whatever was wrong. Meanwhile Ploog had noticed the dry weather and that he could get a pretty decent static electrical shock by rubbing his feet on the hotel carpet, which he amplified by holding one of the hotel's large metal keys – a perfect conductor. Ploog and I had been busy zapping each other and anybody else all afternoon. We'd hold the key close to anything and this big pink spark all blue around the edges would jump out of the key.

Well Ploog chose his moment while Dennis was on the phone to unleash a mega shock to the back of our manager's neck. The spark leapt through space disappearing into Dennis's head. He recoiled and stood there quite … shocked … and then he said quietly into the receiver, 'Excuse me.' And then he chased Ploog around and around the hotel through the kitchen and dining room and through the posh drawing room where posh old blokes were reading the papers and drinking port. Finally he cornered him in the cloakroom and gave him such a punch on the arm that Ploog had trouble playing the drums.

Another punch on the arm then ensued the following night after Ploog flicked a towel at him. Dennis patiently hunted him down and WALLOP! Ploog was playing drums with only one arm for a while.

Dennis became a legend among my brother's band, The Crystal Set: they called him Mr Grit. One day he came over and taught them a lesson. He chopped out a load of cocaine for my brother and his friends. But before they could get up and have it he snorted it all up himself saying, 'You gotta be quick in this world!' It's something me and my brother still refer to as the parable of the slow snorter. A lesson was truly learnt that day.

You know, no one had any idea how much we were earning or where the money was going. I was pretty self-absorbed at the time and trusted in providence that we'd all get looked after. No one ever checked how much of our money went up other people's noses – you've really gotta shake your head in wonder at the greediness and narcissism and naivety that flourishes in the music biz. I was so distracted by all the flattery and bullshit that I didn't notice I was funding Dennis's raging cocaine habit. No wonder he never minded chopping out a few lines for the band every now and then! Still he was a likeable rogue and the source of endless amusing anecdotes; they don't make 'em like that anymore, that's for sure. The tour managers these days are all clean-living types glued to their computer and drinking Starbucks. More reliable but a lot less fun.

Eventually in 1983 we went into the studio to make our third album, *Seance*. I'd written all the songs and demoed them at home on my four track. We went into the studio with no real producers but ourselves and I kind of took over too much. The record was like one big demo. In this regard it's the most Steve Kilbey of all The Church records: I chose the songs and figured out almost everything except the guitar solos themselves, which I left to the players' discretion.

We'd always hoped that at the end of the project Bob Clearmountain might mix it, and I certainly had his rich organic sound in mind when I made the demos, but an officious little twit at EMI and I started to clash. This guy thought he knew what was best for us. We'd been signed to EMI through our deal with ATV/Northern Songs, but somehow now we were signed direct to EMI and this officious little twit wanted to take me down a peg or two. He decided we needed some modernisation and got in the mixer du jour, which was Nick Launay. Nick had done Midnight Oil's *10, 9, 8, 7, 6, 5, 4, 3, 2, 1* and had done a cracking job for them. He'd rejuvenated the Oils with all his slabs and stabs and dramatic new-fangled sampling triggering stuff. Kudos to him. But he fucked up a lot of *Seance* and it wasn't supposed to sound like it does. It's like he did the opposite of what I'd always imagined it would be.

For some reason I was the only one allowed to visit him and comment on the mixes. I went in there one rainy Sydney day – it was dark and overcast and I remember it so well. After chatting up the girls in the art department on the ground floor I went up to the mixing suite on the seventh floor. And there's Nick Launay, all of about nineteen, and the officious little EMI twit himself. And they played me some mixes and I was horrified. The fat bass was now wiry and grinding, losing all of its bottom end and its entire boom boom quality. The guitars were de-emphasised somehow and some parts were missing altogether. It never occurred to me in 1983 that someone would mix our record and actually leave off things I'd recorded to be on there but Nick just did what he liked.

I told them I didn't like it. Nick just stood there with his hundred boxes of outboard gadgetry, uninterested in my reaction. 'This is what I do,' he said, and actually that was true. He was heralding the dawn of the mixer who put you through his process to give you a sound that had his stamp. And good luck to them. But he ruined the mix on *Seance* – as epitomised by the unbelievably stupid sound of Richard's drums on 'Electric Lash'. Machine guns would blush at the rapid-fire electro miasma of Richard's rolls, but Nick was backed up and sanctioned by EMI's ninny.

The others in the band blamed me for the awful fucking sound of *Seance* and reckoned I should've done something but I don't know what. I ended up being the apologist to them for the mess Nick Launay made of the album by mistakenly pinning the record to that laughable era of stupid sounds as opposed to the classic sounds of *The Blurred Crusade*, which exist outside the zeitgeist. Never again did I want a mixer of the day foisted upon us.

I'd intended to put the song '10,000 Miles' on *Seance* but our EMI nong rang me up and we had a screaming match when he said he didn't want it on *Seance* because it wasn't good enough. I said, 'Since when do you decide which tracks go on Church records?' And he spat back, 'If you argue with me I will lock this record up and it will never come out. And that fucking song will still not be on it!'

A lot of people used to say that *Seance* was their favourite album, which makes me happy, but it could've been so much more if I'd relaxed control a little and if someone other than Nick Launay had mixed it. Or even if I'd been allowed to mix it with the band and John Bee. But it never escaped a certain stiffness, and never attained the warmth I wanted it to have. It's harder to create a masterpiece than you think – I sure found that out!

The record came out to some mediocre reviews. We did a half-arsed arty video with Richard Lowenstein, who'd done good work for others but it didn't really work out with us. He seemed oblivious to any advice. A bit like Nick. This is what he did and he was doing it. The song we chose for our first single was not an obvious one, and the video was obscure so it hardly ever got played.

As all this was happening I got a message from Karin asking me to come and visit her for summer in Sweden. It was my first real invitation from her so I booked the tickets and one day in June I flew off to Stockholm. It would be the start of an endless stream of songs that are still flowing on into this world.

10
SMORGASBORDS AND OMBUDSMEN AND MALIBU

It's not about anything. Like all my songs, it's a portal into your own mind where I give you a guided meditation. It's a blank, abstract canvas for people to lose themselves in.

KARIN AND HER friends met me at Arlanda airport in Stockholm and we drove straight to her father's house at Graddo (which translates to Cream Island), a spot outside Stockholm on the archipelago. The house was full of young Swedish types including Karin's three younger brothers: Anders was handsome, quiet and distant; Marten was the friendliest and the kindest; And Olle was the youngest and naughtiest. Plus there were a couple of members of Karin's all-girl punk band and their partners.

They were all lefty, intellectual feminist types – even the guys! I was totally out of my depth. I didn't know anything about the IRA or the Black September movement. I thought the punk days were over and hedonism ruled, but not there in Sweden. I immediately began to behave like a bit of a turkey and probably pissed them all off much more than I meant to, although they maintained a polite Swedish detente at all times. Everyone was impossibly good looking and polite and so fucking Swedish. They spoke Swedish all the time too, which I hadn't really considered. I thought they were gonna speak English with a groovy accent!

Of course being a jumped-up little rock star in Australia meant that now everything was all about me. I couldn't just relax and take it all in. It seemed every time we sat around that big long table in her father's kitchen they were all talking or laughing about stuff I had no idea about. Discussing Swedish musicians and actors and writers. No, I'd never heard of August Strindberg or heard any records by Ebba Gron. Sydney suddenly felt a long way away.

Being the sensitive kind of ninny that I was, that whole trip was beginning to blow my mind. I'd left Sydney in the middle of a gloomy, rainy, dark winter and popped up where the sun shone until eleven o'clock at night. And then at three in the morning this bright grey twilight mist would start up and it was impossible to sleep or even know when you should be sleeping. I felt like I was in a parallel universe; everything seemed just a little strange: wooden butter knives, showers with hardly any water pressure, hard bread, caviar and pickled herring, coffee with buttermilk, and the list went on and on.

Karin and I would go for walks around her father's place. The weather and the scenery was beautiful, it overwhelmed me and I behaved childishly trying to get more of Karin's attention. I mean we were having a nice time but she wasn't bowled over by me, which some stupid arrogant thing in my brain was demanding. I mean for fuck's sake, she invited me on her summer holidays – that meant she liked me. But I needed more reassurance. So instead of enjoying all of that as much as I could I was being needy and sulky. My narcissism knew no bounds. In a foreign land, stripped of the roadies and the groupies and all the flatterers, I felt strangely naked and exposed.

Karin's father Jan came home one day and he and I got along really well. He loved to speak English and had a whole bunch of slightly naughty jokes, which were pretty funny as he sometimes grasped for the English word needed to deliver the punchline. His second wife Gunnel spoke perfect English and Jan would always stop right at the end to ask her the English word for something. Jan always included me in everything and was a very kind and gracious host. We went out fishing on his boat and got on famously. He was a very likeable guy and didn't put any trips on me because I was with his daughter. Gunnel was a really intelligent woman and would discuss literature and stuff with me too, even though I must've seemed a bit of a philistine to her at the time.

Karin herself remained elusive. We were together, but I felt lonely nonetheless. One day we left the country and went into Stockholm where Karin lived in the most amazing share-flat I had ever seen. It was a grand old apartment in a leafy part of Stockholm, with huge windows and high ceilings and a bunch of hip young Swedes. Karin and I went shopping in the Swedish supermarket, which had such a different vibe from the Aussie Woolworths and Coles! Everything in Sweden was muted, luxurious and futuristic. The people seemed homogeneous and sensible, and ever so slightly aloof – like the elves in *Lord of the Rings* or something. We went to the famous Red Room and sat at a huge table quaffing beers that I calculated to be worth 30 bucks each. Everyone was rabbiting on in Swedish and I just sat there looking stupid. At one point this was confirmed when one of Karin's band mates said, 'You look pretty stupid sitting there not knowing what's going on!' Yeah, she sure was right about that.

The more I tried to impress Karin the less impressed she was. One day I played her a cassette of two romantic songs I'd written for her. She didn't say a word. After they were over she jumped up and said, 'Now I'll play you something I like!' And she put on some awful Swedish punk song. No doubt this was good for me, taking off some of my arrogant edges, but it was still hard to take at the time.

We went out to the country to celebrate Midsummers Eve, which is a really big thing on the Scandinavian calendar. At trestle tables under the trees outdoors sat loads of her relations eating and drinking and becoming more rowdy as the evening progressed. After a while Karin and I walked down that long track to the lake where we swam naked in the cold brown water and sat on the mossy rocks talking. I'd never known anything like that feeling before: the magic of the Swedish summer, the beautiful forests that surrounded us, the unfamiliar stars in the northern sky. Sydney really seemed a long way off, and so complicated and dirty.

In the days we wandered through the villages and visited the kiosks where I topped up on French fries and Swedish licorice lollies.

I felt I was being drawn to Karin because of some higher purpose. I knew she felt it too but she just wouldn't put my mind at rest and tell me she loved me and wanted to be mine. Well I mean she probably did say those things but for some reason it was never enough. Maybe it was because we were surrounded by her ex-boyfriends and guys she'd had a fling with somewhere sometime – it was all doing my head in.

One day we went to a restaurant called Bistro Boheme and in the men's room there was some graffiti in Swedish about her: 'I love

Karin in Pink Champagne,' it read. And underneath someone else had written: 'Who hasn't?' Embarrassingly enough I had to ask Karin to translate it. What a total dork I must've seemed.

One day we caught the ferry to Gotland, a small island off the Swedish coast. We stayed with Ann, the singer of Pink Champagne, and her husband Micke. Ann and Marty were also destined to one day have a daughter, Signe, who's a year older than the daughters that Karin and I would eventually have. But then Ann was married to Micke, a journalist at some big Swedish newspaper and they had a great little house where we could spend our days driving about the island and playing mini-golf. This really was the life. The weather in Sweden during a good summer is surely the most wonderful thing ever. The biggest place on Gotland is Visby, which is like a full-on medieval city complete with its own wall and everything; I walked through the old streets and felt like I was in a dream with the blue sky and the dark water of the surrounding sea and the clatter and chatter of this quaint town almost untouched by time.

We spent the evenings outside eating and drinking and I worked on my latest 'thing', which the Swedish call *snus*. *Snus* is this tobacco that you stick in your mouth against your gums. You can get it in packets or just loose, which is kind of messy. The loose kind often leads to this characteristic boot-slap thingy that you see all the time in Sweden as the guys knock it off their fingers on their boot-heels. You're not supposed to swallow it, although I did a few times and it makes you feel verily nauseous. So there I was sitting at the table with my lip bulging, full of *snus*, looking like a right idiot, I'm sure!

Some of the Swedish words sure are funny to an Englishman. There were signs up all over Stockholm in all the shop windows bearing the legend 'SLUT SPURTS'. Wow I thought that was raunchy! The reader won't be very surprised to know that the

Swedish meaning was rather mundane compared to the English. It meant something like 'End of Sale Rush'. Karin's father was a great source of info about Sweden: 'In summer we Swedes hunt and make love,' he said. 'In winter we don't hunt much,' he added.

All the Swedes could speak perfect English except the oldest ones. And yet almost all of them apologise for their *bad* English when they really don't need to. The Swedes like to point out the words they've added to the English language like the two words in the title of this chapter. And all Swedes will tell you about their word *largom,* which means 'just right!' and does that job so well for them. I'd never before encountered such national pride in a word – although when one gets used to it, it is incredibly pithy!

Karin's accent was quite Swedish – more than say that of her mother, who spoke English in a crystal-clear upper-class English accent that contained more interesting vocabulary than most Aussies could shake a synonym at. (And she wouldn't have ended a sentence on a preposition!) But I liked to listen to Karin's accent. She made English interesting for me again. One morning she said, 'Today, I think I will upset my hair.' It was very endearing, although she didn't necessarily like me thinking that.

As the holiday went on Karin and I became closer and closer. Waiting for trains in the country on a sunny day or taking our long evening walks down to the lake we talked and laughed and became friends. Something bigger than ourselves seemed to be pushing us together. It was as though it was fated to be. Karin resisted that more than me at first; she was only 23. I imagined she could've had a whole load of groovy Swedish rock stars and actors for her boyfriends and sometimes I felt inexplicably inadequate. I would've done anything to please her.

It was an ideal summer, like a scene from a film – everyone deserves at least one summer like that in their life. We sat in

Kungstradgarden in the middle of Stockholm and ate cheese and tomato baguettes and drank coffee and beer. The Swedes seem to have an affinity for alcohol and they all drank copiously, even from an Australian perspective. I was amazed and in awe of how much booze they could put away and how many strong cigarettes they could smoke. Pot and hash were available but generally frowned upon; Karin smoked a bit of weed but she could take it or leave it.

Sweden was a funny country when it came to intoxicating substances. You could only buy booze from these Systembolaget places run by the government. You couldn't go in to the shop, pick out what you wanted and take it to the counter. Some lackey would have to go out the back to fetch it for you. Usually the place was packed so you'd have to take a ticket and wait your turn. The system was failing spectacularly if it was trying to keep alcohol out of people's hands: everyone bought up more than they needed in case they ran out over the weekend. And then they'd be back at the bottleshop first thing Monday!

But most people weren't that thrilled about pot. When I first went there they had an ad campaign against the dangers of *hasch*. My my, the damage done by a month of hash smoking is devastating, did you know? Hollow cheeks, acne, greasy hair, missing teeth, bags under the eyes. Looked like those Swedish youth had been in a death camp smoking ice for ten years! But the campaign worked.

One night I went to a party in Malmo, Sweden's third-biggest city. The kids there were so fucking wasted on vodka they were fighting and vomiting all over the place. I lit up a joint and suddenly people started fleeing the party like rats off a sinking ship! 'What are you doing man?' screamed the host of that drunken melee. Someone even jumped out a window to get away from the horror of my joint! I was bemused and contemptuous of their desire to toe the government line while getting as pissed as newts on vodka. Oh the irony!

Though I have a passion for pot I've never been a big drinker – sometimes I'll drink onstage a little to loosen things up but I never want to get drunk. I just can't hold my liquor. I'm a one-beer drunk and I've never been really drunk in my whole life. The scene bores me. But in Sweden I guess I pretended to be vaguely interested in it because everyone seemed to be drinking all the time. *Skol!*

Eventually our last few days rolled around and Karin and I agreed she'd come and visit me in Australia in the not-too-distant future. Just before I left I rang up Marty in Australia and told him I'd had a bad dream that *Seance* had dropped out of the charts. He told me that it had. It was gonna be a struggle to regain our momentum.

After I returned to Sydney I began to brood about Karin. At least it was good for my writing, and I started my routine of going to the swimming pool every morning. I'd walk up to Victoria Road and take the bus into the city. Then I'd walk through the streets and the Domain to the Boy Charlton pool, where I'd do twenty laps come rain, hail or shiny shine, all the while thinking about Karin and Sweden and music. Afterwards I'd go home and try to teach myself Swedish from a book. Eventually she came out to Australia in 1984 and we were a couple for about the next ten years and ending up writing quite a few songs together including, of course, 'Under the Milky Way'.

1984 was a year of marking time for The Church and for me. *Seance* hadn't done very well anywhere in the world and the pundits were suggesting our time had come to an end. I started to believe them. Our gigs in Australia weren't leading anywhere. Instead of advancing the cause and conquering and building and all that, we were merely paying bills and earning a wage. We toured more, doing all the same places, often to fewer and fewer people. The country towns totally didn't dig us and never will, it seems. We were just too 'city' for them I guess. It was certainly demoralising to 'burn' promoters and publicans when we didn't pull a big enough crowd. One night I saw a guy crying as he handed over our fee to the tour manager: 'That's it I'm out of business now,' he sobbed. It made me feel so fucking bad! I urged the tour manager to give him some of the money back but he refused. A few years later in San Francisco I urged a tour manager to give back some dough to a complaining venue owner after we'd done mediocre business that night – the tour manager gave him back half the dosh and everyone involved was furious with my stupid interfering because now our tour was struggling itself. Me and my big mouth!

Our success and the subsequent lack thereof had played games with my mind. Occasionally I took a stab at replicating an 80s sound in my home studio: hence you have 'Constant in Opal', which is a good song, and 'Maybe These Boys', which is a bad song – you know the one the smart-arses mention when they're casting around to find my Achilles heel, my true nadir of songwriting. You can't go much lower than that little two-chord horror to understand what letting the 80s in did to my head. But a few people heard the demo of 'Maybe These Boys' and I got talked into doing it. And so the first and only real stinker of a Church track got onto an EP called *Remote Luxury* that came out in early 1984.

Later that year we would release another EP called *Persia* that contained 'Constant in Opal' as well as a few other cool tracks like 'Shadow Cabinet', which was kind of a taste of things to come on *Heyday*, being composed by the band and not just me. It was the first time the band had written a piece of music that was earmarked to be sung over by me. I was very happy with both the music and the lyrics. The band was moving forward, becoming a sleeker machine: I thought *Persia* was a great little record.

Unfortunately our decision to do two separate EPs was a mistake. Why do EPs? They're neither here nor there, don't you agree?

But now I'm only talking from that stupid commercial perspective. I'd been forced to contain the duality of seeing things from two perspectives simultaneously: that is from my private songwriter's perspective and from a commercial record company's perspective, whose job it was to sell my bloody songs so I could get paid – even if only partially! And looking back I see we did three EPs when we should've been trying to make the golden album that *Heyday* would almost prove to be. Almost but no sugar lamp as one review said …

Meanwhile some bizarre things began to happen for The Church. Out of the blue Warner Bros. Records in the US signed us up and decided to release *Remote Luxury* and *Persia* as an LP called *Remote Luxury* towards the end of 1984.

For a while some nineteen-year-old kid in America had been calling me up and telling me how great *Seance* was and generally being an inquisitive fan-boy type. He was supposedly part of a management group run by a millionaire who wanted to acquire hip groups. From the kid's perspective there were few hipper groups in the world than The Church: we were totally obscure, our records were almost impossible to find in the US, and we were mysterious and all that malarkey.

The kid's name was Marc Geiger. He's now a big agent in LA. And he did actually have a millionaire friend who wanted his own fucking rock'n'roll band to manage. He already had a load of other things but he wanted a goddamn band, and a good goddamn band too. One that was gonna go places and impress people.

And so we split amicably with Michael Chugg and signed up with the millionaire and the young guy. For a while we managed ourselves in Australia and were amazed by how much money was actually floating around, then Marty and I flew over to the US to meet our new management.

We arrived at night, got picked up in a limo and ate dinner with our new guys. There was John the millionaire and Marc the kid and also Ken the BMW dealer. We went home in the limo and it was dark and foggy. I went into a guesthouse and flopped down into a deep, deep sleep. When I awoke the next day nothing could've prepared me for the sight that greeted my weary jet-lagged eyes. John's house was on the side of a hill, very high up overlooking the Pacific Ocean. Below sprawled his gardens complete with a swimming pool surrounded by topless girls. It was a perfect blue morning, warm but not hot. On a set of drawers someone had thoughtfully left an ounce of Humboldt County purple heads and I got busy smoking at once. It sent me off into a dreamy delicious haze. There were other refreshments as well; I'd sure fallen on my feet!

John was a very nice guy. He was affable, generous and easy to like. Where all his money came from, no one ever said, although there were many rumours circulating that it was South American drug money being laundered somehow. I never really knew and I didn't think it appropriate to ask. Once I went into a shoe shop with John and he liked a pair of shoes so he bought twenty pairs of the same shoe in all these different colours. He bought Marty a load of equipment too: a Vox amp and a rare Rickenbacker guitar and a drum machine too. John asked me what I wanted but I wouldn't or couldn't name anything that I wanted him to buy me. I know that if I'd said a Porsche or something he would've gotten it for me, but I was too proud – or silly – to ask.

As wonderful a guy as John was he didn't have a single fucking clue how to manage a rock band. But he wanted to try it out. Hey it couldn't be that hard, could it? Warner Bros. wanted us to lose him almost as soon as the arrangement started. We had a disastrous visit there one afternoon: John and I were both as high as kites after snorting cocaine and smoking that primo Californian weed.

I was so out of it I was unable to talk or say anything! We must've made some impression as we sauntered down those platinum- and gold-lined corridors. Two nitwits, yet complete opposites, out of our depth and both floundering.

On the other hand the kind of guys you met in record companies those days weren't up to much scratch. They seemed so phoney and insincere, like caricatures, always blabbing on with all the industry jargon; it was the exact opposite of why I got into music and I instinctively knew that to get involved in all this management stuff would destroy my creativity. This talk of shifting units and penetrating secondary markets was anathema to me. It was useless me going into record companies in those days; I only ever succeeded in pissing everybody off.

Life in Malibu was grand. There were always loads of pretty girls at John's and plenty of refreshments too. We went to the best restaurants every night. One night we went to a place doing nouvelle cuisine, which I'd never had before. The dishes came out looking awfully sparse – just a carrot, a few sticks of asparagus and a thin sauce. Marty and I complained about it, not understanding what it was supposed to be. Marty was complaining about the dress code too; everybody seemed very dressed up. 'It's a wonder they let us two blokes in at all!' he said, indicating our holey jeans and scruffy jackets.

'They wouldn't have,' said John, 'except that I own this restaurant.'

We spent two weeks with John. He was indeed a gracious host. But Warner Bros. wouldn't come around to him. He wasn't really a manager anyway, he was more like a guy collecting a menagerie and he needed a band. Eventually Karin and I went back and stayed with him for a month prior to the band's US tour, which was coming up in November and December. Again John was a faultless and generous host, but things turned a little strange when a vacancy turned up in the American all-girl band The Go-Gos, who'd lost their bass player.

In 1984 The Go-Gos were one of the biggest bands around, and although Karin wasn't a bass player she could certainly play the bass – and she had rock star looks and a few records and tours with Pink Champagne behind her. So we put in an application and she got a reply and a time for an audition. At this point John got really interested. He started daydreaming about managing one of The Go-Gos and started to believe that this unexpected windfall would wind up in his lap. He imagined all the leverage this would give him and all the status, but Karin didn't get the gig. John was mightily disappointed and we saw his petulant side for a while ... although the dinners and drink and drugs still flowed whenever we wanted 'em.

Then came our first US tour, which was quite an eye-opener in many ways. The rest of the band turned up and we started rehearsing: we were going all over the US and it was gonna be amazing!

11

CRUISING DOWN THIS SHUDDERING HIGHWAY

By the end of November 1984 we finally hit New York City and, of course, we were all bowled over by this most fabulous place. We played a great show at the Ritz and I snorted a line of coke with one of the Psychedelic Furs. Man, I was really making it in show biz now! The Ritz show was a great response just like in London and it really meant a lot to us. A review said that on the night we 'were the best guitar band on earth'. Amen.

We hit the road running in America. At last the Holy Grail of every band ever: the big US tour. But first there was a secret warm-up show at a cozy little cafe in Malibu. It was a small and rather intimate night, even by a secret show's standards. We did OK. It was beginning to dawn on me that we'd pretty much be starting over again. There were a few people at the gig and most of them were very enthusiastic about *Seance*, which was kind of gratifying. Unloved in Australia, *Seance* was revered as a cult classic there. Though it wouldn't get an official US release until 1988 when Arista Records released all our old records in one go, *Seance* was the record that most hip Americans dug the most.

John had secured a lovely old-school tour bus and a lovely old-school tour manager called Mel, who'd tour-managed Aerosmith once upon a time. We had a crew of weird characters as our road crew, and John paid them all top dollar. In fact, during an argument the crew even told us, 'Fuck you, we're working for John, not you!'

And so we set out. The crew were all jaded and cynical, the band naive and enthusiastic. We started out at Fender's Ballroom in Long Beach, California. The first thing I noticed was how in-your-face a lot of the American audiences were. They always wanted more. They were more argumentative. And they made a lot more sound than the Australians when they were appreciative. They waited around longer to meet us and were more persistent in finding us to ask questions. They were essentially on our side. A young guy started pestering me as soon as I showed up; I couldn't believe it. When I tried to ignore him he started threatening me – all this within five minutes of showing up for the sound check!

Afterwards we travelled down to San Diego on that clogged-up highway. Richard and I were tucking into that trippy Californian weed and getting spaced out. The crew were snorting cocaine but they weren't particularly keen on sharing it, which caused some problems when the band wanted to partake beyond the customary freebies. Our hippy demeanour didn't sit well with the uptight coke-snorting crew at all. It was a clash of ideologies, I guess.

Then the gig in San Diego was not that well attended. Morale was terrible as we slunk back to LA to play an outdoor university gig at USC, which turned out to be OK in the end.

Wolfgang's in San Francisco was where I first caught sight of Donnette Thayer, who was there to meet her favourite band – or so I heard later. The crowd was definitely on our side at Wolfgang's and they gave us a really good reception. The next day we went to the Haight-Ashbury district to chase down some old hippies, but there were precious few; though we did find some good clothes shops and record stores.

Then we had our ill-fated gig at The Palace, right in the middle of Hollywood. The Palace was a real showcase gig where big shots from record companies and powerful moguls hung out. For some reason Richard didn't turn up for the sound check and so the drummer for the opening band kindly played the drums in his stead while our new sound guy got the levels right.

Each drum had its own microphone and its own input channel. So the guy drummed along with us for a few songs. Trouble was, the guy played about a tenth as loud as Richard. And so at the gig when Richard sat down and started playing the drums all hell broke loose because his walloping at full strength made all the microphones feed back and howl indignantly while all the bass elements rumbled deep in the PA. It was an awfully inauspicious beginning to the evening and we quickly lost our vibe and kind of gave up, all in front of all the Warner Bros. geezers and our managers and stuff.

Why was Richard late? I don't remember, but we sure hadn't made any friends in LA with our performance at The Palace. Yet up the road in San Francisco we'd been so goddamn groovy. A tale of two cities!

We played two gigs in Colorado; it was snowing and everything there. The dressing room in Denver was in the kitchen and the gig was across the courtyard but the roadies had to run through the snow with the guitars, which would get detuned – especially the 12-string. All the retuning must've been so boring for the audience.

In Chicago we played at Cabaret Metro. We pulled 400 people and they liked us. The tour then wound around the Midwest: sometimes there wasn't a bad little crowd, other times we struggled.

Life on the road was like being in a little army. It had its rules and its regulations. It had its own jargon and jokes. There were two places to travel on the tour bus: up the front or down the back. Everyone knows that down the back is where all the action happens; it was where people were taking serious drugs or seriously plotting or seriously listening to music. I spent many afternoons of my life driving through darkening suburbs and hurtling down highways in dark green beltways. And I sat down the back and smoked the dope that people gave us at almost every show. And I watched America go past out the back of our warm and comfy tour bus listening to Richard's reggae cassettes.

At this stage of the game Richard and I were sharing hotel rooms. We were very marijuana oriented – it was our creed and our manifesto. To smoke and smoke. The pot insulated me from that outside world rushing past in the snow and the rain. The pot distanced me from the audience and the people pushing in to shake our hands and ask strange questions. It extended a warm umbrella for me to shelter under. You could hide within being stoned; life seemed like a cartoon that way.

Richard and I shared our stash most of the time. We'd have a smoke first thing in the morning, then we'd light up after breakfast. Ever so quickly Richard would be doing a charade of someone smoking a joint, which meant he had one rolled up and ready to go. So I'd follow him out into the car park. Then we'd have a few on the bus. Everyone would, often even the driver. Then we'd have one before sound check and one after dinner and one or two before the gig, and then many more afterwards if people were rolling them for us out of their own weed.

Pot has its logistical problems, but Richard was onto it. He kept a healthy stash, but not so much that it'd be some heavy bust if we get caught. The attitude towards pot in America in those days (and to some extent still today) varied drastically from state to state. In some places everybody had it or grew it, in other places it was hard to come by and a bit hush-hush.

The crew had no trouble finding cocaine though. Which they bought by the '8-ball' – that's like three and a bit grams, right? In some states there was also some real music-union malarkey going on. It seemed like there was a union for unloading the truck and a union for putting the stuff into the theatre and another union for moving it to the stage where your own crew could then actually handle it. And somehow we transgressed the rules a few times, and the solution was always that every union demanded its own 8-ball. Can you really believe you're reading this stuff?

Meanwhile our music was getting tighter and harder, and we were developing and learning. Our tour de force was a song called 'You Took' from *The Blurred Crusade*. In the long extended middle section we'd always built up to this climactic spot with everyone hammering away harder and harder. This really came to fruition on that tour and I must say the American audiences really seemed to appreciate that kind of thing – it's a shame we didn't do more of it. We usually ended our live shows with 'You Took', and it left the crowds pretty satisfied that they had seen something special.

But still the audience reaction varied from town to town. We went to some places that seemed very gothic and dark, especially as America went deeper and deeper into winter. I kept thinking of that Doug Ashdown song with the line 'Winter in America is cold'. It surely was and very bleak. We did Cincinnati and Pittsburgh and we went to Toronto where we played the El Mocambo Club, not long after The Rolling Stones had played there.

Seriously though, America does have the best audiences beyond any doubt in my mind; for The Church, at least! Our tour rolled around to Minneapolis where we played at First Avenue, which was a venue that Prince made famous in *Purple Rain*. Disappointingly it wasn't the same dressing room and corridor system that it was in the film: it was just a room side of stage. We got dinner and the vegetarian option for me was spaghetti with ketchup. Wow, that's nutritious!

Anyway, people had been telling us about Minneapolis and this record shop that had given us a lot of support there: *Seance* had been a big seller on import at this one shop called Northern Lights. So we were gonna have a record signing. I'd done a few of these before and no one had shown up and it had been pretty *Spinal Tap* I tell you! So I was rather wary about the idea and didn't believe all the hype. You can imagine I was pretty shocked when we were led into the store and they had 400 people lined up! They gave us a huge ovation – if only every city had been like that we would've been fucking laughing. It was very touching and gave us hope to carry on into the future and towards gigs where they hadn't heard of us or where no one turned up. It helped to boost our sometimes flagging morale.

Yeah if only every town was Minneapolis but they weren't. We saw the downtown collapse and decay in cities like Detroit and Cleveland, with their boarded-up buildings and beggars in the snow. We trod cautiously down unfamiliar terrain and I never wandered too far away from everybody else. We drove out into the snowy wastes of Wisconsin and did three gigs to small but enthusiastic audiences.

In Boston we played a gig at the Paradise Theatre and afterwards someone gave me a huge line of the strongest cocaine I'd ever had. I came out of the dressing room like a bull into a china shop. I was totally off my tree and extremely amorous. In a wildly uncharacteristic move I marched up to some girls still hanging around and pretty much said, 'Do any of you wanna sleep with me?' A pleasant-enough damsel volunteered to take me up on my invitation. 'C'mon!' I said, 'Let's leave right now!' We walked out into the frozen empty streets of Boston and there wasn't a cab in sight. 'We'll walk then!' I said. But the walk was long and the snow fell steadily as my swagger turned into a trudge through the frozen and mushy streets. By the time we got to my hotel we were covered in snow and our boots were full of sludge. Up in my room the girl and I looked at each other properly for the first time: we were bedraggled, red-nosed and both of us wished we weren't there, I'm sure. I said to her that she should sleep in my bed and I took the couch. In the morning we parted grimly. I thought the matter over and there was no real harm done, so it bemused me no end the next time we turned up in Boston to see her waiting with all the other fans. As I got off the bus she loudly declared in front of all and sundry, 'Hi Steve, remember me? I'm the girl who said NO!'

Providence, Rhode Island, was a strange town and a strange gig. The place was so gothic it made Cleveland look like Honolulu: there were all these two-storey wooden houses and strange little shops. We played an afternoon gig at a place called The Living Room. The guy who ran it told us his mum was cooking up a vegetarian treat. And then he sat there and watched me try to eat it but it was truly terrible and was full of every kind of vegetable I hate: eggplant, capsicum, celery and cilantro or anything too oniony. This guy's sitting there asking me, 'What ... you don't like my mother's cooking? She's fed every band who's ever played here and every one of them's loved my mother's cooking!' Wow, you could get into trouble fast in America without even trying. And funnily enough,

I remember the guy and his mother's cooking but I don't remember the gig at all!

In Washington DC we played a rat-infested joint called the 9:30 Club where the rodents were literally running about in the dressing room. Fortunately the audience response was definitely not mousey!

Finally we went down south and hit Georgia and played in Atlanta at the 688 Club where we got a truly wild reception. The next day our manager John rang up and gave me the truly dismal sales figures for *Remote Luxury*. He almost seemed to enjoy giving me the bad news when he used the term 'grand total' – we'd sold a mere 16,000-odd records, which in those days and on a major label was absolutely disastrous.

Ploogy and I flew to LA after the tour – Ploogy was going on to Australia and I was going to Sweden. We stopped in on John at his mansion in Malibu. We had to give him the bad news that Warner Bros. insisted we find ourselves a more experienced manager. Well John got us nice and high and we sat with him in his hot tub overlooking the ocean and suddenly Ploogy blurted it out in his stuttering embarrassed way: 'We don't want you to be our manager anymore, John!' And John, for all his money, sat there and shed a tear or two. It was a poignant moment for all of us. And he let us go graciously after having wasted a small fortune on us, and never asked to be paid back. He was a good guy; he just wasn't a manager, whatever that was.

So I flew to Stockholm where I stayed with Karin at her mother's place in a suburb called Jakobsberg. It was an incredibly snowy winter; Karin's mother's lovely big house was half buried in snow and it just kept piling up and up. It was always dark and outside it was so cold that the moisture in my nostrils froze, giving me this strange crunchy nasal feeling.

I spent my days recording tracks on Karin's brother's Portastudio, a cassette version of my own four track. (The songs all later appeared on some Steve Kilbey bootlegs.) One of Karin's friends had scored me some killer weed and when everyone went out I sat there looking at the black snowy weather and I smoked and fiddled around with the Porta ... Karin's brother Olle added some flute on tracks such as 'Snowman' and 'The Prophet Margin'.

During the day we'd wander down to Centrum where I'd eat chips with bearnaise sauce and drink a chocolate drink called Pucko. At night we'd play Trivial Pursuit with the family. I fared badly at Swedish Trivial Pursuit so it was very nice when I was the only one who knew the name of Thor's hammer. Mjolnir. I knew that from my readings of Norse mythology, which certainly impressed 'em for a little while.

While in Sweden Carrere, in England, asked me to come over and do some interviews to promote *Remote Luxury*, which was going nowhere fast over there. A guy called Matt Snow was giving us all these mediocre reviews, unfavourably comparing us to REM. If he'd done his homework he might have seen we were in operation a clean two years before REM even existed and realised we weren't influenced or even vaguely impressed with them. Some people kept trying to lump us in with them but they had nothing to do with us; we had no intention of being like them, or any other contemporary band. But still this geezer's unkind words in some big English rag hurt my sensitive feelings.

I imagined what Matt Snow might look like and how cool he probably was. I was so not prepared for the chubby little beer-swilling blob who spilled his baked beans and eggs all down the front of his shirt: the beer and baked beans and eggs that my record company had bought him. He didn't want to start the interview until he knew he was getting a free boozy lunch, and he got as much down as he could in our allotted hour. I sat there thinking to myself: such is the power of the press that *this* guy is dictating musical fashion and criticising people's records. *This* comical little man! I was quite affronted by his scruffiness and his greediness. I decided then and there that I didn't care what the English press wrote about me – they weren't the hip oracles I had imagined; they were sad, opportunistic, beer-guzzling blokes, getting free drinks and whatever else from record companies desperate for publicity.

It's astounding how much power these guys wielded. The kids in America all read the English music rags and they could really make you or break you. The English press was the most dismissive of us, although we did enjoy some really good reviews as well as some really rude and uninformed bad ones. And I made the classic mistake of arguing back with the guys who gave me the bad reviews, and it did absolutely no good at all. Eventually my stupidly argumentative interviews would cost us a blanket silence in the UK as they stopped writing about us at all. You couldn't argue with these guys and win: they always had the last word.

But 1985 was a good year for me. Karin and I returned to Sydney, where the two of us lived a very peaceful and harmonious life together. We had everything we needed materially; my jealousy and possessiveness of her had abated somewhat and I was allowing her to be herself. We existed together quietly and happily.

For the first time in my life my thoughts began to turn towards the spirit and I began to haunt Sydney's Adyar Bookshop, now sadly defunct. On wet weekday afternoons Ploog and I would peruse the shelves for things on magic, yoga, drugs and anything strange, weird or trippy. We liked Madame Blavatsky and Al Crowley and we liked Hermann Hesse and Tim Leary and Ram Dass and anything to do with Buddha. We liked astral travelling and lucid dreaming and reincarnation and anything like that. Karin and I had started yoga classes and I was meditating and swimming and getting massages and floating in float tanks. I became very chilled out and very laid back. I was actually happy. I even stopped smoking weed for a few months, and I felt really good about everything. I didn't see the other two guys in the band all that often, and this calmed me down too – the two guitarists and I were constantly arguing about something but with them out of the picture I could relax even more.

I bought a very silly car, a 1959 Renault Floride, which really was a gutless wonder but it did look good. In the afternoons Karin and I would drive to Bondi for a swim, our old convertible rolling through the summery city on our way to the sea. At night we practised yoga in our candlelit spare room while listening to Brian Eno. It was a lovely time, and afterwards I called it my golden period. It would never ever be quite that good again.

Despite everything that had or hadn't happened for us in the US, Warner Bros. still wanted us to make another album. So we got together and decided to write it together. That is, we'd jam stuff out and I'd put vocals over it later. This meant everyone could contribute to the music, and everyone could get a share of the publishing dollar. We decided to try an English producer called Peter Walsh because we all admired the great job he'd done on Simple Minds' *New Gold Dream*. It had a really spacious atmosphere, and some great modern sounds that weren't your usual 80s blather. The record didn't seem obsessed with that horrible huge drum sound everyone in those days thought they had to have. Something in me just said that we should use him …

In those days getting a producer was a bit like telling your mum and dad what you wanted for Christmas, only the record companies were the mum and dad. In this case EMI in Australia and Europe, and Warner Bros. in the US. Just like your mum and dad they'd look into it for suitability and see if they could afford it. Luckily for us Peter Walsh became available and agreed to do it although I never really found out how much he charged. Whatever it was it was well worth it.

It was a cold and wintery day when we began working on the music for *Heyday*, which would contain some of our very best work ever. We'd already written 'Columbus' during a sound check one afternoon at the Newport Music Hall in Columbus, Ohio. We also had a little instrumental jam called 'Poland' that Marty and I had concocted one day at his flat Sunnyhurst in Bondi, as well as some songs we'd each written individually. I had 'Youth Worshipper', which I'd written with Karin, and I had a song called 'Disenchanted', which I'd never liked. Peter had a song called 'As You Will', which I liked, and Marty had a song called 'The View', which I didn't like.

But the bulk of the album would be written together; the music would be composed by all four of us at once. Everyone could come up with their own bits.

There was a feeling in the air that we were going to come up with something special. In a tiny little rehearsal room in Surry Hills we jammed and came up with a load of different bits and pieces. This was the most natural way for us to work. By now everyone was aware of what The Church was, and what it was supposed to be doing and it actually took a lot of the work off my shoulders, not having to compose all the music.

No one really knew what to expect when Peter Walsh turned up. He was extremely young and good looking in a cherubic way. He had longish blond crimped hair and rosy cheeks. He was the very epitome of an English schoolboy and only about 23 at the time. He was very charming and softly spoken and he immediately made friends with everyone in the band.

After we first met we were walking down the street towards Laurie's Vegetarian Diner, which was our favourite haunt and which was still in its original location in Surry Hills then, and I looked over and there's Peter Walsh walking along with Ploog holding his hand. It was some of Ploog's situationist humour again – he just wanted to find out what Walshy would do. At the cafe Peter came over to me and said, 'Richard keeps holding my hand, what should I do?' I said, 'Ignore it I suppose and hopefully he'll get sick of it!' He did and he did, and none of us looked back. Walshy was officially declared to be all right. And we all cooperated with him to the max. His suggestions were never rejected without some thought being given to them. He was one of the lads.

We had some terrific material lined up for *Heyday* and Walshy was pretty impressed with what we laid on him, though none of the songs had any lyrics. Recording the album was a lot of fun. There was a KISS pinball machine in the foyer of the studios and Walshy fancied himself as a pinball wizard – if you read the stuff scratched into the vinyl on *Heyday* you will read about 'the young English knob-twiddler versus the boys from Bondi' ... well that'd be referring to the pinball games in the studio!

The album was very elaborately recorded. Making use of a 32-track system we did more overdubbing than ever before. Walshy stacked up tracks and tracks of 12-string acoustic guitar on everything. Then when vocals came around we stacked up layers and layers of my voice. We decided we wanted some orchestra on a few songs so we drove out and met an arranger who did some scoring on the ideas Walshy and I had. It was a true and unbelievable blast to see the players roll up and get out their music and play. We got in a choir to sing on 'Already Yesterday' and it was beautiful. My only slight criticism of Walsh is that he got his timing slightly wrong: he spent too much time doing overdubs and mixing the first few songs and then ran out of time mixing the last songs. It became a bit of a hurried job, which was a shame but he couldn't change his schedule and stay the extra week that I reckon he could have used. Still, he did a superlative job and we got that soft warm sound that I'd always envisaged.

The album contains one of my very favourite Church songs of all time, 'Myrrh'. I guess this is the song I'd play to someone who said they'd never heard The Church and I had one song to give 'em an overall taste. It contains everything I like about The Church: all the very best bits in one song. The lyrics were written with a hundred books from the Adyar Bookshop swimming around in my head. All the ideas I'd gleaned, all rushing out in one song that seemed to glide along frictionless through the atmosphere. David Fricke in *Rolling Stone* described the lyrics as 'telegraphic' and he called the guitars the 'guitarchitecture'.

With the album recorded we needed a cover and a video. OK, I'd already decided the album was gonna be called *Heyday*. I mean that was its name, and there was no uncertainty to it. It was to do with idea of being unable to tell when one is really in their heyday: in 1985 it felt to me that we'd had some serious highs and lows but maybe our heyday was during *The Blurred Crusade* period, already three years behind us.

It was a wistful and hopeful title and it seemed to suit the music, don't you think? Some titles are just glued on to the music and don't have any real bearing on anything; to me *Heyday* was an organic and natural title. Irony within irony we decided to wear paisley shirts because that's what we'd worn during *The Blurred Crusade* when our star was still in ascent. So we dug out some paisley shirts and posed against a Persian rug. I'm not quite sure where the rug idea came from but it sure made a great cover. A lot of people have told me they bought the album for the cover alone – four long-haired pretty boys looking all delicate and poetic. Yep, the kids loved it!

Next, the video. Warners hooked us up with Larry and Leslie Williams, a young married couple from LA. They flew out to Australia and hung around to get to know us. They filmed me swinging in my hammock in the backyard at Rozelle, and Peter walking along the Bondi cliffs and stuff like that. Then we assembled in an open block in Pyrmont in inner-city Sydney. And again we had a lot of fun. We ran through the song all day and night as Larry and Leslie filmed us, and got us to give off some attitude. They even gave the pizza delivery guy a camera and told him to film us. The result is by far the best Church video ever.

The song was 'Tantalized'. It was about as rocking as The Church would ever get but sadly it wasn't a hit. Still the lyrics are kind of vaguely prescient and the song was a rush of energy, which the video well and truly captured. I for one was a very happy customer.

12
POEMS AND TANTRUMS

My solo albums represent the automatic, raw, unpolished version of what I do – I play all or most of the instruments myself, and I do the engineering and mixing too. Whether you think that's a good thing or a bad thing depends on you. Some prefer the undiluted Kilbey and some prefer it focused through the prism of The Church.

HEYDAY WAS A great album, but I was a very prolific writer and I was writing tons of songs I wanted to get out there. So I decided I needed to make some solo records. My first attempt was a single called 'This Asphalt Eden', recorded at EMI. It cost a fortune and somehow got fucked up in the process.

Then I had a good sift through all the stuff I was recording on my new eight-track machine – there was definitely enough good stuff for an album. Fatboy Studios down the road from me had the same machine I had, and some more gear for mixing. I took it in there and a brilliant guy called Pauly Simmons sprinkled fairy dust all over the bastard. In the end I had a nice little solo album with some good artwork and a local release on the small independent label Red Eye. The tracks were kind of all over the place; I suppose I imagined it was like Brian Eno's *Another Green World* or something ...

Some independent charts had just started up in Sydney and my album went to Number One – gee that felt pretty good, though it didn't really mean a great deal of sales. It made me feel slightly more relevant, but the album got mixed reviews. One said it was 'music for dentists' waiting rooms'. But some people liked the demo feel of it. It does contain some good and real songy songs as well: 'There's Nothing Inside' and a final song for Jennifer called 'Othertime'.

There's some great electronic-type tracks as well like 'Swampdrone' and 'Rising Sun', which is me getting the very most out of my old analog mono synth. And there's 'My Birthday the Moon Festival', which is a weird little number done on a very cheap drum machine. Actually the drum machine part was what most people didn't like: they'd hoped for an album with real drums but I had no way of recording real drums in my tiny bedroom studio in Rozelle! Anyway, I always liken my solo albums to sketches and see my Church albums as paintings. And they both have their own place in the scheme of things.

Around this time I decided to write a book of poetry. I'd been writing loads of poetry while we waited for *Heyday* to be released, sitting at an actual typewriter banging stuff out. The book was called *Earthed*. Yes it was a real hodgepodge of ideas and writing styles. Some of it reads really badly today and probably didn't read much better then. A lot of it is to do with a character called Neumann who is some sort of spy. The whole idea is a little bit of a cop from Michael Moorcock and his Jerry Cornelius character to tell the truth, which is strange because I'd stopped reading Moorcock about ten years before I wrote *Earthed*. But I remember reading in one of the Jerry Cornelius books that Moorcock invited people to take up the tale where he left off. I guess I kind of did.

Earthed is sometimes OK and sometimes it's a bit mediocre and merely derivative – when the book isn't about Neumann's vague adventures it's a kind of exercise in this prose poetry style that I was trying to develop. It was based on the idea of looking like prose but doing the kind of things within it that a poet could do, like huge leaps of the imagination and trans-magical realism. I printed 2000 copies of the book with a little help from Mr Phil Tripp, and sold every one either by mail-order or actually walking around the hip record shops in Sydney and selling to them as needed. It surely must be one of the most successful poetry books ever published in Australia, where selling a hundred copies is considered pretty damn good!

The poems are about all the usual Kilbey preoccupations: drugs, magic, ancient Greece, religion, etc. To make matters even more confusing, I then released an album called *Earthed*, which was an instrumental album vaguely based on incidents in the book. The album also went to Number One in the Australian Indie charts, which was again a nice bit of encouragement. Like the book, the record is a bit of a grab-bag of sounds. There's some very good stuff on there and there's some for aficionados only, you might say. It was like I loved the idea of the album and the book but, typically, I didn't follow through as much as I could or should have. Which is a shame, as it was halfway there, but I wanted the book and record out there much more than I wanted to do the serious work of getting the material ready. I just kind of knocked it all out casually thinking it was very surrealist of me (you know, doing things in an 'automatic' way). At the time I said I'd released the book 'to impress girls in nightclubs', which actually got me a little cartoon in *The Sydney Morning Herald*.

The book got some hilarious reactions. Particularly memorable was 'J Wallace Grubblesnutch', who slammed it with the headline 'Earth to Kilbey, Earth to Kilbey'. Yes I guess it's true: the book was a little pretentious and a little silly in places. On the other hand I've heard from many people over the years who were impressed or influenced by what they found in it. I've even heard from people who were so taken with the poems that they became an archaeologist or a professor in Ancient Greek, like I wanted to ... remember?

Eventually in 1988 Ryco released a CD of *Earthed*, which came with the book reduced to a flimsy little booklet, which took away from its original snazziness. I'd used the best and thickest paper available for the original so the booklet seemed a bit lightweight in comparison, robbing the poetry of some of its gravitas.

Meanwhile *Heyday* had come out to nearly unanimously good reviews in November 1985. Australia seemed to reappraise The Church because of this record. Suddenly our shows were full again and people were excited by what we were doing. We were back on the front covers of the music rags – not as defeated has-beens but as reinvigorated champs. The American music press also began to give us very good reviews, in important magazines too: *Heyday* was generally accepted as a good record right across the board and was getting college airplay.

We embarked on a huge tour of everywhere. Starting off in Australia we played a gig in all the big cities and then some. Then we hit America opening up for Echo and the Bunnymen, playing in large theatres and small halls. Echo and the Bunnymen were a very hip band at the height of their powers and success; live, they were formidable and put on a good show. Their audiences were receptive to us and we definitely made some converts. It seemed there was room for at least two hip bands in the universe.

The Bunnymen had a new drummer playing with them called Blair Cunningham. He was the most friendly of the whole bunch and would actually sit down and talk to us. The guitarist and bassist seemed sullen and unhappy and the singer Ian was never with the others. He travelled on his own and avoided talking to anyone other than his minder – a big Aussie guy called Ted Gardner, who accompanied him everywhere.

Ian wasn't beholden to sound check schedules or anything: he often waltzed in five minutes before the gig started and then no one got a sound check. I noted that his own band were as furious with him as we were. I mean come on, it's great that Ian's on a star trip but the rest of us wanna get a fucking sound check in! Ian did eventually speak to me at the very last gig, though it was hard understanding his thick Liverpudlian accent. He said something about how he didn't think it would work out with us initially but was happy to say we weren't bad for a bunch of long-haired Aussie hippies. Gee thanks!

There were whispered tales of long lines of girls at his door and long lines of coke on his mirror but I never saw any of that. But he was certainly succumbing to his own myth, and I wasn't surprised when the band broke up amid various shambles. He'd made the mistake of thinking he didn't need them, even though he quite patently did. The others then made the mistake of trying to carry on with a new singer, and the resulting album was torture. There was a lot to be learnt from all this – I simultaneously envied Ian and felt contempt for his star behaviour. As bad as I've been or ever could be, I would always turn up for sound checks and try not to let crews and other musicians down.

Throughout the tour a slow smouldering resentment was building up in Marty and being flung in my general direction. It got worse and worse every day. Eventually the oblique and cryptic remarks turned into full-on insults as he began to decide that he hated me. By the time we got to Europe it was turning into an all-out feud. The Church played at the first-ever Hultsfred Festival in Sweden, and in the middle of a song I walked over to Marty to indicate that I didn't know where we were in the song. I was shrugging my shoulders and, laughing, asking him to help me. Apparently he thought I was telling him to get fucked.

A few nights later in Hamburg the shit really hit the fan: he said he wasn't gonna play on the same stage as me. He said he'd do the gig on the side of the stage but not on it. Boy he was an angry little camper that night! He imagined himself Fletcher Christian about to throw off the yoke of the oppressive Captain Bligh in *Mutiny on the Bounty*. In Marty's fevered mind I was every rotten villain all rolled into one. Actually I was a tired and silly musician, who probably had said some stupid things, as well as being wilfully misinterpreted by others looking for something to complain about. As the time approaching our gig grew nearer we said some childish things to each other – bands are a hotbed for hurtful, childish comments; being a cross between a family and a little business you can imagine there was a bit of pushing about.

'Come on,' I remember Marty saying, 'I'd have you for breakfast!'

Not being much of a fighter I had no doubt he could. One of our roadies jumped up and restrained Marty saying, 'I'm not gonna let you hit Killer!' (my nickname being Killer Kilbey … duh!).

When Peter Koppes tells this tale he says that at this point I started throwing grapes at Marty. I'm not sure if I did or not. You'd think I'd have remembered, wouldn't you? Grapes or no grapes Marty stormed off into that good Hamburg night and disappeared. I informed the crowd that we'd be doing the gig as a three piece and if they wanted to go now they could get their money back. No one left. Thank God it was Marty who left and not Peter because Marty's parts weren't as crucial to the songs as Peter's.

We played a furious and punkish set: bootlegs of it are in circulation and you can certainly feel the desperate energy of the night. The next morning I contacted our management and told 'em Marty had gone. It came at a bad time; we had gigs in London already on sale and *Heyday* was in the US charts at about 150. But Marty's simmering petulance had to run its course.

With Marty gone I flew back to Stockholm to hang with Karin and try to figure out what to do next. I rang Craig Hooper in Australia and asked him if he'd like to join temporarily so we could fulfill our commitments – Craig had already played keyboards with us on some Australian tours and was a great player and a very nice guy. He agreed, and even cancelled some Reels gigs (his main band) to do it. It would've been a good thing I'm sure.

Marty was in Stockholm too and I heard through the grapevine that his girlfriend wasn't impressed with his sudden resignation and had advised him in no uncertain terms to get his job back quick smart. So one day he rang me up and we met up at the Bistro Boheme in Drottninggatan, the very one where I had read the graffiti about Karin. We talked the whole thing through: it was, as I imagined, all a storm in a teacup. We both promised to behave ourselves and be nicer to each other for the sake of the band, but the subtext was really that Marty didn't like me or approve of the way I carried on. I, for my part, agreed to stay out of his way and try not to offend his delicate sensibilities.

So what did I do to piss him off so much? Well I don't think I was as bad as some have made out. I smoked quite a bit of weed, and therefore was always going up and down a bit with that; you know how the initial burst of talkativeness eventually breaks down into a blurry torpor? But I only drank one or two shots of spirits during shows. First it was scotch, then it was mescal, and then finally I ended up on Jagermeister or Unicum Zwack, the Hungarian herbal aperitif.

But getting back to those undesirable qualities that would make any band member flee a group in horror: I was sarcastic and negative. It must've been hard for the others to hear me moaning on about our lack of success. Even after we did two sold-out nights at the Marquee Club in London I was still moaning because I wished we were somewhere bigger. The music biz wound you up and fed you all these expectations and I was getting despondent. People were always whispering in my ear, telling me how big we *should* be and how big somebody else was. No wonder I was always in some hyper-competitive mode with every other group in the universe. I was becoming a bit cynical and a bit vacant and a bit unreliable and fickle I guess.

Italy was a surreal experience for The Church. We opened for The Cult, who were quite big there. Just like Echo and the Bunnymen, the players in The Cult were lovely guys but the singer was a real ponce on a stupid star trip. Needless to say he didn't lower himself by talking to the support band. Live, The Cult were just another band rehashing some AC/DC licks. The singer put on a good show but the music and words were empty clichés. It pissed me off to have to support this malarkey and it pissed me off more that the audiences liked them way more than us! Envy and jealousy were definitely alive and well in my mind: they simultaneously hindered me from achieving my goals while goading me forward to keep doggedly trying.

In Italy I became really good friends with a guy from EMI Italy called Ernesto. He had a great big BMW bike and we sped around through all kinds of weather, me nervously hanging onto the back of the bike as we rode about doing all kinds of different press – for a few years back then it constantly seemed like The Church were just about to take off in Italy and Spain. A lot of people really dug us and our record companies dug deep into their pockets for more publicity.

We went down to Rome, the eternal city (officially my favourite city in the world). We ate the most wonderful food and drank the most wonderful wine at outdoor restaurants during the charged Roman evenings. Afterwards we played a bowling game in these special lanes set aside for after-dinner entertainment. Ploogy of course decided on the situationist stuff again, and bowled the balls at the feet of the guys from EMI Italy, giggling while he did it. Luckily everyone ended up laughing when it was determined there was no harm in it.

A few weeks before at a posh Madrid restaurant we'd been eating dinner and Ploog had started flicking his paella at Marty, and Marty had retaliated and flicked a big dollop on Ploog's face. As if this wasn't bad enough, Ploog loaded up his fork with paella, bent it back and let it go. The paella, which held together as it whizzed through the air, sailed over Marty's head and – wouldn't you just know it! – hit a very patrician-looking lady in her 50s who was eating dinner with her husband, who looked like a Spanish nobleman. He was absolutely beside himself as his wife tried to get the gooey rice out of her hair.

Marty could speak fluent Spanish so he translated what happened next: the nobleman demanded 'satisfaction' from Ploog for this grave insult to his wife; I like to think he meant an actual fucking duel. Imagine Ploog with a pistol at seventeen paces; I could've been his second! But our record company guy placated the nobleman by explaining we were a bunch of Aussies and Englishmen and that we were uncouth yobbos not worthy of his ire. The guy glared at Ploog, but was eventually persuaded to sit down and resume his dinner while Ploogy narrowly avoided some real old-world bother.

Meanwhile someone at EMI Italy had come up with the brilliant idea of sending The Church around Italy with a travelling pageant of pop artists. Yep, in the marketplaces of these cute towns we would mime 'Tantalized' to a bunch of puzzled Italians who didn't know what to make of us. Also in the line-up were The Blow Monkeys, and Limahl from Kajagoogoo, and an Italian singer called Sexy Girl who performed with a koala strapped to her back for no discernible reason ...

We turned up in one town on the Adriatic coast and stayed in the kind of hotel James Bond would've stayed in. Overlooking the slightly misty Adriatic Sea, there were crumbling columns on the shore and everything! We all had a dip in the water, which was so warm and inviting. We feasted in the dining room overlooking the sea where we could order anything we liked regardless of the cost. Our English tour manager Mickey constantly strained relations with EMI Italy by ordering those $250 bottles of Vin de Ruff, as he called them. Ploogy, in situationist mode again, started having the drum kit set up stupidly or missing the kick drum to see if anybody in the crowd noticed. I noticed and it looked stupid but I didn't care.

Soon Ploogy began to disappear before the shows. A classic example was when Mickey was sitting backstage sampling another bottle of Vin de Ruff, and the guy from EMI Italy comes running in saying no one could find Ploogy and we're on in five minutes. 'You must find Richard!' the guy is screaming at Mickey.

After tasting the wine again and beckoning the waiter for more Mickey says, 'You fuckin' find him!' In his own way, though, Ploog was protesting against the silliness of miming – I tended to agree.

We had a few days off and Ernesto invited us to his family villa on Lake Como. You cannot even begin to believe how beautiful it is there; words fail even an old Italian-loving fool like me. Karin came in from Sweden and we swung in hammocks, drank even more wine and walked the ancient streets. It was a magical rest even though tensions were always present.

We returned to England and played a triumphant sold-out gig at the Town and Country. England was still keen on us despite a few bad reviews. One guy, Steve Sutherland, who'd sung our praises earlier, seemed to be standing in line to give our albums a bad review. He dismissed *Heyday* contemptuously with some glib putdowns describing 'Happy Hunting Ground' as sounding like 'Felt stumbling through a Big Country rehearsal'. No it didn't actually ... the cloth-eared ninny.

Talking of disasters, I have to mention our gig in Stockholm at the Moderna Museet. Man, of all the places for something to go wrong! We were headlining this hip outdoor gig in the middle of Stockholm in summer. We should've fucking aced it! We turned up for the sound check and they had a brand new magnificent PA. The guitars were very loud but it was a very big stage so that was OK. They also had a very powerful monitor system that allowed me to hear my own voice above the drums and guitars. We played a few songs and I got it the way I wanted it, with nothing in my monitors except my own voice. We sounded great.

Another band was in line to sound check. The technician swore he wouldn't touch my monitors; he didn't need to – he had enough channels on his own desk. Sorted, I went backstage where everyone was jubilant. Karin and all her family were there, as was Marty's new girlfriend Ann and her family. We were finally going to claim Stockholm as our own. It was such a perfect day; we smoked some Swedish hash and waited to go on, confident we were about to slay 'em dead. Yeah right!

We walked on stage to much applause. Everyone knew we had Swedish girlfriends and spent a lot of time there; they were willing us to succeed! But it was not to be. The first song 'Myrrh' started up. That incredible beginning as it gets more and more intense, symbolising to me a body vibrating as the soul departs in astral travel. The imminent take-off. It sounded fantastic ringing out over the Moderna Museet gardens. But as I got near my microphone I realised something was terribly wrong. The guitars were both coming out of my monitors at an earsplitting level. It was excruciating; I could hardly get near the microphone to sing. Then I discovered my voice was not in the monitors at all. It was the very opposite of what I needed – I couldn't tell if the audience were hearing my voice either; I couldn't tell anything over the roaring racket of the guitars. Apparently it sounded perfect out the front. But slowly I got angry and despondent and then bitter and surly when the monitor guy couldn't or wouldn't get the guitars out of my wedges.

The audience started slow clapping and calling out 'COME ON!' It sounded fine to them; they couldn't understand the hell my ears were in just trying to cope with the noise. Eventually Marty attempted to swear in Swedish and it went down like a lead balloon. The sound onstage finally came good for the last half hour of the show, but by then we'd lost a lot of the audience's goodwill and they started leaving. We'd really made a mess of it through no fault of our own. I wasn't a hero among Karin's people like I hoped I'd be: I was still the guy who always managed to blow it.

Then we headed back to America, where good reviews and goodwill from the Bunnymen tour had actually translated to a tangible increase in audiences. We killed it again at the Ritz in New York and our travels took us to San Francisco where I again encountered the incredibly seductive Donnette Thayer, a big-time Church fan and all round gorgeous babe. I certainly succumbed to her many charms that night! We both had partners but ... wow she was a very cool American woman. She was incredibly pretty and feisty, but it wasn't so easy to stay in touch in 1986 so that was it for a while.

So The Church wended its way back to Australia and did another umpteen gigs that were all well attended. We had new clout and new authority. The Aussies had handed us a new mandate to rock. For me, the old days of snottiness and arrogance were replaced with a trippy wonder and a desire to recede as a personality and bring music itself to the forefront of my work.

The press gave us a second chance, and a new wave of critics sprang out of high school worshipping us the way the old guard Aussie press never did. We'd kicked a goal with *Heyday.* We'd stayed in good places, drunk the finest whiskey and the best wine. We'd partaken of nice drugs and had met nice women. In Australia we had a new confidence and strength.

In those days established bands used to tour with an up-and-coming band that the agency chose to open for you. One such band was The Venetians, who were a new romantic band who were vaguely threatening to make it, but our audiences always hated them. This amused me to no end because The Venetians were a very jumped-up bunch of characters and took the game oh so seriously. They were a nice enough bunch of guys, but individually they were quite catty and bitchy. Even worse than The Church!

Their drummer Tim and I were never friends; to me he seemed the most stuck up of the whole lot. He was a good-looking young guy and he sure had all that complicated technology sorted out. I am ashamed to say I enjoyed standing offstage seeing them go down so badly. Their songs were shockingly awful 80s blather. They were trying so hard to be something that they simply weren't – these guys should've opened for Duran Duran, that was the field they were in. It's a strange thing indeed that Tim would come back into my life. I never picked it, he certainly didn't seem like Church material at the time!

And then we got some bad news: Warner Bros. had dropped us. Gulp! Who was left?

13
STARFISH AND CHIPS

I was constantly battling the zeitgeist. Everyone was trying to make us oh so 80s but The Church were not an 80s band – even though we began in the 1980s we were trying to be a classic rock band.

IN 1987 ARISTA Records offered us a contract. It came entirely out of the blue; they just rang our manager one day. Just like that. Unsolicited. It was like waiting to catch a minnow and suddenly you got a whale on the line. I believe our manager asked for a lot of money and that may be true but very little of it came to the band. Instead we got to fly to LA and make an album with these two big-shot producers, Waddy Wachtel and Greg Ladanyi, at a place called The Complex, a huge set of studios all fitted out with the latest knobs and whistles.

We were accommodated at the Oakwood Apartments complex on Sepulveda Boulevard, and those of us that drove had cars hired for us. Ploogy and I shared one apartment, while Marty and Peter shared another across the garden. There were swimming pools and gyms and all that kind of thing. Arista had a vision for us and they thought Waddy and Ladanyi were the right ones to help us sell records in the US.

I had a funny feeling something good would come of it. I mean I knew we'd clash with these guys, whatever they wanted to do with us; we were argumentative at a basic cellular level, with each other and everyone else too. We each knew what we wanted from our music and compromising sometimes brought grown men to tears ... We just weren't into all those embarrassing 80s touches, like the whacking great snare drum punctuating the song with a massive wallop or the corny machine handclaps or the wimpy Mickey Mouse keyboard sounds. We didn't like bass guitars with no heads, mullet hairdos or skinny ties. Or anything to do with new romantic, heavy metal or country and western music for that matter. We had a sense of ourselves coming from greater traditions. And we consciously and unconsciously understood what was and was not to be included in The Church.

Waddy was a famous sideman and musical-director type. He brought a lot of energy and a lot of discipline with him. He was pale and skinny and had a big mop of frizzy red hair and ran a band like a sergeant major drilling his troops. He usually had on a pair of John Lennon–style glasses too. He looked like a Furry Freak Brother come to life and acted like one too; he had a prodigious appetite for drugs. The blow never seemed to knock him around or distract him. He fucking batted on regardless. He must've had the system of a horse to endure the total chemical hiding he gave it every day.

On the other hand Greg Ladanyi couldn't handle the stuff with such aplomb. He was all over the shop on the blow. Suddenly enthusiastic, suddenly deflated, suddenly and usually angry. He was about the same age as Waddy, round the 40 mark I guess. But he wasn't travelling as well. His relationship with each member of The Church was troubled – he gravitated towards Marty at first and they were friends for a time until Marty strongly disagreed with him over some guitar idea. Then he and Peter clashed and he hurt Peter's feelings, unnecessarily I thought. Ploog, he just couldn't fathom.

My relationship with the producers was complex: I'd decided to let Waddy guide me and see where that got me ... at least for a while. I'd made a conscious decision to listen to whatever he said and not immediately kick back. My whole musical life I'd instantly rejected any suggestions as to how I might improve things. I decided, as a situationist exercise almost, to put my cool hip self into this LA mainstream rock guy's hands and see what strange thing might emerge.

I could never really figure out what Ladanyi was supposed to do – he was like a vibe merchant I suppose. He'd come rushing in the room after having a line or two and run around clapping his hands exhorting, 'Yeah! Yeah! Yeah!' But he didn't make much attempt to hide his contempt for us. One day he was reading *Rolling Stone* and he yelled out to Waddy, 'Hey that fuckin' Roger Kaputnik is engineering Springsteen's next album ... Fuck! Why haven't we got that gig?' Greg looked despairingly around the room at the bunch of unknown Aussie hippies he was stuck with.

'And you're here wasting your time with a bunch of unknown nobodies,' I said.

Our eyes locked and he smirked, half in embarrassment, half in triumph. 'Exactly!' he muttered.

Anyway, Waddy was drilling us in this weird building in Santa Monica. Around us were troupes of actors and people making films and rehearsing and all kinds of things. The first morning we were to begin rehearsing I was lying in my Oakwood Apartments king-size double bed when I was woken by a diabolical racket. Alarmed, I jumped out of bed and went to the window to see where the racket was coming from. It was a rumbling, pounding, booming, shouting racket that I couldn't comprehend at all. It was the first time in my life I'd ever heard rap music coming out of a car with a souped-up stereo system! And it shocked me. I was truly horrified to think of what it must've sounded like in the car itself. And what wreckage their ears would soon be in.

We'd arrived in LA with a bunch of songs we'd written individually or collectively back in Sydney just prior to coming over and now we spent a month drilling them down at this strange rehearsal place. We stood there and played those frickin' songs over and over and over. Most had no lyrics; we drilled 'em as instrumentals. Waddy was there like the experienced pro taking in a crop of rookies – he was one of those classic characters who seems tough at first, but gradually reveals a heart of gold as things progress. He and I started to get along fine and became better friends as things went on.

At these drilling sessions all the focus seemed to be on the drums. Waddy was always searching for some elusive rhythm or timing or something. It was so important to him, though I couldn't quite figure out what he was looking for. I sure was as tired as all fuck of playing those songs over and over. By the time they got on the record almost all the life had been beaten out of them: we played 'em as we had been drilled to play them. Tight and lean, with no surprises – especially in regards to the drums. No speeding up. No slowing down. Don't vary the wallop or crash. Hit evenly. Richard was demoralised by all this and rightly so. All the marvellous flair and improvisation he'd shown on *The Blurred Crusade* and *Heyday* was now denied him. He was to act as a human drum machine.

Of course we should've stepped in; maybe if we'd been in Sydney we would have. But in LA I was so stoned and dazzled and preoccupied with everything else I just let it go. But Richard was falling victim to that nasty syndrome that happened a lot in the 80s, where bands get a top American or English producer and the first thing they do is sack the drummer. The 1980s did not suit drummers like Richard: he was a wild intuitive drummer; he didn't play drums according to these new restricted tightened guidelines. He couldn't have even if he'd wanted to, and it was at this point that he began to go under.

So while these rehearsals were easy – though tiring – for me, they must've been really tough on Richard. Waddy was meticulous and noticed every last thing everybody in the band was playing. If I made the slightest fumble or flam or slur or stumble he'd give me a piercing stare. But Richard took the brunt of his meticulousness. He could never escape or hide or deny the little mistakes he made; Waddy was used to working with these LA session drummers and he expected a drummer to be able to do his bidding exactly to the tee. And here we had Richard who played by feelings and had always done a fantastic job that way. Before this no one had told him exactly what to play and exactly how to play it and not to deviate from it. Richard was a guy who sat down at the kit and let the spirit of the music take over. He was right brain and Waddy was left, it was practically impossible for them to meet in the middle.

Meanwhile one night we were driving along and Ladanyi said, 'Hey Kilbey, when're we gonna do that song they sent me on your demo tape? It's not such a bad song actually, I think we could do something with it,' he said.

Embarrassingly enough it turned out he was talking about 'The Unguarded Moment' ... the real finished version! I told him that was actually a song off our first album and had even already been a hit in Canada in 1982. When he realised his mistake he still tried to persuade me to re-record it for *Starfish*, thinking we could, with his help, record a 'good' version of it. Ha ha!

Meanwhile our days consisted of eating the best Mexican food and smoking the best Californian grass, as well as snorting cocaine with the producers. I don't know what the LA music biz is like now but then cocaine was everywhere – we were all snorting it whenever we met anyone who had it, though the band never usually had their own supply. None of us were obsessed with it, though none of us said no either in those days. It sort of came with the territory and the studio. There was always a line to be had and they used to chop it up on the little flat bit next to the mixing desk. A few times the supply got interrupted and Ladanyi lost the plot. One day he said to me in all seriousness, 'Kilbey have you got any cocaine because I feel a real bad attitude coming on!'

Another time someone procured a real big batch real cheap. I remember it was a kind of grey colour and that should've been enough warning – but hey I've seen heroin and cocaine come in a variety of rainbow colours and still found them to be efficacious. Anyway one little line of that grey cocaine made me feel weird-sick for three weeks after. It was weird enough at first but it got weirder and sicker later on, like sunburn. I knew enough from that first snort to leave it alone. Not Waddy and Greg, though, they went for it hard all day and night. The next day Waddy showed up but Greg didn't – he wasn't there for about a week. When he did show up he was grey-skinned and slack-jawed. He just lay there groaning and could hardly manage anything at all. After half an hour he was gone. But Waddy was unfazed and kept snorting that grey cocaine: 'Fuck it!' he said. 'Might as well finish it now I've paid for it.' And so he finished it all by himself.

As well as blagging coke from whoever had it, me and Ploogy were smoking pot like demons. One day we met this weird guy on the street and we went around his apartment where he played us music and showed Ploog how to freebase cocaine. We'd never seen freebasing before. I tried to intervene but was coming off as uncool so I just smoked the guy's dynamite pot like a hypocrite and shut up. I avoided the guy from there on in but I think Ploog kept in touch. He wasn't a bad guy but he was a wild character and not a good influence on Ploog. Not that any of us were – especially when you keep in mind Ploogy was only 24 at this stage and still very much a kid from Adelaide easily led astray.

Eventually we began recording the album proper. We set up in a huge room that looked like it used to be a basketball court and, just like in rehearsal, we played the songs over and over and over looking for the right take to suit Waddy's elusive criteria. This was much harder work than we'd ever endured before. Nobody had ever driven us this hard and I still think it was probably unnecessary. We seemed to hammer all the life out of every song.

We worked on and recorded nine songs. There was a tenth as well, which our manager had asked us to record, which was 'Under the Milky Way'. Marty and Peter weren't that interested in it really. I wrote it in 1987 one night on a piano in a little flat out the back of my mother's house in Smiths Lake. Karin had helped me write it. I'd cut the demo on my eight track at home, and that was pretty much the finished version. Richard really liked it too and agreed we should try it. Ironically he never got to play on it. It never got to be rehearsed at all actually since Waddy and Greg didn't like it either, but we recorded it because our manager insisted.

Greg said I should do it on my own in the little midi studio inside The Complex – they had a new-fangled Synclavier workstation, which in 1987 was the top synth/sampler/sequencer in the world. There, a guy called Welles and I mapped out 'Under the Milky Way' and put on bass, drum machine and keys. (The sound in the solo is a backwards African bagpipe, which we put in there for a joke.) Welles and I worked away on the song while the other guys did other things in the big studio. Later Marty and Peter put the guitars on it. For drums Waddy decided it need a guy playing drum pads. He got in Russ Kunkel, who was one of the most famous session drummers out there at that time. Russ was a lovely guy, and he and Waddy spent a long time getting the drums and percussion just right; I really have to give that to Waddy, he helped get the beat of this song perfectly right. But at that stage of the game 'Milky Way' was the black sheep of the record. Nobody really liked it that much. Not even me.

When the bass parts were all done I was free to roam around LA and get into trouble. I hooked up with a few old girlfriends: one was Grace, who one day brought peyote over and we both went tripping inside the Oakwood Apartments. I jumped in the swimming pool and was totally out of my tiny mind. When I remembered to breathe I popped my head up to the surface and there was pretty little Grace sitting on a banana chair waving and smiling. She seemed to be having a good time. I, on the other hand, was troubled.

Later we went back to my apartment and it was a wonderful warm night perfect for romance. Instead, I spent the night apologising for what white men had done to the rest of the world. You see Grace was an Asian girl and I was experiencing some serious white guilt! So I apologised and apologised for hours. At first she was understanding, then bemused, then downright confused and bored as I banged on and on. I wonder what she made of all the nonsense I was spouting that night; it surely must've ruined her peyote trip.

Meanwhile Donnette Thayer knew I was in LA and would come down and visit me from San Francisco, where she lived with her boyfriend. They were in a band called Game Theory together. Donnette was one of the most alluring women I've ever met: she was sweet and languid and very intelligent. When I met her in 1986 she made it very clear she would always have time to see me. She made it perfectly obvious that I was her number one musician/songwriter/whatever. She was like a devotee and her ardour was hard to resist.

Yes I already had a girlfriend but I guess we had one of those open relationships. Donnette, however, didn't have an open relationship but she was prepared to see me no matter the consequences. She treated me like a real rock star in a way no one had done before, goading me to be reckless and stupidly confident. She could justify all my excesses and foibles. She made me feel like a hero. She turned up at the Oakwoods one day and I was made dopey by her petite sexiness and her tricky mind. Although I was her admired idol she teased me and provoked me all day long about almost everything, 'Go on, Steve, you're the rock star!' she'd say all the time. She kept hopping on my lap, and insinuating herself all over me. Her body was lithe and light. She smoked and drank and swore and took sleeping pills. She always seemed slightly tired and vulnerable, like Marilyn Monroe, or at least that's what I always thought. And, in her one-piece black costume down at the Oakwoods swimming pool, her figure blew Andre the sixteen-year-old pool guard's mind: 'Boy Steve you're lucky having a girlfriend like that!' he'd say as she swam through the blue water.

Donnette and I went to restaurants and cafes and smoked the pot she brought me from her mother who seemed to have some good connections. We talked about making a record together and I played her a few songs I'd written that weren't for The Church, which we earmarked for a new joint project. Later we'd go on to make two albums together that I really still enjoy listening to, called *Hex* and *Vast Halos*.

Back at the studio when the music was done it was time to lay down the singing. Greg suggested that Peter and I go and have singing lessons in Hollywood and we both said yes just to spite him.

Singing lessons proved to be bizarre. There on Hollywood Boulevard up a few floors in the elevator was our singing teacher, Mark. I won't say his last name ... maybe he's still there. But before he was a singing teacher he'd been a beefcake actor playing Samson in Italian biblical epics. Then, though, he sat behind a white baby grand playing scales for his pupils to sing. 'La la la la la la la la la,' he would sing and play as his voice traversed up the octave and back.

Then suddenly he'd stop and turn around and say, 'Hey Steve, do the girls in Australia like to give head?' An odd question, I thought.

He regarded me earnestly waiting for my answer. 'Ah gee, uh, yeah Mark, I guess they do I suppose ...' I stuttered. What the fuck are you supposed to say to a question like that from a singing teacher on Hollywood Boulevard who used to play Samson?

Mark seemed cheered up by my answer. You could see him seeing himself arriving in Australia and all those head-giving women lining up to welcome him. 'They do, do they?' He said thoughtfully. Then suddenly we went back into the scales: 'Try this! La la la la la la la la.'

We'd sing for a couple of minutes then he'd say, 'I had a woman come in here yesterday. She said, "Mark I'm the queen of the blow job." So I said, "Honey get down on your knees and defend your title!"' He let out a big guffaw before returning to scales. 'Try this ... la la la la la la la la la. Hey Steve, do the girls in Australia have big tits?'

I decided to humour him. 'Oh yeah Mark!' I said, 'and not only that, they sunbathe topless on my favourite beach, Bondi.'

My singing teacher gazed off into the distance imagining all those naked Aussie bosoms turning a lovely golden shade under the southern summer sun. 'Topless,' he repeated, and rolled the word around in his mouth as though it was a delicious lolly. Our whole lesson he swung back and forth between his twin obsessions of fellatio and mammary glands.

'A man shouldn't get too many blow jobs, Steve.' He said most sagely. 'Steve, promise me you won't get too many blow jobs!' I promised solemnly to heed his advice. 'That's what's wrong with all those big record execs like the guys at Arista,' he said. 'Too many blow jobs! It sucks the life out of 'em,' he sadly opined. 'Now try this: la la la la la la la la la.'

Eventually he confided to me sadly that his marriage had fallen apart. 'Oh that's no good!' I said.

'Yeah, some guy fucked my wife and farted on my sheets,' he said. Wow! That sounded dismal! I went outside and waited for Peter to have his turn. When he came out Peter said Mark had said exactly the same things to him. And then he proceeded to do the same through every lesson we took with him – what a character! Greg said our voices had actually improved but I imagine it was a placebo effect; I never learnt much, but that Mark guy was some hilarious piece of work.

In the meantime I was beginning to write the lyrics for the album – as I said, most of the songs were just instrumental pieces. It made Greg nervous to work this way. He'd been asking for lyrics ever since we arrived in LA. When I didn't have any he was surprised. 'What are you gonna do ... just make 'em up?!' he demanded incredulously. He couldn't see that that was exactly what I was going to do.

The stay in LA had definitely started to come out in the lyrics. One night we were having late-night sandwiches and chips at Canter's Deli, a famous place for minor stars and their acolytes to hang out. A big cowgirl type approached me as I was leaving. Her opening line was a classic: 'Whoever your girlfriend is I can fuck you better than her,' she said. Back at her place (out of mere curiosity) I went into the bathroom for a pee. Standing there I heard something kind of scratchy. There was a rustling sound behind the shower curtain and I pulled it back to reveal a great big lizard sitting in the bathtub blinking at me. I jumped out of my skin and lost my nerve. Could that have been the catalyst for the lyrics of 'Reptile', one of my favourite songs from *Starfish*? It was all grist for the mill.

One day I went into the studio and more or less automatically wrote the prose poem that we put on the *Starfish* sleeve. It didn't have much to do with the music or anything; just being so far away in space and time from my childhood in Canberra made me want to reassure myself. Writing about certain people and places and events always brought me closer to them, like writing these very words is doing now. I began approaching times long gone into the past as I sat there and wrote this piece and I tied it together by having the word *Starfish* in there. (I told you I wouldn't be revealing the meaning of my songs like they're a code that's meant to be analysed and unpacked.)

I'd already decided that 'Starfish' was the main contender for the album's name, it just felt so right to me. For a million reasons and absolutely none. Not everything has to have a sane rational reason behind it, especially in rock'n'roll. Although Arista still demanded an explanation – they wanted to call the album 'Under the Milky Way' but I wouldn't budge. Neither would they. Finally I wrote them a long letter about why *Starfish* should be called

Starfish. It was the most intense pseudo-poetic bullshit polemic that, hilariously, nobody could disagree with it. So I got to get my way. Blind 'em with science I always say!

A lot of people responded very positively to my nostalgic poem on the sleeve. I'm glad I wrote it. It showed another intimate side of what I do that perhaps might surprise given much of the sarcasm, irony and sophistry within the lyrics on *Starfish*.

After having had a bit of a breakthrough with *Heyday*, my lyrics had gotten more 'moderne' and a lot darker. On *Starfish* I was depicting a bleaker world than *Heyday*, which now seemed to be more naively optimistic. The album starts forebodingly and moves through different shades of melancholy – except for Marty's 'Spark', which was youthful and exuberant, and Peter's 'New Season', which was tranquil and soothing. One song, 'North South East and West' was all total LA stuff. 'The numberplates that rhymed' (BILL and JILL I think) were on two BMWs outside some mansion. '(Restore your lost soul for) two dollars plus toll.' You sure heard that phrase a lot. 'To a wolf from a lamb for just half a gram.' Guess who that was about? 'Wear a gun and be proud but bare breasts aren't allowed.' The US must be mad, I thought! But 'North South East and West' was also the band itself: four members moving in different directions …

Sometimes when The Complex was booked out we'd go to other studios around LA. One hot afternoon I arrived at another famous studio in the valley to find the door locked. I hammered on the door and a voice came over the intercom telling me the electronic door was jammed and that someone was coming to fix it. Could I wait?

A grey-haired guy in sunglasses was also waiting. 'Fuckin' door!' he said. 'But what can you do?' So I sat down in the warm LA sun and had a chat with this guy about the weather and Australia and guitars and stuff. After a while the door jerked open and admitted us both into the air-conditioned world inside. We shook hands; he went to his studio and I to mine. 'Nice to meet ya!' he said as he walked away.

When I got into my studio the guys in there crowded around me asking, 'How was Neil? What did you and Neil talk about?' Fuck! I'd just spent the last 30 minutes talking with Neil Diamond. And I never even suspected I was talking to one of the greats ... damn! I could've laid a copy of *Starfish* on him ... you know, he just might have dug it!

Other famous people I met were Jackson Browne, who kindly lent us some amps – Jackson was impossibly boyish and incredibly gracious. Linda Ronstadt was another one I talked to without realising who she was. The Complex was a mecca for those Californian-sound musician types. I met some geezer from Toto as well, who was horrified that I'd neither heard of him nor gave a pinch of pelican's poop for his band. I hate the kind of pompous stuff they played but they were all mates of Waddy and Ladanyi.

In the end doing the singing wasn't particularly hard. Ladanyi was sometimes a pain in the ass demanding to know what this or that meant in my lyrics – 'Hey Kilbey,' he'd demand, 'what the fuck is an exquisite fuckin' corpse?!' But before I could explain he'd cut me off mid-sentence saying, 'Yeah yeah, I knew nobody could understand any of this shit.' But we got it done. Their modus operandi was to record my vocal takes across six tracks: it took a lot of singing for them to narrow it down to the six tracks they wanted to work with. And then they'd mix and match in a process called comping the vocals. They'd take a word here, a phrase there, maybe just one syllable. It was a long, involved process. A lot of what you hear on *Starfish* is singing pieced together from numerous takes ... strange, isn't it?

Finally we went back over to the other valley studio to do the percussion. Ploogy and I both loved to do the tambourine and the shakers and the eggs. When we got there, there was a huge box of percussion instruments, the likes of which we'd never seen before. Ploogy responded by trying to play just about everything at once. 'Why don't you just pick up the whole box and shake it?' the engineer drolly suggested.

With the album done it was time to do the mixing. This is the bit where they combine all the ingredients to create a sonically pleasing concoction. I thought the mixes were OK; they weren't anything spectacular, but they weren't terrible either. They were kind of dry, safe sounds. The mix didn't stand in the way of the music like Nick Launay's work on *Seance*, though it didn't enhance the music the way Bob Clearmountain's lovely mix on *The Blurred Crusade* did, either. But it was clear and easy.

I didn't really like the roaring lions in 'Destination' but there you go. How Waddy arrived at that I'll never know. I do know that they mixed the record at the highest possible volume that the human ear could withstand ... Unlike Clearmountain, who mixed really softly and refused to even be in a room with loud music, these guys had it pumping around the clock. So we'd goof off around LA of a day and drive in at night to hear our record coming together. Of course we had input into the mixing too – sometimes our advice would be heeded, sometimes not. But that's how it'd always been and I had long accepted it.

After a while Waddy and I sat down to sequence the record. This was very important in the days of vinyl, when the first and last tracks on each side had added emphasis. I'd already decided that 'Destination' should start the record: the lyrics were set up for that purpose. I suggested 'Milky Way' for the second track but Waddy said, 'No man, you don't want people hearing that one too soon.' So we put it second last. Eventually we had things juggled around.

After settling on the order the guys from Arista and our manager came in to hear it in the studio. We played them all our favourite tracks. Greg Ladanyi was actually trying to sell them Marty's song 'Spark' because he thought it had energy and maybe to spite me. I thought 'Lost' or 'Reptile' could be singles, though I had a sinking feeling the album had no single. The big shots all nodded their heads in agreement that this was a good album; I mean, they weren't all that jazzed by it, but they certainly weren't disappointed.

'Play 'em 'Under the Milky Way',' someone said through a patina of Californian pot smoke. Then those familiar chords started up on two double-tracked acoustic 12-string guitars. The voice came in, 'Sometimes when this place gets kinda empty,' the bass, the drums all came in … everybody knows how it goes by now …

When it finished the room was silent. Suddenly they all swung around. Our manager had a very strange look in his eye, which must've been something called avarice: 'I think we can get this song on the radio,' he said as his eyes glazed over. The guys from Arista were up and shaking my hand, 'That's a hit Steve,' said the head honcho Clive Davis, who I was a little bit in awe of. Each guy from each department at Arista shook my hand and said 'We'll make this a hit!' From that moment on there was never any doubt that 'Under the Milky Way' would be a hit!

When they'd gone the mood in the room was strange – no one, not even me, had seen that one coming. Except maybe Richard, who sadly didn't even play on it. It was as much a surprise as anything else ever was. Over the years there's been some revisionism over that song: most people working on it at the time considered it the weakest song on the record; it was the public and Arista that made the damn thing such a hit. The Church were merely onlookers.

We had no idea that it would revive our fortunes and one day be considered a classic and a standard with hundreds of cover versions all around the world. What did *The Guardian* call it, an unintentional anthem? You gotta love that about the music biz – every song is like a ticket in a lottery. And The Church had just gotten real lucky!

14
A HUNDRED AND ONE GIGS

It was incredible to feel the power of a US record company. It was like being lifted up by a huge wave and pushed skyward towards the Billboard heavens and the greenback pastures where our hearts had so longed to be. Or maybe I'm only speaking for myself… We never sat around discussing what we all hoped to get out of it – I don't know how much the others actually longed for success. And success affected everyone differently.

WE HIT THE ground running in 1988: 'Under the Milky Way' was a bona fide hit single in Australia and especially in America – the rest of world never took it on so much, but it didn't matter because America was the goal of every band that ever strummed a guitar. We'd always been determined to conquer America, but when it happened it wasn't how I imagined it would be …

Despite our success with *Starfish*, which went gold in the US, there were some serious cracks appearing in our band. This time it was Richard at the centre of the disruption; his behaviour was becoming increasingly bizarre and erratic. Then he brought his girlfriend from Sydney on the road, which nobody wanted. She was a total wet blanket and we didn't want her on our friggin' tour bus walking around in her dressing gown and slippers! Richard promised to send her away but every morning she was still there. Sometimes he tried to hide her in his bunk like a stowaway. She'd complain if we were doing an encore because she was tired and wanted to go to bed: 'Ohhhh, ya not doing another one are ya?' she'd moan as we went back onstage at New York's Beacon Theatre to play another boring old encore. She should've stayed at home.

Richard was losing interest in drumming – his playing got faster and faster and more and more iffy. He and I began to really clash, initially over the girlfriend, but eventually over everything. We'd been pretty good mates for a while but this was the beginning of the end. It may sound childish but it's best when the band hangs out a bit together on tour and when making records – develops a bit of camaraderie and all that kind of thing. Richard's isolating himself with his girlfriend wasn't good for the tour or the band. He became more and more disconnected from us and the music, and then drumming itself. By the time the tour was over his drumming had descended into a quite unpredictable shambles. Just when we should've been slaying them we were crumbling apart like fools.

The tour began in the UK, where we acquired a big Estonian giant of a man called Big Mike. He was a wry and funny guy and sometimes he had to provide a little muscle. We started off with two sold-out gigs at the London Marquee again but our triumphant return was marred by someone hiring a toothless middle-aged stripper to celebrate – or ruin – someone's birthday. I was fucking furious that someone had spoiled our night with that tasteless malarkey!

Then we jetted straight to LA for a showcase at the Roxy. Everyone who was anyone was there, including Greg Ladanyi, who told me he now understood what The Church was all about. It was a pity it hadn't occurred to him while we were making the record! Marty bought a cheap Rickenbacker copy and smashed it onstage. It exploded spectacularly in a shower of sparks and plywood. Maybe it was a little premeditated and a few people must've seen it coming but still it was effective. Afterwards some of The Bangles lined up to meet us but I was so exhausted I hid in a closet to avoid talking to anyone. It was only the third gig of the tour.

After recording at KCRW in Santa Monica we flew to New York where we impressed the pants off of all the bigwigs at Arista at a gig at the legendary venue The Bottom Line. It was a very accomplished show and Clive Davis gave The Church and our new album *Starfish* the two thumbs up, which meant that everybody at Arista was focused on us for a while.

In New York we did a load of photo sessions and interviews. Suddenly it was all happening *for real*, like it did in the movies and *Spinal Tap*. Everyone at Arista was so nice to us. For such a left-of-centre band as The Church to get into the charts was an accomplishment for everyone: the band, the label, the crew, the management and all the rest.

It was a real honeymoon period for Arista and The Church. Everyone was on a little winning streak. It was our first record together and we were shipping serious units: we doubled *Heyday*'s sales in just a few weeks. And more than mere sales, the American critics were full of respect and praise. Everyone in America loved *Starfish*! A hundred kids in garages were already cranking out 'Reptile' on Saturday afternoons. 'Under the Milky Way' was everywhere: it was on *Miami Vice* for crying out loud! Somehow the song was defining 1988 for everybody, it was a soothing balm in airways saturated with the pop miasma. The song was ambiguous and indefinable, like it'd slipped in from another dimension. Everyone who liked it could congratulate themselves that they liked a cool song slightly left of centre.

On a big promo tour we hit Amsterdam and Stockholm and then Milan in Italy. We went down to Rome to do a TV show and recorded 'Destination', 'Milky Way' and 'Reptile'. The guitarists had a huge meltdown over the amps they were supposed to use, which weren't up to their usual standard; there was much arguing but they ended up using the studio amps in a performance you can see on the internet if you like.

After the show there was a bunch of fans at the gate outside the TV station. A curvaceous Italian woman who looked like she was straight out of a Pasolini film was hoarsely shouting 'STIV STEEEV!' I walked over to talk to her and was swamped by a load of kids asking for autographs. Seeing me looking overwhelmed, she grabbed my hand and pulled me away.

'Mr Kilbey, have a nice night and be in the lobby by 2pm,' boomed Big Mike's voice over the general melee. I jumped on the back of the woman's scooter and we zoomed off through the sunny streets of Rome. You know, I remember sitting in the cinema or drive-in with an uptight Canberran girlfriend watching these earthy, buxom Italian women with their deep laughter and their stormy passions in movies like *The Decameron*, but never did I ever imagine I'd be in Rome being hijacked by such a creature.

I didn't know where the fuck we were going and I didn't care. We rode around. She showed me to her friends. One guy wasn't so happy to meet me. We smoked hashish and drank wine. Back in my hotel room she applied herself to the rites of Eros with impressive physicality. She didn't speak a lot of English; it wasn't especially necessary. She had an enormous appetite for laughing, and my Anglo squareness amused and bemused her. She put on my green suede jacket and my green suede boots and in nothing else marched around the room doing a lewd impression of me onstage. The seventeen-year-old Steve sitting just below the thin veneer of the pop singer was pretty impressed. I was living the life!

We hit Valencia and Madrid. We sold out some big venues and just like in Italy our star was on the rise. We did TV shows and interviews, and there were the slightly harsher ladies of Spain. Marty could speak pretty good Spanish, and passable French and German and eventually Swedish. I always envied him this instant leg up in whatever country we were in: his Spanish was so good they even interviewed him in Spanish on some shows. He was a real babe magnet in Spain, the ladies tried to devour him. I was a little jealous sometimes but I was kind of used to it and we tended not to go for the same girls anyway – it was always nuttier girls who liked me. Marty was a very obvious pop star and attracted obviously gorgeous women.

Sometimes someone in the group trod on someone else's toes, romantically speaking, but it's par for the course in bands I imagine. It's funny how distant those days seem – a huge city every night and the attendant women. It seemed so life and death at the time: you'd meet a woman one night and the next morning swear you're not gonna leave her. Until someone threatens you get on the fucking bus or else! You'd spend the day teary and mopey but by 2am there'd be a new senorita or fraulein to laugh and drink with backstage.

We had a couple of Aussie guys on the crew, Trevor and John, who were as Aussie as Aussie can be and whom I immediately began to stay up late with all the time. After a few weeks of jetting around from Finland to Italy, Amsterdam to Minneapolis, some of us were getting a little frayed around the edges. John was always partying. I ordered him to get some rest but he didn't listen. Every day he was more and more tired and every night he was going out partying with a new girl he'd just met … needless to say they were usually very attractive women.

Then one day up the business-class end of a Finnair flight John broke down among all the businessmen flying from Helsinki to Stockholm. What a sight he was crying among the suits and buttermilk breakfasts! Pulling his long hair over his face as he sobbed out of sheer exhaustion. What a bloody carry-on!

Yet I wasn't to fare too much better. We were going to Minneapolis to visit some huge vinyl warehouse where they were doing good business with our records. They wanted us to walk around and meet people and make polite chat – not one of my fortes in those days! After flying from Europe I checked in mid-morning to a beautiful art nouveau hotel and was trying to meditate when the most strange and terrible feeling swept over me like the very hand of dreadful doom. I was having a panic attack. I'd had one once before, just before the final external exams of high school. Convinced I would do badly I'd begun to hyperventilate until I was in a total state of madness and panic. My parents had called the doc then and he'd had me breathe into a paper bag while he rolled up my sleeve and gave me a sweet shot of intravenous valium. I'd been stunned and intrigued by the rush of the mainlined hit. With lightning speed the drug had spread out, calming and numbing everything. I'd gone from sheer panic to a dreamy tranquil state in seconds. The delightful velocity of the injected stuff and its transformative powers had not been lost on my teenage psyche.

There in Minneapolis – my suitcase full of wrinkled shirts and old socks, books and cassettes exploded open on the double bed – I felt like I was no longer able to keep the outside out. It was like I was losing myself in some awful cold unfeeling void. Just like the roadie on the plane, now I was crying. I hadn't been much of a crier up to that point, so crying for no reason was quite a shock. I felt like I was gonna implode.

My door was unlocked and my manager Mike Lembo came in. 'Why are you crying?' he said. 'Your record just moved five places up the charts!' My blubbering and wailing gave him the best idea he ever had: he ordered up a stiff double brandy from room service.

The shock of the brandy gave way to a warm and sleepy impulse as the panic began to subside. 'Mike, I can't fucking go to the warehouse tomorrow!' I said.

'I know,' he replied.

We went to see a doctor in the Minneapolis hospital. He examined me, softly banging my knee with a little hammer and peering into my ears and eyes. He called my manager in and said, 'This man must have at least three weeks' holiday right now!'

'I know,' Mike responded again.

When we got back to the hotel I was still shaken: 'I can't do that fucking warehouse thing!' I said to Mike before I went to bed.

'I know,' he said again. 'But you have to!'

At seven o'clock the next morning they dragged me out of bed and drove me to the warehouse. I was so unbelievably worn out that I was shaking and moaning. Along with a delegation of Arista staff I toured this bloody vinyl warehouse or depository or whatever it was and shook the hand of every last bastard hanging around. Everyone wanted records signed and photos taken. They were good, well-intentioned people in the Midwest colliding head on with the wimpiest, most tired pop singer they'd ever seen. I was so fragile I would've made Keats seem like Schwarzenegger. I was getting angrier and quieter as we made our way though the place, but the people seemed oblivious to my suffering: they just wanted a picture with the guy who sang 'Under the Milky Way', and they didn't give a damn if he was a sullen, sulky twit in his green jacket and green boots and hennaed red hair. Boy, I must've looked a treat that day!

Another huge gig ensued at the London Town and Country Club, which is largely memorable for a big black bouncer telling my mother to fuck off because she didn't have the right coloured bracelet. She eventually got in and said, 'Son a big black man just told me to eff off!' My mother was visiting England at the time and was pretty impressed with how big we were there. She couldn't believe the fad for stage diving and nor, actually, could I.

The Church hit Paris for a mediocre show and mediocre turnout. Our record company guy there scored us some hash, so Richard and I got off our trees. After Paris we flew all the freaking way to Adelaide and then Melbourne and Sydney before flying out again to Montana, which was like that real old-fashioned America we used to see on Disneyland, the one hardly touched by progress. We worked our way down the coast after we did the Commodore Ballroom in Vancouver and did great business in Seattle and Portland.

And then we went to San Francisco, where a couple of fateful meetings occurred ... As we were coming down the coast I was talking about all our weird and whacky friends in San Fran we'd be seeing, like talking to this old gay fan who used to fucking question me about tiny details of record releases when I wanted to be getting chatted up by women. I said aloud that I hoped this guy Rodney wouldn't be there to pester me. A few hours later as we drove over the Golden Gate Bridge we were listening to the radio and they were playing 'Under the Milky Way'. When the song finished the guy dedicated it to Rodney, who'd recently passed away from complications due to AIDS. Jesus I felt like such a jerk!

Anyway we were told *Melody Maker*, the biggest rag in England, was going to put us on the cover and it was gonna be terrific.

They were flying over Steve Sutherland to interview me, and then he could watch us totally slay the Fillmore West. You remember Steve Sutherland, the guy who gave us all those bad reviews, even for *Heyday*? I could recite his pans and jibes almost word for word; boy did I have a bone to pick with that guy!

So Sutherland shows up at my hotel and he's a little weasel of a geezer. And I made a huge mistake: I thought I could rip into Sutherland and his bad reviews and that he'd print it all. In the flesh he was a spineless, chinless little man and again, just like Matt Snow, I was surprised how such talentless, gormless, beer-swilling blokes could dictate musical tastes all round the world. But all my words were for nothing. He was politely amused by my attack but despite the fact that we spent a few hours doing a photo session and everything, Sutherland just didn't run the story at all.

So we lost our front page on one of the most influential rags ever because I wouldn't be nice to this character or play the whole game. I should've learnt my lesson from Stuart Coupe! At the time I didn't realise it but this was a severe blow to our chances of world domination. If only we were bigger in the English press, it would've cross-fertilised with our US popularity into a nice thing! My arrogance really fucked that one right up.

On the same afternoon there was a knock at my door and there stood Donnette – it was as if a veil had been lifted from my eyes. She was undeniably sweet and gorgeous. She moved like a cat. She had the coolest American accent like a female beat poet. She was super smart and she was very funny and irreverent. She also made it clear that she adored me more than life itself as she curled herself around me like an orphan kitten. Remember I'm just an overgrown boy from Canberra! I'm standing outside myself and I'm in a nice hotel room in San Francisco and I've just had an argument with *Melody Maker*, and now this woman is treating me like I'm the god Apollo. Donnette had a way of making me feel so damn good about myself: she constantly rewrote my faults as virtues.

Donnette totally understood me. She was a real soothing gorgeous honey and she swore eternal fealty to me but she was no stupid groupie: I loved the fact that Donnette loved what I did so much. Her devotion and her seriousness suddenly centred me in a lost universe of onwards rushing events. Although I'd hung out with her quite a bit before, that afternoon she suddenly rushed into my head and it changed the course of my life forever.

The gig that night was a ripper, the San Francisco audience re-anointed us. Sutherland was there looking smug as he drank with the Arista guys, knowing he was never going to write about that gig and its two encores at the legendary Fillmore. My big mouth had ruined us ever getting good press in England. But I didn't know that yet and Donnette and I spent an incredibly romance-soaked night together, and the next morning all over San Francisco kids were walking around in Church T-shirts. It felt like a fairytale.

Donnette slunk off back into her life with her boyfriend and Game Theory. By day she worked as a chemist testing water or something while The Church worked our way down the coast getting a pretty good reaction wherever we went. The more I thought about Donnette the more I wanted to see her again as soon as possible. I started ringing her every day from my hotel and we would talk through her lunchtime about music and the cities I was seeing. Her very inaccessibility made her even more desirable.

I'd fallen in love with being in love, again. It was a sweet and motivating drug to be running on; I was high and low riding its roller-coaster rush. All my songs took on a new poignancy. I started to live only to talk to Donnette each lunchtime. Now all my memories of that tour are filtered through the elation of my crush on her.

It was a crazy time. I had certainly lost my head but we toured on regardless. We had some super-long drives on our nifty little bus with its double bunk beds – man, you crawl in there at the end of a long night and wake up the next day somewhere else entirely. It was an especially cozy feeling on a wet rainy night zipping along warm and safe, oblivious in your little curtained-off bunk, hearing only the road sloshing by outside.

Donnette and I cooked up a plan for her to come and spend a few nights with me in New Orleans. As this gig got closer and closer the anticipation of seeing her drove me forward. In Dallas we played a free gig and pulled a record crowd but we didn't go down that well for some reason. In Houston I called Donnette from the rooftop pool during a spectacular thunderstorm – life had taken on mighty new dimensions: I'd be seeing her the next day. The gigs were fading into the background of my life. As we drove towards New Orleans every song playing on the radio was charged with meaning. Every tree and bayou was portentous of romance. She was flying in a few hours after The Church arrived. In the meantime we checked in to a fantastic hotel, old and dimly lit with rooms that were soft, calm and inviting.

At the airport my desperation to see her reached fever pitch. I watched literally everyone disembark the plane before Donnette finally emerged. She looked so damn good: lithe as all get-out, a fragile and slightly tired beauty.

That night everything was charged with an incredible intensity. Before the gig we'd squabbled with the opening band called The Mighty Lemon Drops, who'd been named the best band in the universe by *NME* and weren't that happy about opening for us Australians. On that night we played at the legendary Tipitina's in New Orleans and Peter Koppes accused The Mighty Lemon Drops of eating all the chocolates that we requested on our rider.

I do believe he may've been right because a general brawl broke out over the missing chocolates with people pushing each other around until Big Mike waded into that fight and The Mighty Lemon Drops, um, melted away.

The gig was a corker. Richard picked up on my desire to impress Donnette and played a real blinder! I watched her in the audience all night. I sang the songs to her. It was a magical evening like from a romance novel. I've always been a showoff; it's in my nature. Remember the gigs in the lounge room with Russell miming on the tennis racquets while I impressed some girl in the imaginary audience? Well this was that little dream in reality.

We caught a cab away from Tipitina's and it was the heaviest rain I had ever seen in my life. Everything about that night inspired the song 'Louisiana' – the black rain falling in the night and all that. I sat in the back of the cab soaking up Donnette's adoration as we drove through the impossible deluge. Ha ha, I was a true rock star! We had an uber-romantic few days. We walked around the French Quarter and drank hurricanes. We swam in the pool as the rain poured down. We lay in bed listening to the torrent fall steadily. When she flew back to San Francisco I was in a real daze of melancholy, albeit syrupy sweet melancholy. And so during my first big tour of America I was distracted by this thing with Donnette, and consequently all the gigs went past in a bit of a blur.

Then I made an enemy for life with some big shot from Arista when, informed of our latest sales figures, I casually said, 'Oh, is that all?' The guy figured I'd be ecstatic and grateful. But my blasé answer made me appear ungrateful; it was like a slap in the face for Arista and all the people there. What should've been exciting news had been tempered by our manager's constantly telling me inflated sales figures to hype me up, so that when I heard the week's sales figure for real it was only the same as last week's inflated figure.

I think it was 150,000 at that stage; *Heyday* had only done 60,000. This guy – who'd vaguely be the subject of 'Pharaoh' on our next record – later rose to power elsewhere and has hated me ever since. He was so angry with me for saying 'Oh, is that all?' that he stood outside our next gig and complained that we went on too long, that my singing was flat, that Richard's drumming was too fast and that the guitars were too fucking loud!

Next we went to Montreal, which was a real blast. Marty bought himself a pair of boots with all these silver buckles up the sides that cost a small fortune but when he wore them at the gig no one could hide their laughter at how ridiculous he looked with his pants tucked into these ostentatious monstrosities. We never saw those babies again, thank God! They were a solid manifestation of the 80s zeitgeist, containing enough chrome and leather to build a martini bar. Meanwhile Marty's attitude towards me still fluctuated wildly, although he was careful to keep it under control, as was I.

Now that the group was almost hitting the big time no one really wanted to rock the boat too much. Everyone more or less knew on which side their bread was buttered. Having said that, Marty had thrown a hissy fit at the Orpheum Theatre in Boston ... It was an important gig but his self-righteousness held sway as he leaned against a column and occasionally strummed the odd barre-minimum chord. He was angry with someone or something so everybody suffered for it. He just couldn't understand that you didn't take your personal problems onstage with you. And if you upset him he might just ruin the gig to spite you! Peter and I never had and never would take a personal thing out onstage, but Marty just couldn't help himself if his sometimes-fragile sensibilities were offended.

Once in 1984 he didn't talk to me for a month because I had laughed at his white knobbly knees the first time I saw him in a pair of shorts in Cairns. As the group got more famous he fancied himself more of an 'artiste'. It was a long way from the Nick Ward days!

Donnette joined me again in Minneapolis and our torrid affair resumed exactly where it'd left off. We filmed a video of The Church playing an old theatre called The Guthrie – rivalries were running high between Marty and Peter, who could also be a bit petulant. The director sat us all down and outlined his plans to shoot us individually stressing that if the camera wasn't on us at any particular time we should just carry on. 'We'll be filming everyone individually at different times,' he said. But when the filming started and the camera was on Marty, Peter took off his guitar and left the building in a huff; it took a while to locate him and get him back on the set so filming could continue. Anyway, if you watch the video for 'Reptile' you can see Donnette down the front dressed in white and rocking out!

Our stature was definitely on the rise in Chicago, where we did well at the Vic Theatre. Then we jetted out to The Netherlands, where we had a great chance and blew it at Parkpop, a big Dutch festival that was being filmed. We were having a bad time on stage, and Marty stupidly and rudely put his towel over one of the cameras as they were trying to film him playing a solo. That was the end of any goodwill for us in that part of the world! After a bunch of dates in Germany we ended up in Denmark at Roskilde Festival where an angry INXS were waiting for me because of some casual remarks I'd made about them in some music rag. 'We're a real band playing real music,' I'd dribbled on, 'not like INXS, or bands like that, hanging around airports with models on their arms!'

INXS were playing the festival and they were mad as hell. Spider, their Aussie roadie, came to our tent and told us that Andrew and Michael wanted to fight me! Oh dear, me and my big mouth again. Andrew and Michael soon wandered over, 'Come and have a beer with us in our tent, Steve,' Andrew said through gritted teeth.

'I don't drink beer and I've got all the drinks I want,' I said politely.

'Look just come with us to our tent!' he said.

Michael Hutchence stared at me myopically yet disdainfully and said, 'Come to our tent for a beer!'

'Look I'm not going to your fucking tent!' I replied. And they both stormed off and the fisticuffs were narrowly averted thanks to Spider's warning through the roadie grapevine.

The Church went on to do a mediocre set while INXS were a huge hit with the gigantic crowd of over 80,000 Danes.

After this I took a month off in Stockholm where I bit the bullet and I told Karin about Donnette – it turned out she also had a little scene with a well-known singer in another band. He'd even been coming around to our place to see her! But she'd let him go and now she wanted me to let Donnette go too.

Karin and I and my two brothers, Russell and John who'd flown in from Australia, and her brothers all went on a strange holiday rambling about on these walking tracks up in some Swedish mountains above the tree line. Sometimes we even saw reindeers wandering about. At night we stayed in these kind of dormitory places where you make your own breakfasts and dinner. Coming off that heavy-duty tour and then walking along in the middle of nowhere with all these brothers was quite a jolt. No wonder I was restless and stupid then! It took a lot of adjusting just to go home after a long tour, but this was an extreme opposite.

My brothers had a blast in Sweden even though the Swedish summer gave them both hayfever. Karin and I stayed with her maternal grandmother and ate genuine old-time Swedish fare like nettle soup and homemade fresh-pressed juice called *saft*. We went for long bike rides in the surrounding hinterland of Katrineholm, south of Stockholm, and everything about that summer was golden and glowing. We stopped and ate lunch in lovely little places. It was an idyll and slowly healed me a little; the US show-biz thing and all its hoo-ha drifted away as I biked along in the beautiful Nordic summer with verily not a care in the world. This was the good life too!

And then suddenly summer in Sweden came to an end. I was back in the US where our record was doing pretty good for a bunch of Aussie hippies – it wasn't knocking Prince off the charts but it'd definitely done solidly well by anyone's terms. The record company was happy with us.

We embarked on a big tour with some strange bedfellows … there was Peter Murphy, the singer from Bauhaus, who was out on his own with a backing band. He was neither good nor bad in my opinion. We hardly spoke in person; he had an attitude like The Mighty Lemon Drops. He thought he was too damn big and famous to be opening for a bunch of Aussie hippies, but fuck it we had a hit single and he didn't! So someone talked him into opening up for us on a double bill. I guess it wasn't surprising that there wasn't much of a crossover. His fans sometimes left when we came on – once I famously quipped, 'That was the biggest retreat of the Goths since the fall of Rome.'

I remember a slight melee in a dressing room that involved Peter Murphy and someone else until Big Mike stepped in and Murphy ran around the room all distraught and melodramatic screaming, 'Keep that man away from me!' Ha ha! It was difficult to forget this scene when you saw him onstage coming on all vampire and naughty.

Weirdly enough Tom Verlaine was also on this tour: my former hero and idol as both a guitarist and lyricist. But Verlaine was mooted to ride on Murphy's bus. The afternoon before we started the ride out to Phoenix there was a knock at my door and there was the 39-year-old shy, goofy, boyish Verlaine. He'd come to see if he could borrow my acoustic guitar. I'd just bought a brand-new black Guild 6-string acoustic guitar – it was the love of my life until some bastard stole it in New York a few weeks down the track. Verlaine was a charismatic geezer with his whole old-fashioned New York eccentric genius thing and when he picked up my guitar to check it out, he played one note and I could immediately tell it was Tom Verlaine from Television handling my little axe! Verlaine's prowess on the guitar was astonishing to everyone in the band. He could do tricks, imitating seagulls and trains complete with a Doppler effect. He did all his sounds without any effects pedals, just old-fashioned manipulations of an electric guitar and an incredible familiarity that went far beyond even Peter Koppes'. Verlaine was one of the best electric guitarists the world has ever produced. Individual and original, a real innovator! His lyrics too were fucking fantastic. Some of the couplets on the Television albums are among the best in rock'n'roll.

After playing the guitar for a minute Verlaine asked if he could ride on our bus. He said he'd met Murphy and didn't care for him or his music. Verlaine also knew we were all huge Television fans; our bus seemed like a much more attractive proposition for him, I'm sure.

As the tour wore on I became increasingly fascinated with Verlaine. He was nothing like I'd thought he'd be. He was always totally wired on caffeine and nicotine. He drank one coffee after another and smoked one cigarette after the last, all day long. He didn't partake in any other drugs or alcohol. He didn't need to because he was flying on the coffee and tobacco.

He was also a real ladies man. He often had 'little sweeties' lined up in several cities. He attracted gorgeous female admirers but sometimes his choices in women puzzled me. One night he was leaving a theatre with a girl done up entirely in goth clothing, including vampire make-up and the whole nine yards. I didn't think Verlaine would be into this kind of chick, but there you go.

He rang my room one night in some hotel. 'Ah Kilbey, I'm sitting down here in the foyer with some divorcees and wonderin' if you could, ah, take one of 'em off my hands?' When I got down there Verlaine was chatting up two middle-aged women who'd never heard of either of us before. I guess I did my job of keeping one of them company while he showed the other lady to his quarters. Another time in a hotel bar he said, 'That woman over there must be a lesbian!' When I asked why he replied in all seriousness, 'Because she isn't looking at me!'

On board our bus Verlaine was quite a hoot. He always washed his socks in the hotel, and then hung them out to dry on the heating vents on the bus. The whole bus was decorated with his drying socks while he walked around not wearing any at all. For some reason it gave a vague impression of him being homeless or something. One day I met him in the corridor of the hotel at Virginia Beach; he told me he'd been talking to the young pool guard and had made a big impression on her, he could tell. After my swim I talked to the same girl, who told me about a weirdo with no socks! She was surprised to learn he was a famous and brilliant musician.

One early morning we checked into a hotel in Rochester, New York. Verlaine rang my room. 'Uh, Kilbey, come on let's go for a walk and have breakfast!' We went to some diner – it was freezing cold outside – and had eggs on toast and shared a plate of fries. Afterwards Verlaine made me pay 50 cents more because he said I ate more of the fries than him. And he had calculated the difference. He was always very mean and penny-pinching – quite literally.

After breakfast we walked through a forest until we came to this reservoir where we accidentally blundered onto some kind of deal or shakedown between a bunch of black guys and a group of Italian-looking types. They shouted when they saw us emerge from the trees, and started running towards us. Verlaine instantly assessed the situation and was off back down the slightly snowy forest slope hissing, 'Come on!' The guys were shouting and pursuing us; I could hear them crashing through the trees behind as they entered the forest somewhere back up the top. Verlaine looked like an antelope as he hurdled trees and bushes with his long legs. Eventually the pursuers gave up, and I met Verlaine at the bottom of the forest where the cars zoomed by on the highway. He was smoking one of those little cheap cigarettes and seemed totally unfazed. What a hero!

He did us the great honour of coming on and playing encores with us after a few nights on tour. We did 'Cortez the Killer' by Neil Young and 'Is This Where You Live' and 'You Took'. It sounded amazing with him. Three totally different lead guitars at once. It was a dream come true: I will always remember those nights with Tom Verlaine playing. They were career highlights.

Meanwhile Donnette and I had been cooking up a plan to make an album together. She'd given me a tape of her singing, and a few songs really had a lovely melancholy feel. I thought we should make an album of sad weird songs and she would sing it. I'd acquired an Ensoniq keyboard for the purpose with a built-in sequencer, and every night after the gig was over I got out my keyboard and wrote pieces for what would eventually turn into *Hex*. And the next day I'd ring her up and play them to her over the phone. We'd decided that when the tour was over we'd record in New York and stay at Mike Lembo's place – working on the music every night gave me a way to discharge all the energy I'd built up during the performance.

I started to write some really great new tunes that would be on our record.

The shows were mostly good and we were going down OK; not slaying 'em in the aisles or anything, but OK. Richard had really lost interest in drumming by then, which paradoxically meant he sped it up – perhaps in an effort to finish the gig as quickly as possible.

Outside the Michigan Theater in Ann Arbor, Michigan, I got into a spot of silly bother. I'd walked outside the gig during sound check and the door had closed and locked me out. I stood there and the fans began to converge on me. Someone asked for an autograph and I didn't have any paper so I autographed a few one-dollar notes from my pocket. The rumour spread that the singer in The Church was giving away money outside the theatre and a load of people began pressing forward with their hands out demanding money. I quickly ran away and two guys pursued me demanding at least a memento. But I had nothing to give them – my pockets were empty. One of them demanded the piece of gum I was chewing; I thought that was crazy and I spat the gum on the ground. And lo and behold the two stupid guys fought over my piece of chewing gum! The mind truly boggles at the inanity.

Eventually the long tour was coming to an end. The American winter was coming down the line hard. Everything seemed harsh as we travelled in the darkness and snow, just trying to get around. At the very end of the tour we hit Brazil, some gigs in Sao Paulo and Rio. We were shattered. The cocaine was a dollar a gram and the pot was free. There were naked hookers running around one night. There was poverty and there was hope. I saw a kid without any legs dragging himself belly down across a pedestrian crossing with his hands. I saw entire suburbs of beggars who lived in rubbishy shanties. We were followed everywhere by little urchins selling Chiclets gum. Everything was incredibly cheap; breakfast with everything and juice and coffee was one dollar.

The shows were only just OK, and Richard just wasn't trying anymore: we played some really big places but they were only half full. The promoters were disappointed and maybe the crowds were too. It's an uphill battle when the drummer isn't trying, like flogging a dead horse. Brazil did not go nuts for us.

So we reached another fork in the road where we misunderstood the power of the press: how to go more gently because after all you need them more than they need you. The Brazilian record company was very excited when we arrived because they'd scored a coup – we were to be on one of the most widely watched TV shows in South America, one that went to every country there! We were to be interviewed by the host, who was flying in from Argentina especially to talk to us. Exposure on this show and their playing our 'Under the Milky Way' video would help us crack the continent. The host apparently really liked the song and we were extremely lucky to get this kind of break; the record company people were over the moon.

But they'd underestimated our ability to snatch defeat from the jaws of victory.

The appointed night came and we assembled at a beautiful and cool restaurant up in the Rio hills overlooking the city and the beach. The host turned up and she was about 40, haughty and beautiful with a deep and harsh-sounding voice. She was dressed entirely in white leather. We sat down outside in a courtyard and she asked her first question through an interpreter: 'Almost everybody in South America is a catholic and we are interested to know why you call the band The Church.' Before anyone could answer Peter jumped in with a joke he'd been working on for a while I guess, but oh man he picked a terrible time to test it out.

'Because it's easier to spell than ...' and here he made an unintelligible sound while shaking his head. He sounded like a wounded bull. The host demanded an explanation from the interpreter. He gave her the Spanish answer with the bull sound at the end shaking his head just as Peter had done. Furiously, she snapped her fingers and in a minute she and all her entourage had driven off while the minions were packing up the cameras and lights. The record people were writhing and tearing at their hair. 'You don't know what you've just done!' they moaned. Now 150 million viewers wouldn't hear 'Under the Milky Way' on the most prestigious show in town! We had blown it again. What a bunch of clowns! Now imagine if I'd been nice to Steve Sutherland and Peter hadn't made his little joke. Yes, go on ... imagine ...

At the last gig of the tour Richard gave away parts of his drum kit and the microphones as well, which would've been a nice symbolic gesture if they'd been his! But they belonged to the promoter, who had hired them out to us, and he was not amused at all.

The whole thing ended in a mediocre shambles. Richard and Peter flew back to Australia and Marty flew to Sweden. I was flying to New York with a bunch of the crew to make my record with Donnette. That gig was the last real gig Richard would play with us: the band had lost its cohesion. We'd burnt ourselves out with all the accolades and all the arguments and all the drinking and drugging. The late nights had taken their toll on all of us. We'd developed a kind of rock'n'roll hubris and the universe *was* watching.

15

EVERYTHING IS GOING WRONG, ALL MY SONGS ARE COMING TRUE

So there I was in New York with a handful of our crew and we were all in a taxi driving away from the airport laughing and carrying on like the tour was still going on. We drove along for a while dropping guys off. And then it was just me and one more guy. And when he got out of the cab and walked into the freezing black New York night I felt a sudden stab of loneliness.

ALONE SAVE FOR an anonymous driver, I sped uptown to my manager's little flat. The spare room was dark and tiny and the window looked out at the bricks of next-door's block. I felt that old black panic coming down again. Again I resorted to a few brandies only it didn't work as well this time around. I went to bed a bit tipsy and wobbly and tired. When I opened my eyes the next day I couldn't tell if it was night or day; it was uniformly dismal and dark. I thought of my home in Rozelle where it would be summer and full of light. All I could hear was the sound of distant pipes groaning in the building. I seriously had to ask myself, what the hell I was doing there?

Donnette joined me a few days later to make the record, which we did at this sixteen-track place Mike knew about where we could get a good rate. I had all the songs ready to go on the sequencer and we wrote the words together as we went on down the track.

The first song we wrote the words for was 'Diviner' – we came up with some cracking verses I think:

High after the summer
Find all the wells are drunk dry
Miles and miles of star burn
Branded on the hide of the night
Diviner
Low, before the winter
Loser, these vessels are full
Drop between drop of moonshine
Slipping on the surface of our day
Diviner, water under dark
Diviner, rock ceiling fossil pool
Diviner, blind transparent fish
Diviner, seek the liquid dark

With the whole record I was trying to capture the sound of our infatuation: the sound of elation and romantic melancholy. Never before had I been so obsessed with a record I was making – I knew every little last thing on there because I'd played every instrument and wanted the record to be as pure as possible.

The Ensoniq had its own quirky cheap sound. I intended to turn that into a positive; anything I come across I can always find a positive side to it, at least musically. (It was this ethos that would eventually lead to 2012's *Garage Sutra*, which I recorded entirely on my laptop just to show you can do anything with just about anything!)

The time Donnette and I spent together making that record was punctuated by a bout of food poisoning that had us both vomiting and hallucinating for about three days. It was the weirdest and most horrifically trippy experience; I'm sure a big chunk of that made its way onto the record.

After we finished recording each night Donnette and I would sit in pre-dawn cafes drinking coffee and discussing our record. We had a little argument over the line 'Ann rides upon her big white horse', which Donnette insisted should be 'Ann rides up on her big white horse' because Americans would never say 'upon'. We were both in love with our fledgling record and thought about every last detail. I experimented with sampling Donnette's vocals and flying them back into the song. I was constantly excited by all the possibilities of sound and music: my American love affair had given me the energy to realise my vision of the dreamiest, saddest record ever.

Meanwhile many of my friends didn't understand what I was doing in New York making a record with this woman. People in Australia rang up and asked when the fuck I was coming back home. And I didn't know the answer; I was afraid of the answer. I had a home and a girlfriend there and my family and friends, but I was under the spell of love and New York, and it was a potent combo for me to rise above.

One night Donnette and I went to bar to see a comedian. The comedian stopped mid-line when he saw us sitting there in the audience. 'Boy, lady,' he said, 'you sure got something going on with this guy, haven't you?' It was pretty obvious; we were in New York together hiding out from the whole world.

Eventually Donnette had to go on tour with her band Game Theory and return to her boyfriend, who I guess by now must've known something was going on between us. A few times I'd rung her number in San Francisco and this guy had answered – I listened to his voice asking who this was and he seemed like a really nice bloke, not that that stopped me from poaching his girlfriend. I guess he'd always known she had her fixation with me and he just sort of moved aside without much of a fight.

A few days after Donnette left, Karin arrived from Sydney. Of course we had a lovely time and no I wasn't enjoying having two girlfriends at once at all! In fact the whole thing began to immediately break my heart and wear me down and scatter my resources even though I know I'd created the whole mess myself. Karin couldn't be too angry with me after her own indiscretions, and Donnette was in the same cheating position as me. We were all dismayed by all of this. Yet there Karin and I were having such a nice time: we were very good friends and there was no pressure or ultimatums from her. Time went by and when she went back to Australia still nothing was resolved.

Meanwhile a stroke of great luck saw Bryce Goggin agree to mix *Hex*. He was a young genius engineer and a friend of Big Mike's and he did the whole album slightly on the sly. He did an amazing job of bringing the melancholy and splendour of the album to fruition. Thank you Bryce, it still sounds good to this day!

Then in a bizarre twist of fate I somehow ended up going on tour with Donnette's band. I borrowed Mike Lembo's car and drove around a bunch of their gigs with Donnette – the band couldn't afford accommodation so they'd stay in their fans' living rooms while Donnette and I stayed in luxury hotels every night.

One night I was even brazen enough to attend the gig; this was while 'Under the Milky Way' was still languishing in the lower charts but our video was on MTV regularly so the audience recognised me and a big whisper went rippling through the crowd with everyone turning around to gawk at me sitting there. Game Theory's singer Scott Miller saw me and for some reason quickly ran through a short medley of Church numbers. I guess he did it to show the folks how easily it was done, because Scott's songs were very complex with a million twists and turns. His versions brought a new fragile aching bathos to my songs as he sang them back to me sitting there. Even at his gig I'd unwittingly become the centre of attention.

So Donnette finished her tour while I moped around New York in the poverty and snow and darkness. It was nearly Christmas. Every day I saw this same homeless guy who lived in a cardboard box outside Mike's place and he'd smile. One day he got out and wished me a Merry Christmas and a Happy New Year. I said that was very nice of him. 'Well, seeing we're neighbours it's the least I can do!' he replied. There really was an extraordinary number of beggars and infirm homeless people hanging about New York in 1988 – one day I gave a big black guy ten dollars instead of one dollar and Donnette went back to the guy and demanded he give it back. She grabbed hold of the ten bucks trying to reef it out of the guy's hand: what a sight he was towering over her, she so tiny and tenacious as all hell. I had to pull her away and calm her down. Wow, I'd never seen anything like that before. She was like someone from a Wild West town – especially with a few drinks in her, when she turned into a real little Annie Oakley!

At Christmas time Donnette and I flew out to Denver, Colorado, to spend Christmas with her folks. However you may imagine that was going to be, you're completely wrong! Donnette's mother reminded me of Madeleine Stowe, the actress. She must've had Donnette at an early age because she seemed incredibly young and youthful. She had a boyfriend called Roger who I think might've been younger than me. She was unbelievably cool and hip, like a beat generation woman, and her sense of humour was wry and cynical. She made me welcome in their small suburban house and for Christmas I got a huge bud of Colorado's finest weed. And let me say it was snowing within as well as without the house! We went to Mexican restaurants and hot springs in the mountains. It was such a lovely Christmas with none of that pressure you find at a regular Christmas. It was a real cool yule. They looked after me well and I'll always remember it. Now I was having a real dilemma as I really struggled to decide what I wanted to do next, but some sense of destiny or fate was still pushing me towards Karin. I think I realise now that it was the necessity of my first set of twins coming into this world; Karin and I could both somehow sense them out there waiting to be born! And this somehow kept us together. So I reluctantly parted company with Donnette and went back to Australia where some normality was waiting for me at home; where I was still expected to wash the dishes and put the rubbish out.

The Church took time off in 1989 and Karin and I did all our usual things but there was a tension in our relationship now, and a new sense of mistrust and suspicion. We fought a bit and Karin was angry when she found me still in communication with Donnette, who'd left her boyfriend to be with me. Only I wasn't there ... I was back in Sydney pursuing a vague feeling of destiny but still calling Donnette and writing to her.

One day Karin suggested that Donnette come out to Australia. Wow, it looked good on paper: I was a proper paid-up pop star now and I was going to have my own ménage à trois. Donnette stayed for about two months and it certainly was a tumultuous, torrid time, and I was really fucking knackered by the time it was all over. It had proven nothing and merely added a new bitterness in my various personal dealings. I was not cut out to flout social mores; all the jokes and derision and sheer envy during those troubled times did my tiny head in. Yeah, I had two girlfriends at once for a while; you try it and see how happy it makes you. There was a lot of bitching going on, I can say that!

Eventually Donnette went back to the US. I stayed on with Karin in Sydney. It was time to record a new Church album. Eventually we would head back to LA to do it with Waddy Wachtel, though not Greg Ladanyi, who was too much to cope with again. But first we did a charity gig for Tibet under the pseudonym 'Starfish' – Richard fucked that gig up deliberately in a few spots; he was light when it needed heavy and heavy when it needed light. I was so fucking angry after the gig that I swore I'd never play live with him again.

It was kind of strange we were going back to Waddy; the year before at a gig in Nashville The Church had had dinner with John Paul Jones from Led Zeppelin, who'd wanted to produce us, but apparently our manager stopped that happening because he didn't think JPJ had a track record as a producer. It was a shame that didn't happen. Maybe he could've inspired us to have done something better than the utterly ordinary *Gold Afternoon Fix*.

It was an uninspired group that gathered at Fatboy Studios in Rozelle, a tiny little eight-track facility where we could rehearse and record before I'd put the vocals on at home. Richard had well and truly had enough of playing: he could rarely be bothered, and when he did he'd stop and laugh and say something like, 'Oh you guys weren't really serious about that, were you?' Unwittingly or not, Richard was sabotaging everything we did. It was so demoralising.

After a few days of knocking out mediocre music Richard was waiting for me all excited. He and his girlfriend had an idea – he'd stop playing drums, and he and his girlfriend would cater to the entire band for $1400 a week. A veggie lunch, a veggie dinner and protein shakes; Richard even had an idea of a sample menu and the kind of dishes they'd be presenting each day. This proposition filled me with horror. We were possibly on the verge of cracking the big time if we could just knuckle down and get it straight. And yet here was Richard more interested in cooking food for us than being our drummer! I asked him what we should do for drums. He said to use a drum machine to write the songs, so we did that a bit too.

At the same time – being a complete overachiever myself – I was working on yet another solo album, which was in fact intended as my masterwork after the last patchy solo record, *The Slow Crack*. I wanted to make something that would show the scope of my huge ambitions: to make music that sounded like it came out of the Bible or something. The latest Ensoniq sampler would do the trick nicely with its big realistic sampled sounds and I embarked on the feverish recording of *Remindlessness*, which I worked on any hour I wasn't working on The Church. It's easy to see which got the best of my attention. *Remindlessness* is rich in all the things that *Gold Afternoon Fix* is lacking: imagination, love and inspiration. I poured it all into *Remindlessness* and saved the dross for *Gold Afternoon Fix*. What a stupid, wilfully moronic thing to do!

So eventually we all schlepped back to LA to make our new record. Richard was not into it at all. Waddy picked on him and he crumbled under the constant attention. And no one did anything to stop it happening … we all had our own nice little apartments and our nice little rent-a-cars to drive and a nice weekly wage.

Donnette immediately moved into my apartment. Richard imported his whining girlfriend and we didn't see much of him after that. Peter had a girlfriend too, and she moved into his place. Marty was expecting a baby, if I remember correctly. No one's mind was on the record; we'd come up with some OK songs, but the feeling was gone. Whatever magic was on *Starfish* had vanished entirely leaving a very ordinary follow-up record.

Some people tell me they like this record and to stop running it down in public, yet it remains out there in all its disappointing-ness. And that's what happens when nobody does anything! Nothing ventured, nothing gained, as the saying goes. Richard actually only played on three of the songs, the other tracks were Waddy reconstructing Richard's parts from the demos on a drum machine. He did a bloody good job on that, but the record has a leaden, predictable feel. There was scarcely a drop of life left by the time we'd recorded every song from the drum machine up. Richard should've tried a bit harder and Waddy should have gone a bit easier on him. And I should've said something. They were both wrong and they were both fucking up what were a mediocre bunch of songs to begin with! In retrospect I would rather the songs were sped up than the dull ordinariness we ended up with. That album has less vibes than a mausoleum and is totally un-psychedelic.

Of course there are some good songs there. We'd been together long enough to know how to go through the motions. I blame myself for being interested in everything except actually focusing on the record – the others needed me alert and intrepid, but my preoccupation with women and all the rest of it had me down and fumbling around. So I just let it all fall apart.

Eventually Richard and I finally fell out during this period over something petty like divvying up a bag of weed. He said a few things I couldn't get over, and I kicked him out of the band. The others didn't seem to object that much. It was pretty apparent he didn't want to be in the band anymore. He still hung around for a few months and collected his wages and drove around with the girlfriend ... and we had his photo on the album too for the sake of continuity.

(As I write this in 2014 Richard and his son Irie are sitting in my lounge room in Bondi. We're doing a run of shows together with Mark Gable from The Choirboys and Richard's drumming is as good as it ever was, when it was at its very best. And we are friends again. That's the most important thing.)

Meanwhile back in the boring old studio we were recording the album arse-about-face and I was just letting it happen. I'd just made *Remindlessness* at home and it was a bitching and hip record, so now I could just sit back and do all the things that I knew wouldn't be very good, especially recording the bass guitar on its own and first. That really was a lame-brain idea and it was part of Waddy's ongoing obsession that things should be perfect. So I did the bass on the songs to a drum machine and a guide guitar. And Waddy sat there always totally zoomed in on my fingers. Was that a slight slur, squeak or slip? 'Do it again, Kilbey!' Waddy would order for the thousandth time, which was just not the way to make a groovy, classic record! So I did my bass like that and then the guitarists did their parts like that. It's a perfect record ... perfectly boring.

The lyrics had lost the *Starfish* magic too. We'd lost our edge, even though it sounded like a well-made record. No one was that unhappy with it, but it sure wasn't what the doctor would've ordered for success.

The band did a few expensive videos featuring casts of thousands and baby elephants that probably cost more than the album. Then someone from Arista conceived of giving someone else at Arista a shock by making a hoax video. They'd play them the hoax video and get a great angry reaction and then, surprise, surprise ... here's the real one, ha ha! So I strapped on my guitar and walked around singing 'Metropolis' as they filmed me barging into various rooms and meetings with all these different actors trying on clothes and in the canteen and all that. Naturally I liked the hoax video much better than the real thing, and when they realised how much I liked it they destroyed it!

But look at Jay Dee Daugherty playing drums in that 'Metropolis' video, miming along to the drum machine on the record. Jay Dee had been recommended by Tom Verlaine as the best drummer you could get, and Tom wasn't far off the mark. Jay Dee played with us for about three years and was always together and powerful. He didn't have the incredible ups and downs of Richard Ploog, but he was a totally solid and dependable drummer and a very nice guy too.

Jay Dee came out on the road with us to support the album, which was floundering in the middle of the Billboard charts. Everyone thought it was OK but OK wasn't OK for us anymore. We needed to be more than that; we didn't have any great laurels to rest on. We did a big world tour that lost a load of money. The band was playing pretty tightly with Jay Dee pounding out the songs every night with real purpose, but we'd lost our momentum. Someone said we looked more like a firm of accountants than rockers. Everyone was having a good time, but it felt like a last hurrah – it was the same old circuit as *Starfish* but the audiences felt the stagnation within us. *Gold Afternoon Fix* just wasn't what anybody bloody well wanted, and yet here we were spoon-feeding 'em great lumps of this stodge when they probably wanted something off *Seance* or something.

Donnette came out to some gigs but our romance wasn't going so smoothly anymore either. Our record had gone absolutely nowhere. Nothing was really working for me, but I just couldn't see it. Perhaps on that tour I indulged more in all the things that were on offer than I ever had before – the others largely did too.

There was a feeling of cynicism in the air, a real bitterness. The road manager agitated against our management all the time and our management didn't really have a clue how to stop our malaise. Except to write 'another song like "Under the Milky Way" ... but not like it as well'. Riiiiight. Then everything would be fine.

There were some great and splendid moments on that tour though. We did well in London, where Marty met All About Eve for the first time. They'd lost their guitarist and Marty took the job. Why not? We were all happy for him to do it. The Chicago Navy Pier was another incredible gig. People had to find the tickets, which were hidden around different parts of the windy city as part of a radio giveaway thingy. So yeah, there were some good shows with good crowds.

We won a few battles on that tour but we'd already lost the war. Everyone went home except me, who stayed on to partake of more touring with its nebulous and heartbreaking delights. I flew and drove around the US with one roadie and strummed my guitar and entertained various ladies in my room: it was starting to be as though quantity *was* quality. And then I eventually went home too, to discover that Karin was pregnant. We joked about her having twins until we went to the doctor and they detected two heartbeats on the ultrasound. Karin was laughing and crying at the same time. Me? I was confused and dreading the idea of fatherhood. I wasn't that pleased or happy at this sudden turn of events, although I couldn't admit it, only to myself.

And then one day I hooked up with Grant McLennan from The Go-Betweens and he had this drastic impact on my life while I waited for my kids to be born. Grant and I had actually first met up in New York during the harsh winter of 1988, when I was hiding in Mike Lembo's flat. He'd played in a bookstore somewhere promoting a record and we'd gotten on really well. I saw the stripped-down

Go-Betweens play at The Knitting Factory and they killed it. I was so proud of this Australian band and how good they were.

Later on I ran into Grant at a party and we tried to cook up an Australian supergroup involving me and him, Paul Kelly and Neil Finn. They never joined us but Grant still had me. The first day I went over to his run-down share-house in Bondi Junction and he played me ten new songs straight off the bat before I could get a word in edgeways. He announced each song as 'a very beautiful song I've just written' – and man he was banging out some songs. The last one he played me was indeed beautiful. Called 'The Man Who Died in Rapture', it was about Jesus. Grant sang it looking up to the light streaming in the window, and to me at that moment he seemed like a saint. I was truly touched by his religious outpouring all wrapped up in a neat descending chord progression.

'Wow Grant, are you a Christian?' I asked.

Grant's demeanour changed in a second. 'Nah,' he said, 'I wrote it for a competition.'

So Grant and I started to write a bunch of songs together. It was a real eye-opener how easy it could be if you had a like-minded soul to work with. We started recording in a studio in Balmain, which we got cheap because it was going out of business, and it was a load of fun. Grant was everything one could hope for in a musical comrade: he was funny and debonair and quite the raconteur with lots of funny stories about Nick Cave and the early days in London with all the Aussies there. Grant loved a cigarette, a glass of red wine and a cappuccino. He loved to read the newspaper and go shopping to buy loads of novels that he'd probably never read. We became fast friends and we hung out together a lot, writing songs and taking pot shots at everyone else's pretensions.

The *Jack Frost* record was a lovely record, one of the best I've ever made. I was a good collaborator in those days; I had lots of schemes up my sleeve for writing music – something like my own version of Brian Eno's Oblique Strategy cards, which help writers overcome blocks in their creativity. Grant and I could always complement each other. If I could come up with an idea then Grant could finish it off; I was much closer with Grant in those few months of meeting and recording than I had ever been with the guys in The Church. We did some live shows too and they were very well received. Australian *Rolling Stone* magazine named *Jack Frost* the best Aussie album of the year. You'd have thought that we were all set for success, wouldn't you? But then things never work out the way you think they will. Or not for me, anyway.

16

THE START OF THE ASH, THE END OF THE FLAME

On heroin your dreams and visions will be complex, labyrinthine and intriguing. Behind your eyes are swimming empires of golden warmth spreading out to limitless horizons. Poetic visions come tumbling out of your mind. Such sweet warmth, such inexorable grooviness. Such an easy easy path … such a beguiling spirit hiding her cruel face …

ONE NIGHT GRANT and I were sitting in a pub at Bondi Junction drowning our sorrows … only I was on lemon squash. Grant said, 'Fuck it, I'm gonna get some heroin!' Really? That sounded perfect. I'd never had heroin before but that night I was willing to give it a try.

We drove around to Paddington where Grant had some dealers known as 'the girls'. I chucked in a hundred dollars and Grant went into the house for a while before emerging with a smile on his face. We went back to my place in Rozelle; Karin was away in Sweden.

The twins were very much on their way. Grant took out a little baggie and tossed it to me. 'Here, have a line of that,' he said.

If you knew Grant you would've thought him the cleanest-cut guy you could ever imagine. And in many ways he was. He avoided swearing and he was very polite to young girls and old ladies. I guess that's what made it all feel somehow safer. A million things were running through my head but it seemed that if Grant was using heroin that maybe it'd just gotten a bad rap like all the other drugs that had been demonised by the lying, tricky Western governments. I chopped out a line and snorted it. It was the beginning of a long and terrible affair that only petered out after eleven years.

My first snort was nothing spectacular, because at first heroin is a subtle drug. It'd take me a while to recognise and then crave its nebulous effect. But I'll tell you now the essence of how it worked on me. All my life a nagging voice had been telling me I was no good, and now that voice shut up for the first time. I felt comfortable. I felt cool. I felt detached. I felt like I was a child just in from playing outside all day, pleasantly drowsy after a nice warm bath. All my worries and anxieties receded. I followed daydreams across the screens of my mind and everything was all right. All those rotten deeds you did, all those sneaky games you played, all those nasty things you said, all that jealousy and envy – with heroin all of it is suddenly silenced. I was calm and I was happy.

After a while you might start to nod your head a bit and find yourself in a shallow dream-filled sleep. Time elongates then. Time has no meaning in this world. You might be born somewhere and grow up and live a life and get married and have sons and fight in a war and then you open your eyes and realise that only 30 seconds have passed in the real world.

Like all drugs, heroin begins to start up a dialogue with you and it whispers beautiful words in foreign languages that you want to get to know so badly, ever so badly. It will become apparent why heroin is called the White Lady, a gorgeous creature with a chequered past. Hell, nobody understands my White Lady. It's been said that she has fucked a lot of people over but now she's come to me and I can see it was all lies because she is soft and sweet. I feel like I'm in on the most private confidential joke when I snort her up my nostrils and taste her drip down the back of my throat. How I love to chop out those big white lines of smack on a jet-black piano, and roll up a 50-dollar note to sniff her up.

Wow, instant serenity! Bonhomie on a stick. You start to lust after it, you start to desire it. You start to become obsessed by it. You love to hear the mention of its many names. You love to put your finger in your pocket and nudge that fat little bag of smack sitting so snug there.

In next to no time at all, I was connected. The stuff found its way to me of its own accord. Suddenly I was living in a house in Surry Hills where I had installed a 24-track studio with the aid of another guy ... and a lot of people were coming by this house to use heroin there. It was a little heroin mecca for all kinds of people. I had loads of people to go and buy it for me. I was well cashed up at that point too. I had a couple of hundred grand I guess just lying around in the bank and nothing much to spend it on. Jesus Christ I'd come by all this money so easily; did I even really deserve it? There was some poetic irony in wasting it all on something so sweet! My thinking was already becoming addled. I had a dirty little bedroom in the three-storey terrace where my studio was now located. I'd go up there and take out my heroin and commune with the great white spirit.

At first there were no side effects: there were no catches. The White Lady had been given a bad reputation for sure; maybe all those guys shooting up had a problem but not us snorters!

I wondered why people had to put heroin in a needle when it was so nice just to take it up the nostril. I had all these great new friends and they all liked heroin too – it's like they all suddenly came out of nowhere to be with me and help me spend my money. That was the honeymoon phase when I was a heroin proselytiser and turned people on left, right and centre.

When The Church toured in Tasmania we met a guy in Hobart who'd send you a little canister of opium if you put some money in his bank account. And so I regularly began to get little packages from Tasmania. The opium and the heroin were two sides of the same coin: the opium was dreamier. I smoked it and I ate it and I drank it in strong cups of treacle-tasting coffee. Then I lay around listening to music or went into my studio and began to work on what would become *Narcosis*. I became interested in describing the heroin state in music and words. I wanted to reproduce that profound dreaminess and sickly-sweet heavy feeling of being down, down in some deep place.

So far so good. I'd snorted a load of stuff and hadn't had any bad reactions ... until the day I was walking through town and feeling kind of weird like I was having a hot flush or something. Then all of a sudden I broke out in the most unbelievable sweat. By the time I got on the Balmain bus I looked like I'd fallen into a swimming pool. It wouldn't be the last time the sweat would ooze and flow from my body like a river. With heroin it'd eventually happen every day whether I was high or if I was withdrawing. It was always a both-ways bet on sweat.

Which is when I started to think I'd better get off the stuff. I went back to my real house in Rozelle and was shocked to find that I couldn't sleep at all, even though I desired it more than anything. Time passed so fucking slowly a minute would seem like a year. All the voices in my head came back with a vengeance.

My legs and arms were aching a fair bit too. It was like growing pains only amped up a few notches. My nose wouldn't stop running, and when I sneezed I'd get this kind of cold electric shock that'd be followed by shudders of revulsion. I still couldn't sleep even after a few days of shivering on a couch watching late night TV. But everything had a strangely alien unpleasantness attached to it. Everything was raw and hurting. Music that I loved suddenly hurt my ears. TV shows and video clips brought on a burning restlessness and blinding, white-hot anger. Reading a book was impossible; I couldn't concentrate. Water felt like it was burning my skin. Heroin entices you with beauty, and she keeps you with an unbearable ugliness that no one can face. The toughest, most brutal thug becomes a whimpering child in the face of the stuff. Sometimes the stuff lets you think you have a bit of freedom, but you have none. There's no leeway or grace period when you deal with the stuff.

But the problem is not the stuff: it's the absence of the stuff. It's when you can't find or afford it. And it's expensive. A gram is 300 bucks and I could easily do two grams a day then if I was stupid enough, and I often was. The stuff is highly illegal and suddenly you're up against a whole new side of the law that as a mere pot smoker you may not have encountered. If you keep going, you'll be frisked and searched and patted down and maybe handcuffed and led away. If you still keep going you'll become friends with thieves and prostitutes and homeless guys and all kinds of weird people from other walks of life.

I had no control over the stuff. If I bought up big for a cheaper price I could get five grams for $1200 – that's one gram free! – but it never worked out for me in actuality. I could never control myself with something that I loved so much, though love seems a funny word to apply to a drug, I admit.

Was I really some unspeakable fiend for pursuing this chemical detachment and then hiding from its hideous withdrawals? Or was I just some poor bloke who'd encountered his nemesis not in gambling addiction or alcoholism, but in the wicked poppy that has destroyed so many lives? Illegal or legal the stuff has you figured out – it reads your mind and listens in on your plans to get rid of it. It stands in freedom's doorway as you try to leave, mocking your pathetic efforts to be free of it. Every habit is worse than the last and comes on faster. These are the unfailing equations I learned to abide by and expect.

Back in Rozelle in 1991 and I was still writhing around on the couch in the front room of 91 Mansfield Street, and feeling so worn out and shattered. Just think, I could've gotten up and walked away from the whole thing right there, and there'd be barely a distant memory left. But I pursued it until the damned thing pursued me.

I'm sorry to say I probably gave it two weeks and then was back sniffing the stuff. Only I'd learnt my lesson and then had a strict regimen of Saturday nights only. Which quickly deteriorated into Saturdays and Wednesdays only. And eventually all the other days got added in as well ... Sure enough I got another nasty little habit sniffing heroin and smoking opium, the twin dreamy undoers of men. Again and again I went through the entire trauma of withdrawal, and again I soon enough got back in the ring to take another shot at it. But it always floored me. So that was the recurring pattern of my life for a while.

Eventually I stopped trying to withdraw. I did everything within my power to keep on going by hook or by crook. I left no stone unturned to score. All of my modest means were at the stuff's disposal – and it demanded every last cent I had. If I'd earned more it would've demanded that as well. I would only face the true horror of withdrawal a few times after that, and those episodes made the Rozelle days seem like a picnic.

Meanwhile the twins' birth was approaching in June. And The Church was working on its undisputed masterpiece in the shape of an album called *Priest=Aura*. Arista recommended Gavin MacKillop to produce it. We liked his work, so he flew out to Sydney at the end of autumn that year. Gavin was a very cool and funny Scotsman and we immediately got along and saw eye to eye on almost everything.

The Church had spent a few weeks in a rehearsal space in Ultimo having extremely productive and revealing songwriting sessions. I was still in my honeymoon phase of smoking opium, and the music was flowing out of me and everybody else. Peter fooled with the stuff for a while too. Marty and Jay Dee did not, but the opiated feeling was reflected in the music. Jay Dee was a fantastic collaborator and fitted in perfectly to our songwriting method. We came up with all this good stuff so quickly and effortlessly, as if by magic. It was the opposite of the turgid *Gold Afternoon Fix* writing sessions. We were on fire, killing it song after song. It was strange how easily the music was coming to us so quickly and completely. It was like scooping songs out of another world.

We recorded again at Studio 301 in Sydney. Gavin was a wonderful producer: he was across every aspect of the music, and really became a big part of what we were doing. Everything sounded so big and spacious. Gavin pulled great sounds and worked really hard on this record. We knew we were making a masterpiece. We knew it would probably be misunderstood, that it might take some time before people could see how good it was. For me, this record blew all the other Church records right out of the water – it was everything I wanted to do with music. Thanks to opiates I did momentarily catch that dreamy, slowed-down warmth on some of the tracks of this record. It was a new grandeur, a new authority ... a new era.

I made a stylistic decision to play only my Fender 6-string bass on *Priest=Aura.* This gave it a completely different feeling from a regular, deeper, more indistinct bass guitar. The 6-string bass is like a hybrid of bass and guitar though really it's neither. It actually has a very limited application, but I milked that guitar for everything it was worth and it gave *Priest=Aura* such a different sound.

(On the brand new Church album being completed at the time of writing, I have been playing a 6-string bass again. And on those tracks people have been saying that it reminds them of *Priest=Aura* – that's how strong the association is.

Another factor contributing to the unique sound of *Priest=Aura* was Marty's new use of a volume pedal on many of the tracks. Without the normal attack of a guitar he sounded a lot more ambiguous in the music and so everything had a lot more room to breathe. Peter came up with some excellent new things, with some tricks he had up his sleeve. And Jay Dee rocked!

When it came to the lyrics I hit a new level, which I wasn't going to be able to get back to for quite a long time. The honeymoon period with the opium and the stuff was still lingering on, at least creatively. It'd be a lie to say I didn't initially find those drugs useful in chasing after words. I don't ever know where the words come from for songs; I just listen to a piece of music and words start coming together in my head, as if from nowhere. Sometimes I have to give things a little push along with my thoughts, but with *Priest=Aura* whole songs would just download into my head. As soon as I started I knew I was on one big roll because the words were streaming to me as quickly as I could write them down. Every song had its own special thing going for it. I can't really describe it much more than that: the magic happened and the music and the drugs and the experience all came together and I wrote some lyrics that I still haven't surpassed in all these intervening years.

Aura was influenced by the Gulf War, but it went far beyond that and incorporated all sorts of mentions of all kinds of things from all over the place. I was seeing things from a new vantage point, and it gave me a temporarily broad perspective. 'Ripple' was nasty and cynical; it had a new directness and a new acerbity. 'Paradox' was about the honeymoon with the stuff, really trying to drum up that floating feeling. 'Swan Lake', about the imminent arrival of the twins; 'Lustre', a song about some vague wickedness or another; 'Mistress' is probably a bit self-explanatory; and 'Kings' is a marvellously historic song in which I think I prove that the ancient world was probably more groovy than you think.

The bizarre tale of the 'Disillusionist' was where the callous cynicism of *Gold Afternoon Fix* gave way to some real rottenness that was half me and half imaginary me. Ooh what a naughty boy that 'Disillusionist' is! And the heartbreaking 'Old Flame', one of The Church's most tender and sad moments. Then there's the daunting gloom rocker 'Chaos', in which all the anxiety and loathing starts to come out and finally the album finishes on 'Film', a noir movie soundtrack just waiting for the visuals to go with it.

Priest=Aura had it all: the sound, the vision and the implications. It was the 'big music' you sometimes heard people talking about. The album got some mixed reviews – surprisingly it got a few good ones in England, which was in the grip of the shoe-gazer musical movement (if you can use such organisational terms for such random things as rock'n'roll!). One reviewer said the record would have the shoe-gazers running back to mummy to ask for more effects pedals. But *Rolling Stone* in the US slagged it with a really bad two-star review. (Ironically, *Rolling Stone* re-reviewed it and gave it four stars in their big record review book. The second time around it was praised as the frickin' masterpiece it always was.) It was just too far out in 1992 for some dense people to grok something so elegant. Its failure helped to undermine me a little bit more.

At the same time I was working bit by bit on songs that would become *Narcosis*, my next solo record. These songs were like a parallel *Priest=Aura* world only with even more emphasis on the heroin and opium. The reverbs were cavernous and the voice and lyrics were disconnected. The opiates were obsessing my thoughts and feelings. The lack of them became a sore spot in my whole life – Grant and I were using together and a nastiness appeared in our relationship.

I was spending a lot of time at the Surry Hills house in Albion Street. It was a monster three-storey terrace with a bunch of different people living there when I first turned up: there were punk drummers and students and ordinary working people who just had a room and kept to themselves. It had four or five bedrooms. Grant and I would have the stuff and walk around writing songs; sometimes we'd go out onto the footpath and accost passers-by with snatches of Dylan tunes. I'd try to chat up ladies on Grant's behalf, much to his excruciating embarrassment. Grant would sit on the step puffing imperiously in his strange sideways manner. They were wry and slightly bitter times.

Narcosis came out and did absolutely nothing. It struggled to even get a review amid the clamour for grunge and Britpop – things that now seem antiquated although *Narcosis* does not. It was a great record and I released some different versions eventually adding more tracks. It was a document of my great fall from grace, and still makes riveting listening if you have the nerve.

On the 7th of June 1991 Anna Miranda Jansson Kilbey and Elektra June Jansson Kilbey were born by caesarean section at Sydney's Royal Prince Alfred Hospital in Camperdown. A placental test showed they were identical twins. They were both tiny premature kids and they struggled a bit at the beginning. Both their grandmothers were there, one from Sweden and one from just up the road at Smiths Lake. As Anna Miranda was being weighed and blood-tested she let out these little weak cries. A familiar voice came on the radio, which was playing somewhere in another room. It was my brother Russell singing his latest single 'Thrive' on 2JJJ. I hoped that was a good omen.

The twins soon turned into wonderfully healthy little girls. We called them the Twillies, which is a cross between the Swedish word *tvilling* and the English word twin. I sometimes even called them the Twilliepops, which later led to them being called *Popparna* (the pops) in Swedish. They say a loved child has many names: as they learnt to talk, Miranda named herself Minna, and so the family has always known them as Elli and Minna.

Fatherhood was a big set of mixed emotions for me. I loved the kids with all my heart, but Jesus Christ they were hard work. Of course Karin bore the brunt of the hardest parts, and as a mother she was cheerful, practical and thorough. She was also quite fiercely independent and decided to get out and get away from the kids as soon as she could safely do it. So she'd go for a little stroll for an hour leaving me with the two little screamers. It was good for all of us, I guess. For a while when Minna was first born she'd suffer no one but Karin to handle her. One afternoon Karin went out for a little walk and Minna started crying, and soon I had our neighbours in our house all trying to console this tiny baby screaming at the top of her powerful lungs. The moment Karin returned and took her in her arms the crying magically stopped. Sometimes it's hard being a father.

Unfortunately by then heroin had her hooks deep into me. In fact, I shudder to think about these awful days. It's quite an upheaval to write much of the story from here on in … It doesn't come lightly or pleasantly like the earlier chapters: each memory fills me with shame and revulsion and sadness in differing amounts. As I look back on myself, helplessly floundering and starting to lose everything I had, I don't know if my feelings towards that man are anger or scorn or pity. As I sit here I want to rush into the past and give that idiot a great big fucking clout. A thick ear, as my mum used to threaten me with. My life started to unravel in a hopelessness that was not tragic so much as embarrassing. Heroin didn't make me glamourously thin; it made me podgy and flabby. It didn't curb my appetite; it gave me a hankering for sweet milky custardy things. But that was the least of it. It did worse than just damage your looks.

Because I had a partner and family and responsibilities I was suddenly enmeshed in an instant set of lies as to where I was going, why it had taken so long, and how much I was spending. At first when I was just dabbling with the stuff I'd been quite candid about it but as it took hold and dragged me down I began to lie my pants off. And after a while, as the stuff takes hold, the addict starts to enjoy telling lies and he'll enjoy maintaining complicated fantasy worlds that anyone on the outside will immediately spot as a web of utter lies.

Very few people can use the stuff and not turn into a naughty fibbing ne'er-do-well who'll say almost anything if it involves a fix at the other end. Yes, a fix! Because by now I was shooting the stuff up into the big vein in my right forearm that I never before even knew existed.

On the top floor of my house there lived a lady called Katie, an ex-doctor who'd been chucked out of the profession because of some malarkey with – you guess it! – opiate prescriptions. And she had a boyfriend called Tim who was in jail for importing the stuff. Katie gave me my first few shots. And later on when my big veins shrank away she helped me find other veins to shoot. Katie was a lovely woman and brilliantly intelligent; apparently she'd come top of her year finishing medical school. She was not your usual addict. She administered shots in a precise doctorly fashion, dispassionately commented on what was actually going on as she did. 'There!' she'd softly exclaim as the needle probed my vein, a tiny flash of crimson blood appearing in the solution without even being pulled in. 'OK, here we go,' she'd say as she expertly pushed the disposable syringe's plunger down, discharging its contents relatively painlessly into my vein. After whipping the needle out she'd ask, 'How's that?' with a wry smile.

A lot of people have tried in many different ways to explain the feeling of a shot of the stuff. I'll have a little stab at it myself I suppose, although it really is quite an ineffable feeling. One famous Australian songwriter who was once on the stuff said something about people being scared to mention that heroin can have quite a quasi-spiritual feeling to it, and I must agree. The first shot was quite the revelation. I had fallen in love with heroin by snorting it but injections took me to another level. It suddenly occurred to me that sniffing it was a terrible waste … just like Katie said. From then on I'd rarely do that because as soon as the injection was in my blood I felt that sweet, sickly-soft bash as your whole system reeled in the most delightful way. The taste of the stuff appears at the back of your throat and for some reason this bitter chemical taste is most delightful! Instead of the creeping euphoria of a sniff, the shot delivers instant gratification. It rushes through your body and mind, taking away all aches and pains and bad feelings and self-doubt. Katie and I would then smoke a joint and drift off in a disembodied haze in the gloom of her tatty room.

Tim came out of jail and he wasn't at all like I'd expected. He was already in his 40s and had been an opiate addict his whole adult life. He'd been in and out of jail but was the gentlest, most charismatic and softly spoken guy who looked at the whole thing in a sadly philosophical manner. He'd endured a thousand cold turkeys and always came straight back to the stuff. He couldn't and wouldn't ever have one day without it if he could help it. But he wasn't a thug or a pusher or a whining cartoon junkie. He was a decent, intelligent bloke who just happened to be addicted to something that was just about the most illegal thing you could ever think of.

The very word heroin scares many people, and that's partly because the media and the laws have whipped up an unnecessary hysteria. Tim's problems with the stuff were all legal problems. If the stuff were actually legal most junkies' problems would recede to being merely the medical problems that injecting drug users must expect to find when pursuing their course. And that's enough to cope with, without all the other carry-on with police and customs and the underworld one must enter to find it in the first place. There is no actual reason to compound the misery of the addict. He is already suffering enough.

For a while I managed to make as much as I was spending. I got a big advance for my publishing from Sony, and I got in a few production jobs. One was Canadian songbird Mae Moore, with whom my relationship eventually soured towards the end of the record because of my habit. You can read all about it on her retrospective album if you want to get some more details. Another record I produced was Australian chanteuse Margot Smith, a truly gifted woman, albeit already on the path to alcoholism when I met her. I got to produce half her debut album *Sleeping with the Lion.* I co-wrote a chunk of it with her. Margot came in and drank her wine, and smoked my pot and snorted my stuff. She was a real wild child who had an appetite for anything that was going. Her talent was impressive and her singing was sublime but it was obvious she was doomed if she didn't stop drinking, even at that early stage of the game. Meanwhile Karin and the girls spent more and more time in Sweden. I didn't blame them for wanting to be there because I was starting to become a real mess: a sweaty unreliable fool.

The Church had done a tour of Australia that made no money. Peter was disgruntled and left the band for a while. There were no bad feelings, not even a discussion; he just upped and left. Jay Dee stayed on a little longer, though we had nothing to really offer him. Eventually Marty and I were the only ones left, and we reconvened at the studio in Albion Street with Dare Mason producing. There, as my heroin addiction worsened and deepened, we came up with the strange record called *Sometime/Anywhere*. It was OK but my honeymoon with the stuff was over and it wasn't particularly helping me anymore. The album is passable, but I'd run out of steam. Compared to the wonderful *Priest=Aura* it was an unsatisfactory affair in every department. It remains an unlistenable oddity to me – every song feels like pain.

Thankfully Marty wasn't judgmental of my addiction. He ignored it as much as he could, only occasionally offering a wry comment. But I was starting to become truly miserable and wretched. I'd run out of money, so I started borrowing it and pawning my not inconsiderable guitar collection down at the local hock shop to keep up the raging habit riding my back. Everyone was angry and disappointed with me, myself more than anyone.

Eventually Karin moved permanently to Sweden where she might as well be, seeing as I'd lost the plot. The 'stuff' was the only thing I had any real loyalty to, and I became a shadow of my former self. Groups came to the studio to hire it out and I'd demand the money upfront in a very unprofessional way. I was running down all my resources. I was out of control. The stuff now had me completely by the balls and the pleasure had gone out of it for the most part. I was merely running from the horrors, and sinking lower and lower in some bizarre midlife crisis.

I still kept making records though. I still kept plodding on against the odds ... but the stuff had well and truly corrupted my friendship with Grant, and in an ironic twist Grant's own problem with the stuff had worsened in direct proportion to my own. We'd score and use together, and like all drug buddies we ended up squabbling over our dealings. I had more money than Grant, and I'd buy more and use more and sometimes unnecessarily rub that in. Heroin makes people cruel and callous. Grant was shady and deceptive in his dealings with the stuff too. The outside world hadn't twigged that he was using, which is exactly the way he wanted it, but it's even harder to play the role of the incognito junkie.

During this ugly and final phase of our friendship we made another Jack Frost album. Tim Powles, whom you might remember as the drummer from The Venetians, was then a drumming gun for hire around Sydney. The Venetians had long since fallen apart, and Tim had played for everybody since then – including some of Australia's biggest bands who you wouldn't have expected. His drumming was totally solid and he was a reliable, no-nonsense type of character. He'd already done some drumming on *Sometime/Anywhere* and we'd been impressed by his work, so we got him in on drums and wrote and recorded a bunch of songs.

The songs are hard and tough and sad numbers.

Grant and I really outdid ourselves on the *Snow Job* record. Grant was shocked when he saw the cover art I chose after the album lay around unreleased for a while. It was of Buddha and some chick in lotus position, and Grant blushed and stuttered and blushed and stuttered some more. Inside the record there's Grant wearing a beanie and two sets of shades, and me on the nod on my couch. The record did very little and garnered few reviews when it did come out. Grunge and Britpop ruled the airwaves and there wasn't any room for Jack Frost I suppose.

Things constantly churn over in the pop world, and The Church were considered passé if they were considered at all ... but I was too far gone to notice. I was on a losing streak and had no expectation I would win. Heroin was beginning to knock the hubris out of me.

Something had to do it; it might as well be the stuff.

17

MORE SONGS ABOUT KRISHNA AND SMACK

This chapter charts my fall and my redemption, which has been my arc and necessary parabola. For some reason I had to go through all that to get to where I am now. A sadder, yet wiser person … and it's all been something quite peculiar. I mean, you couldn't make this stuff up, could you?!

IN THE MIDST of the mayhem and wreckage of my life I encountered a small island that gave me some refuge. In my house in Rozelle I had a bit of a library going on, with all kinds of books in it. Many different people had stayed in my house when I wasn't there, house-sitters and people just crashing there and things like that. Anyway, someone had left a load of Hare Krishna literature in there. One day I discovered a book about Sri Prabhupada, the guy who brought the Hare Krishna movement to the West. I was immediately captivated and went on to devour all the Hindu and Buddhist books I could find in the library. And then even beyond that I got the *Bhagavad Gita* and the *Mahabharata* and the *Ramayana* and finally one morning after getting a large cheque

I went and scored some stuff and then I went and bought the 24-volume *Srimad Bhagavatam.* I lapped it up just like I'd lapped up Greek and Norse mythology as a child, and Latin as an adolescent, but this was different.

As preposterous as Krishna may seem to a Western mind, to me Krishna became more and more real ... and closer and closer as I read and tried to understand the subtle paradoxical nature of Hindu cosmology. I also read Buddha's *Pali Sutras* with great relish, feeling the soothing tranquility of his words. All of this moved me and reached me at a deep level. It was consistent with the world as I had found it. And Krishna was a god you could really fall for and long for until you found devotion all around you.

I read the *Bhagavad Gita* with commentary by Sri Prabhupada, which is a dialogue between Krishna and his friend Arjuna as they stand prepared to take part in a great war that's about to engulf humanity. Arjuna has confessed he's lost his appetite for fighting: he is loath to kill his friends and family on the other side. In a beautifully poetic treatise called 'The Song of God', Krishna instructs Arjuna on how to live. At Arjuna's insistence Krishna eventually reveals himself in his universal form, which is too impossibly huge and awe-inspiring for a human being to take in. Krishna returns to his normal form and Arjuna rejoins the battle enlightened and clear about the course he must take. The *Gita* can be considered as an equivalent of the *New Testament* – it definitely has the spiritual advice and the solemnity.

One day I was apparently standing in my paisley dressing gown drinking vanilla custard and reading Hindu literature when Stephen Cummings rolled up to make an album with me that would later be called *Falling Swinger.* He wanted to work with me because he knew I could bring something different to his usual trip, which was becoming a bit stale to him I guess, so I was surprised when he turned up with a bunch of his Melbourne cronies – the same ones who'd helped him make all the stale stuff he was trying to get away from. They were a smug little bunch of characters, and we didn't get off to a good start. Instead of trusting me Stephen would always ask them their opinion, and their opinion was often the opposite of mine causing long pointless stalemates. Throw into this complicated mix my brother Russell, who was now living at Albion Street with his girlfriend Amy, and one Simon Polinski.

At the time Polinski was one of the most troublemaking little geezers you could ever imagine, and also my engineer and co-producer of this record. He never missed an opportunity for some sort of insurrection and was a thorn in my side as well as Stephen's. He was and still is an excellent engineer, with just enough lovability to get him through his relentless shit stirring. But overall, as far as Stephen and I were concerned, it was two cultures clashing.

Like Tom Verlaine, Stephen was out of his tree on nicotine and caffeine; you never saw the guy without a cigarette and a fucking cappuccino. He was so on edge he was already into the middle of next week! He was jittery and jumpy, and reminded me of a red setter I'd once seen in an electrical storm. I, on the other hand, was lazy, sleepy and always distracted by the stuff, whether it was obtaining the finances for it, administering it, sleeping off its effects or waiting around for it to show up. I was never at my best back then, and was never giving 100 per cent.

I'm ashamed to say that some aspects of Stephen's stories are true: there was a ten-year-old boy, William, who delivered the heroin while his mother sat in the car. Everything went through this kid, like 'Mum said you can't have any more credit until you pay the $150' or 'Mum says this one's slightly small so she'll give you a bigger one tomorrow.' It was far from an optimal state of affairs I admit, but it was this or nothing, and nothing was now intolerable.

Nevertheless Stephen Cummings and I eventually produced a record, which was successful on his own terms and within his own parameters. Unfortunately we tried the trick again sometime later with the same bunch of hangers-on, and the same arguments arose only that time they ended in tears … Here I have to contradict Stephen's version of events and most emphatically state that the tears were his and not my own. And the album was *Escapist*.

And so I continued shooting heroin, drinking custard and reading books about Krishna. Eventually *Sometime/Anywhere* came out and we went to America for a promo tour, where I carried on my pursuit of using the stuff – sometimes ending up in a city empty-handed and having to do gigs as sick as a dog. Other times getting lucky and overindulging, being stoned and sloppy on stage. As the tour wound its way towards the final gig in Las Vegas a guy from Arista arranged for me to go into Exodus Recovery Center in LA as soon as the tour was over. I had one last big night with the stuff and flew to LA early the next day where a man met me and drove me straight to Exodus. I was frightened out of my mind; it seemed like a death sentence. I knew I was about to go through the most terrible upheaval I'd ever faced in my life. I couldn't imagine how bad it would be.

I don't remember anything about the first three days there. I was given some incredibly heavy barbiturate that just knocked me out 24 hours a day, and if I vaguely woke up they gave me some more. The next three or four days after that I began to wake up but I didn't really know who I was or where I was or what I was doing. I wandered around the rehab – which was really just the wing of a hospital and its tiny courtyard filled with cigarette-smoking patients – completely disconsolate and shocked in my hospital gown. People from Australia rang me on the telephone; people I'd been friends with for years, but did I know who they were?

The slime was oozing out of my body in every possible way. I was vomiting up pure bile, and it scorched my throat. I spent a lot of time lying on the floor beside the toilet convulsing. Sleep became the most desirable thing in the world, but it was totally denied me. My brain didn't have the chemicals to sleep – and it wouldn't have them for several weeks to come. I was so hungry but every time I tried to eat something it made me violently ill. I was so tired I would've given everything I had just for one minute's respite.

Eventually after about a week this gave way to a searing depression, while my bones and muscles ached like a bastard. It was the worst hell imaginable. I became angry and defiant, and plotted to get out of there. I talked to other inmates about getting the stuff brought in. I was rude and didn't cooperate with staff and began to demand valium and klonopin pills. I tried to ring some numbers but the people on the other end had been told not to answer – on pain of their lives. Marty and our then-manager Jeff visited me a couple of times but their stays were brief. I watched them drive away, envious.

One fateful night it all became more than I could possibly bear. I was alone in the room I was sharing with a guy from Porno for Pyros. He wasn't there at that moment though. I was just sitting on the floor feeling totally wretched, totally used up and burnt out: every fibre of my being was screaming out for the stuff. My stomach was spewing forth this green chemical slime, a cold stinging sweat bathed my body, my legs and arms ached like I was on fire. I hadn't slept or rested or drifted away for one moment: the insomnia was worse than all the other things put together.

I'd continued my reading of the Krishna literature while I was in rehab; Donnette also visited me and brought me more books on the subject. I found reading these books a tiny comfort during the state of agony I found myself in. My mind was brimming with Krishna.

In the NA and AA meetings we had in our little unit (attendance was compulsory) I'd heard a phrase being bandied around that God would never give anyone more than they could handle, and I'd read the same sentiment in the Krishna literature.

Sitting there I decided I'd had more than any person could possibly deal with. There was no refuge left to me but God. Instinctively I assumed the position known in yoga as the child pose: my face on my knees, I crouched down flat on the floor symbolically showing the entire universe that I'd run out of ideas for myself and was surrendering totally and unequivocally to whatever was out there. Not a single shred of me remained that wasn't part of that surrender. It was mental, spiritual and physical. It was a 100 per cent unconditional scream for help – that or let me die.

Instantly it filled me – warm, sweet and healing, and I immediately understood that it'd always been there and was always there all the time. It hadn't come to me; rather, I'd let it in. It was more real than anything else. It completely blotted out the horror of the withdrawals, the squalid little cubicle where I currently resided. I was connected, it was mainline deep and it extended unlimited grace and mercy to me. The warmth didn't communicate with me in words, it didn't name itself and it didn't judge me. It simply filled me. My ego hadn't intervened this time, ruining things as it usually did during previous spiritual exercises.

Feeling suddenly delightfully drowsy I lay down on my bed and at once fell into a delicious dream, the most wonderful dream I've ever had and most probably ever will. In it I was in a beautiful country setting next to a river dotted with proud swans. Exotic flowers were in bloom everywhere and the brilliant sun gave out warmth but didn't burn. I was chatting with Krishna, the dearest friend anyone could possibly have. It seemed like we stood there talking for years and years in some gorgeous, endless afternoon.

When I woke up I discovered I'd been asleep for only twenty minutes, but feeling completely refreshed I got up and wandered about the wards offering words of encouragement to those who'd recently arrived as well as attempting to talk others out of their plots to either break out or have the stuff brought in. My behaviour seemed so suspicious that the staff drug-tested me on the spot, but of course their tests came back negative.

Unfortunately my ego had also reawakened and I began to visualise situations where my new-found godliness could come in useful. Over the course of the following hour my gradually expanding ego squeezed the warmth right back out of my head, but even though the wonderful feeling was gone its memory and the certainty of God enabled me and gave me the strength to get through the rest of the gruelling rehab that lay ahead. God has never returned to me since, despite much chanting, a bit of meditating and a fair bit of yoga. That's because I've never been able to summon the surrender necessary to properly open up to it. My surrenders since then have always been accompanied by the doubting voice of the devil, but maybe I can handle it.

The reader will be disappointed to read that this still wasn't the end of the road for the stuff and me. No, I went back to Australia eventually and slipped back into my old ways just to see what it was like. Yes, just to see what it was like! I already knew what it was fucking like but I still had to have another little try. The hubris was still within me; I thought I could master the stuff even though nobody else ever has. I thought I'd learnt my lesson but no, I hadn't. I slipped back into it slowly but surely. Which led to another six years of addiction and sorrow and loss when I could've walked away right then …

I sold my house in Rozelle and moved to Sweden where I bought a lovely little apartment in fashionable Sodermalm so I could be closer to Elli and Minna, but it was all for nothing as I just carried on with the stuff there. If anything I was worse than ever. An endless parade of rogues and thieves and prostitutes and dealers flowed through my life like characters in an awful story.

A couple of times I got nicked by the coppers there, and I also had a couple of near misses. Once, a copper chased me and another junkie along a street after we'd both just scored from the guy they'd already nabbed. We ran as fast as we could but the young giant of a copper gained on us quickly. I had two caps in my mouth and I wasn't going to spit them out for anything. Two 500-krona caps that would keep me all right for two days? No way! Being sick scared me a lot more than being arrested. At the end of the street I went one way and the other junkie went another way and, the good Lord be praised, the young copper went after the other guy and not me. I got home sweating and puffing and exhausted, my heart going boom boom boom, but I had my stuff!

Another time I got run over on Gotgatan because I was looking at the traffic the wrong way, the way you do in Australia. But Swedes drive on the other side of the road. I knew my dealer Janne was in the pub across the road, and I was anxious to score after having just pawned a guitar up the road. I was feeling rather poorly because it'd been a while since my last fix. (You understand why the word 'fix' is so very apt; I sure needed to be fixed as I fell apart without the stuff.)

Anyway, I ran across the road and was hit by a grey Mercedes. I put out my arm to ward off the car and there was a crack and I was tossed into the air. I crawled off the road and sat in the doorway of a shop. A guy immediately came out of the shop and told me in my wretchedness to piss off from his shop.

The driver from the car had stopped and soon the cops and ambulance were at the scene. The cops wanted me to press charges against the driver, who they said should've been going slow enough to stop, but I didn't want to cause the guy a load of trouble when it had actually been my fault. The ambulance guys said they reckoned my arm was busted and I had to go to hospital but I didn't want to go to hospital or press charges – I just wanted to see Janne and go home and have a bloody fix! The cops said that if I could lift my arm above my head then I could go home, so with an almighty groan I lifted my arm above my head. The cops and ambulance people had a quick conversation and decided to let me go. The driver of the car was so relieved he slipped me a few hundred krona and told me to buy myself a drink. Somebody later told me I could have seriously sued him and his insurance company would've had to pay but now it was too late. And at the time I just didn't care.

Everyone went away and I walked on down to the pub and scored from Janne, who was still waiting for me. Then I went home to my lovely little flat and had a lovely little fix. My arm was throbbing a bit but it was nothing compared to the feeling of withdrawals. Well that was all good until a few days later when my arm turned completely black. I had to go into a hospital and have it re-broken and reset – now that was painful: stupid and very painful!

And so I blundered on and on. Sometimes finding some money and indulging in the stuff big-time, and sometimes just scraping through by the skin of my dodgy English teeth. What a miserable grovelling excuse-filled existence it was, trying to rake up 500 krona every day (about a hundred Australian dollars) and travelling around Stockholm in the dead of winter meeting dealers in kiosks and churchyards and on train station steps.

In my three years there I had hundreds of dealers, all of whom would come and go or suddenly disappear. There was Juan the Spanish guy, who always had very good stuff but then he'd suddenly disappear without warning. There was Leffe, a taxi driver who married a junkie prostitute and thought he could supply her the stuff and keep her out of the game. But it didn't work out: he ended up addicted too and she kept on turning tricks. I turned up to their place one day and the police were everywhere and Leffe's wife hurried towards me and said, 'Leffe hung himself today. You cannot go in there!' Of course I was devastated but I still had to sort out my sickness. Instead of being shocked by his death, I saw it as just another damned inconvenience.

Then there were Carina and Janne. Coincidentally I'd known Carina long before all this, when she was about thirteen. She used to hang around with Pink Champagne and I think they might've actually had some legal guardianship over that poor waif. Her father and brother and many of their friends had raped her throughout the greater part of her young life. She came to find that the stuff switched off all those memories and allowed her to just *be*. Fifteen years later she'd become a hardened prostitute who worked so she could take the stuff. And took the stuff so she could work and forget the horrendous memories of unspeakable things that'd been done to her as a child by those who should've loved and protected her. She spent a terrible life in and out of jail and rehabs, until she passed away a few years back.

Her boyfriend Janne really loved her and cherished her. He was a two-bit dealer in and out of jail his whole life trying to forget his own demons. Together they had a semblance of a home life in a flat in the suburbs where they had a dog and everything. They just happened to be heroin dealers, but they were kind and generous people who loved each other and had found each other. There was no way those people could ever get off the stuff.

As recently as two years ago when I was visiting my daughters in Sweden I caught sight of Janne hurrying through a crowd at Skanstull subway station. Still doing some hustle, but by the looks of him things weren't working out so well; Janne was a good man with a good heart doomed to a life of persecution by an idiot system not interested in damage control or harm reduction.

Sweden, with all its great socialist innovation, still had the most draconian knee-jerk response to drugs. They even refused to have a needle exchange program to help prevent AIDS, obviously preferring to take some hard line on drugs that was popular with the voters rather than actually showing some compassion for Stockholm's thousands of heroin addicts. As I got to hang out with Carina and Janne more and more I met their coterie of friends, most of whom were in the same professions as they were. I found all of them were using the stuff to forget nightmarish childhoods or escape their memories of atrocities committed in the war-torn Balkans. I was the only one among them who'd drifted into the stuff for hedonistic reasons. If those people who'd been so terribly let down by society needed their nepenthe then I believed they bloody well deserved it. If they could've gotten their stuff the way other people could get alcohol then they would all have had normal, productive, happy lives. It was the illegality of the stuff that made their lives impossible.

In the end the routine was just sordid monotony. Getting the money and scoring. Over and over. As you can imagine I wasn't doing a good job of being a father to my kids at this time. I was a hopeless, flaky, unreliable idiot. There isn't really anything else to say. I'm deeply embarrassed and ashamed by my behaviour and am eternally sorry to my eldest twins.

That said, on a cosmic level something *was* going right for me. The arrogance, the hubris, the lack of empathy were now somewhat mitigated. I understood how it felt to lose and lose and lose. By the time it was all over all I had left was a bass guitar and a rusty car – pretty much what I started out with.

I look back now and realise it was just something that had to happen. I had to learn to eat some humble fucking pie because it was good for me. On tour in New York I got busted buying twenty bucks worth of stuff and was slung in jail for an afternoon and a night. From this harsh example I learnt to value freedom a bit more and learnt how complicated getting a bust can be when it comes to passports and customs and things. You bring down a lot more attention on yourself and everything is suddenly harder. I still get pulled over and interrogated, and it still scares me and fills me with unease. Luckily I got off with community service, spending a day cleaning a train downtown for my debt to society.

So I left Sweden in 2000 for a couple of years in America after having met an American girl on tour in 1999, and had another pair of twins. Early on in my time there I weaned myself off the gear with a bottle of methadone, which stopped the very worst of the withdrawals. I was no happy camper and didn't realise at the time that heroin was finally behind me. I worried about drifting into it again, and spent about a month in some dull purgatory, not violently ill but not particularly well either. I felt old and achey and uninspired and had a lot of trouble sleeping at night, but what could I do but just keep going as the hurting hours trickled by like molasses?

Then one day I made a pivotal discovery. I was walking along a beach near where my two new daughters – not even two years old – were sitting with their mother. One got up and ran towards me and the other called out to me in excitement. And then it struck me: for the first time in ten or eleven years I was happy without any chemicals in my body. I was calmly contented and quietly happy. I searched my heart for thoughts of heroin; I was shocked to see the obsession had verily lifted. I was no longer in love with the stuff. I would never care about it again. I'd done my time and had learnt some things about being a decent human being that I might not have learnt if I'd just carried on being cashed up and successful. At the end of it all I'd sacrificed a million dollars and houses and studios and guitars and equipment. I'd lost the love and respect of many people, including my family and friends, some of whom decided to give me the benefit of the doubt, and some who didn't. I certainly fucked up The Church's chances, and I fucked up my chances at ever being a record producer, which I could've been good at.

In return I had my hard edges knocked off. Man, I was Napoleon-in-rags and I dealt with some hard-arsed bastards out there! Somehow I'm a better person for it. I regret the destruction but I don't dwell on it. I did my time in hell. And now it's over.

OUTRO

The music comes pouring out of The Church. Why couldn't it always be so easy?

It's 2011 and I'm standing on stage at the Sydney Opera House. Everything is going unfailingly right. The Church are playing with a 70-piece orchestra conducted by the charismatic and flamboyant conductor George Ellis. There's a sold out standing-room-only crowd in front of me, and they seem to be really enjoying themselves. Once again George Negus has introduced us to the audience. We've flown our friend Patti Hood over from the US, and she's playing harp to my right and smiling. The songs sound astonishingly incredible with the orchestra. The arrangements are beyond cool. Tim Powles has put a lot of work into this, along with George Ellis, and our songs come alive again but with all of their new elements. It's absolutely magical.

Yeah, I'm standing on stage and I'm playing and singing and yet I'm outside myself watching it all happen. The voice goes on singing, the fingers go on plucking at my Fender Jazz Bass, the body keeps moving, the foot keeps tapping.

But as I always explain it to people and myself, just because you can play bass guitar and make up songs doesn't mean you're a natural born leader of men, does it? It'd taken me a long time to learn to let it all just happen and not try to control every aspect of every thing. I was at last at home with myself. It felt nice to bask in the spotlight and receive a little bit of peer acknowledgement.

It was a long way from some of my other lives, but since 2002 I'd been living at Bondi Beach doing yoga and swimming every day at the Icebergs ocean baths. I was pretty close to being vegan. I was pretty damn healthy. I'd taught myself to paint. I had numerous musical collaborations on the boil all over the place. I was acting in plays and doing seminars and all kinds of things. I was writing a blog and writing poetry. I was constantly busy and constantly in demand for something or other. Artistically, I was completely fulfilled and I felt needed and loved by our incredible fans.

Then, an added bonus: in 2012 Elektra and Miranda formed their own band, Say Lou Lou, and released a stunning debut single right out of the blue. The song had all the qualities I'd tried to inculcate in my own songs – mystery, melancholy and melody. It was a feeling of the baton being passed on to the next generation.

Acknowledgements

I would like to thank my kind patron and friend Kevin L Keller whose idea this book was in the first place.

I would like to thank my publisher Fran Berry for having faith in me and my editor Rose Michael for her invaluable contribution.

I would like to thank my kind patron and dear friend Kip McClanahan for spiritual advice and belief and back-up.

I would like to thank my good friend John Tehranian for all the good legal advice and for being such a cool lawyer.

I would like to thank my great mate Dave Rundle for all the amazing help he's given me over the years.

Lastly, I would like to thank my mother Joyce without whom etc, etc: she really is the most excellent mother a geezer could have!